P9-BIN-565

Tales with Tails

# Tales with Tails

## Storytelling the Wonders
## of the Natural World

**Kevin Strauss**

**LIBRARIES**
UNLIMITED
*A Member of the Greenwood Publishing Group*

Westport, Connecticut • London

**Library of Congress Cataloging-in-Publication Data**

Strauss, Kevin, 1969-
  Tales with tails : storytelling the wonders of the natural world / by Kevin Strauss.
      p. cm.
  Includes bibliographical references and index.
  ISBN 1-59158-269-5 (pbk. : alk. paper)
  1. Environmental education—Activity programs.  2. Nature stories.  3. Storytelling.  I. Title.
GE77.S77   2006
372.35'7—dc22      2006007467

British Library Cataloguing in Publication Data is available.

Copyright © 2006 by Kevin Strauss

All rights reserved. No portion of this book may be
reproduced, by any process or technique, without the
express written consent of the publisher. An exception
is made for reproducibles, which may be copied for
classroom and educational programs only.

Library of Congress Catalog Card Number: 2006007467
ISBN: 1-59158-269-5

First published in 2006

Libraries Unlimited, 88 Post Road West, Westport, CT 06881
A Member of the Greenwood Publishing Group, Inc.
www.lu.com

Printed in the United States of America

The paper used in this book complies with the
Permanent Paper Standard issued by the National
Information Standards Organization (Z39.48–1984).

10 9 8 7 6 5 4 3 2 1

# Contents

## Part 1
## Nature and Stories

# Part 2
# Environmental Stories

# Preface

*Imagination is more important than knowledge.*

—Albert Einstein, physicist

*In the end we will conserve only what we love. We will love only what we understand, and we will understand only what we are taught.*

—Baba Dioum, Senegalese conservationist

When I began working as a naturalist at environmental centers in Vermont, New York, and Minnesota, I enjoyed taking schoolchildren outdoors to teach them about the plants and animals there. While I loved showing children how to use water insects to determine how clean a stream was and how to track deer through the forest, there were times when I felt something was missing. Learning the science of plants and animals sometimes helped children and adults care about the natural world, but it didn't always work.

It wasn't until later, in graduate school, that I figured it out. Those outdoor science classes did a great job of teaching children environmental science. They gave students a chance to exercise the logical, mathematical sides of their brains. But although those classes provided students with ample scientific reasons for why they should conserve water, turn off lights, or care about animals, they often didn't give students enough experience and perspective to help them care about making changes to protect the natural world. These sixth-grade students hadn't been alive long enough to see how pollution in a nearby river can kill the fish that live there, or how development in a forest might mean fewer homes for deer, owls, and foxes. What's more, if the goal of environmental education programs was to motivate children and adults to take better care of our natural world, educators were aiming programs at the wrong side of the human brain. Cognitive scientists often describe the left side of the brain as logical and mathematical, the side that helps us compute a restaurant tip or figure out why a lawnmower won't start. But it isn't the part that allows us to care about things. The right side of the human brain is the center of language, imagination, creativity, and emotions for each of us.

I realized that if I wanted people to care about the natural world, I needed to talk to both sides of their brains: the logical side *and* the emotional side. The science activities in environmental education programs have already done a good job of answering the "How nature works" and "How humans affect the natural world" questions. I needed to find something that will answer the "Why should we care?" question. That's where storytelling comes in.

Imagination helps us understand the "why" of things; it taps into the emotional side of our brains and gets us to care. Stories help do that in environmental education programs. Through stories we can see animals as creatures not all that different from ourselves, or we can see an example of what happened when people didn't take care of their environment.

After I began experimenting in using traditional and original stories in my environmental education programs, I saw changes happening. Children who were tired or restless focused better. Kids who could "take or leave" stream study suddenly took an interest in backswimmer bugs after hearing a story about why bugs live in the water. Suddenly my programs seemed to be "firing on all cylinders." I had found the missing piece.

Storytelling is not a silver bullet. It's not a Holy Grail that will fix any problem in education. But it is an important tool that you can use to help children and adults connect with and care about the natural world.

As a naturalist, I believe the opening quotes from Albert Einstein and Baba Dioum sum up why we should use stories to teach people about the natural world. What we don't understand, we often fear and abuse. What we don't value, we will someday lose. I believe that storytelling can be a bridge between our increasingly urban culture and the shrinking natural world. Stories can show us how to get along with the natural world and how to learn from the mistakes of our ancestors. But most important, I hope that the stories in this book get people to think and talk about the plants, animals, water, and land of this world not merely as inanimate "resources" but as the community in which we all live and grow.

## Telling These Stories

I believe that stories are for sharing and that they only truly live on the tongues of tellers. Please tell these stories. When you do tell these stories, please credit the nation or culture that first gave us that tale. When telling one of my original stories, please mention me as the source of the tale. If you would like to record or reprint any of my versions of these stories, please contact me at www.naturestory.com and Libraries Unlimited for permission.

# Introduction

## Purpose

In recent years we have seen a renaissance in both the art of storytelling and the use of storytelling to teach about the natural world. *Tales with Tails: Storytelling the Wonders of the Natural World* is a resource for teachers and naturalists who want to use storytelling to teach about the animals, plants, and ecological systems in our world. It is also a guide for storytellers to help them find and craft stories to more effectively teach ecological concepts like "Everything is connected" and "Diversity is the key to stability."

The goal of this book is to give you a clear definition of what makes an enjoyable and effective environmental story and to provide examples of such stories. It also gives you, as a naturalist or teacher, guidelines for how to adapt or create brand new environmental stories for use in nature centers, schools, and libraries.

As I gained more experience in the world of storytelling, I realized that many storytellers don't know a lot about the natural world. There are also many naturalists and classroom teachers who know little about the art and practice of storytelling. This book is an attempt to serve both audiences.

## Stories *and* Science?

As both a scientist and a storyteller, I am sometimes asked which field is more important. To that question, I always answer "yes." Traditional stories and research-based science have at their heart the same basic goal: finding truth. But they each use different tools and different languages to get there. I see research-based science and metaphorical stories as the two legs of our understanding. Take away either, and our understanding topples to the ground.

Folktales and myths use a metaphorical truth to help us connect to and care about our world. They answer "why?" and "so what?" with metaphorical and symbolic answers that connect with our emotions. Research-based science explains how the world works and speaks to the logical side of our brains.

When I tell a story like "How Birds Got Their Colors"" (Chapter 8), I always discuss how that story gives us a "story reason" for why birds have different colors on their feathers. Then I ask the audience if they know of a "science reason" for the same thing. Often students are familiar with the importance of camouflage for some birds. In two minutes I can connect the metaphorical story with hard science and hold them both up as important ways to understand our world.

## Ways to Use This Book

I have divided *Tales with Tails* into two sections. Part 1 provides background information on what an "environmental story" is and basic information on environmental education and the art of storytelling. Part 2 contains more than 60 "environmental stories," organized by the animals in the stories or by the ecological concepts that they demonstrate.

You can use this book in several ways. If you are just looking for an environmental story to use in an Earth Day or Arbor Day storytelling program or as part of an environmental science lesson, turn to Part 2. You can also look through the "Story List" (pp. xiii–xv), which is organized by topic.

If you have a lot of background in education but are a beginning storyteller, see Chapter 3, "A Crash Course in Storytelling." It will give you the basics you need to find, learn, and tell a story. If you are a storyteller but don't know much about environmental education or ecology, see Chapter 2 for "A Crash Course in Environmental Education Concepts and Values." Also be sure to check out the nature facts sections throughout Part 2. They provide basic biological and ecological information about the animal and plant characters in the stories in this book.

For the more experienced storyteller, Chapter 4 provides guidelines on adapting or creating new environmental stories, and Chapter 5 contains guidelines on developing effective animal characters and dealing with the challenges and advantages of anthropomorphism in animal stories.

If you are a classroom teacher or naturalist who would like to add some new activities to your next environmental education lesson, check out the activities at the end of each chapter. The activities are primarily geared to older elementary and middle school students, since that is the stage at which most schools offer their environmental education and environmental science programs. But you can adapt many of the activities for younger and older students. Chapter 2 describes how to integrate storytelling into your environmental education or environmental science lessons as introductions to, conclusions for, or illustrations of environmental education concepts like "habitat," "adaptations," and "interconnections." Chapter 2 also defines and explains the environmental education concepts described in other sections of this book.

Since environmental issues and story resources change quickly in our high-speed information age, I have designed this book to be a doorway into the world of environmental storytelling. To that end, I will be providing regular updates of environmental storytelling resources on my Web site, www.naturestory.com.

My goal as both a naturalist and a storyteller is to connect people and nature through stories. If you are holding this book, I suspect that is yours is as well. Welcome to the journey.

# Story List

Within each category, the stories are listed in the order in which they appear in the book.

## Animal Stories

### Mammals

### Birds

# Earth and Sky Stories

# Ecological Concept Stories

# Part 1

## Nature and Stories

# Chapter 1

## Using Stories to Teach about the Natural World

### Truth and Story

Long, long ago, Truth walked the world as an old man. Everything about him was old: his hands, his face, even his clothes. His skin was wrinkled and his clothes were so ragged that some said that he wore no clothes at all. When he would arrive in a town, he would walk up to the first person he found and say, "Hi, how's it going?" But the response was always the same. The person would look at the ground, turn, and walk away.

"I don't understand, wouldn't people want to hear what Truth has to say?" said Truth to himself. "When I am not around, people always talk about wanting to hear the Truth. But now that I am here, they avoid me."

Then Truth saw a large crowd assembled at the edge of town. They seemed to be listening to someone with great interest. He approached the crowd, thinking that surely someone there would want to listen to him. But as he approached the crowd, people quickly looked away and hurried off. The only person left on the street was the speaker, and her name was Story. Story was dressed in fine, colorful robes. Her clothes had every color of the rainbow. They had fabrics that sparkled silver or gold in the sunshine. They even had colors that changed as she moved, going from red to blue to green as she talked. "I don't understand what is going on," said Truth to Story. "Why don't people want to hear what I have to say? Perhaps it is because I am old." "No, look at me. I am old as well, and people still listen to me," said Story. Then looking at the state of Truth's clothing, she added, "perhaps the problem is that you are just showing a little too much of yourself. Come home with me and I will give you one of my beautiful robes to wear."

So Truth went home with Story and put on one of Story's bright-colored robes. Then the two of them went walking arm in arm down the street. Truth noticed that now, rather than seeing people turn and walk away, people were coming up to talk with them. Truth and Story were invited into a house for dinner, and they spent many hours talking with the family there. And that is how it is today. When Truth walks naked in the world, people turn away. But when Truth walks with Story, they are invited into our houses and into our hearts (story from the Jewish tradition).

# Definitions

The story above lies at the heart of why I believe storytelling should be a part of any environmental education program. But before we get started, we need to make sure we know what we are talking about.

- **Story:** a narrative of an actual, fictional, legendary, or mythical event
- **Storytelling:** the act of using voice and body language to communicate a narrative directly from one person to another

    In my mind, storytelling is much more than just words or gestures. In the process of telling a story, a storyteller takes mental images, translates them into words and body language, then transmits them to the minds of listeners. Storytelling is actually an act of co-creation. The teller transmits the images, but the listeners play an even more important part. They create the story pictures in their own minds. As the audience reacts to a story, a storyteller adjusts the story, making each telling of a tale a unique, living experience.

- **Environmental storytelling:** using the power of spoken word narratives to teach about the natural world and our ecological relationship to it
- **Environmental story:** a narrative that teaches either something about the animals, plants, and natural wonders of our world or an environmental education concept like diversity, sustainability, food chains, or adaptations

# Why Tell Stories?

There once was a famous Rabbi who, rather than preaching in the temple or giving people advice on the street, would always tell them stories. One Sabbath, a young man came up to the Rabbi and said, "Teacher, I like hearing your stories, but I was wondering . . . when were you going to get around to teaching us something." The Rabbi looked at the young man for a while and then a smile crept across his face.

"That is a very good question," he said. "In fact, it reminds me of a story . . . " (story from the Jewish tradition).

It is clear from historical records that people have been telling stories at least since the beginning of recorded history and civilization. But people were probably telling stories long before that, ever since humans developed the ability to communicate. What's more, most people use some aspects of storytelling every day of their lives. When we talk about how our day went or describe a favorite book, we are telling stories. Anything so well ingrained in our lives must be there for a reason and must come with benefits, otherwise humans would have stopped doing it long, long ago.

## The Effects of Storytelling

- **Storytelling is fun.** It is a captivating, economical, nonelectronic form of entertainment accessible to most people regardless of income or educational level. This is the primary reason that most people tell and listen to stories. We enjoy the experience.

- **Storytelling builds language and comprehension skills, the precursors to literacy and creative writing.** Very young children CAN learn new words from stories. Older children learn narrative patterns of beginnings, middles, and ends. Children and adults who tell and listen to stories exercise the creative parts of their brains (Brand and Donato, 2001). This "imaginative exercise" helps students and adults write literature and solve problems more effectively (Haven, 2000).

- **Storytelling is an effective way to teach lessons.** Human brains seem to retain material put in story form much better than a list of unrelated facts (Haven, 2000; Weaver, 1994).

- **Storytelling is a gentle and effective way to pass on lessons and values.** "One upon a time . . ." is far more powerful than "You really shouldn't . . . ." When someone gives you advice, especially unsolicited advice, what's your reaction? You normally get defensive, put up barriers, and ignore it. On the other hand, if you hear a story about a foolish bear and what happened to him in a similar situation, you are much more likely to heed the warning.

- **Storytelling helps to build bridges among people.** While humans have set up many barriers to divide humanity by race, gender, income, geography, and sexual orientation, many stories have themes that remind us that humans are much more alike than we are different. Stories from China and Kenya that are more than 500 years old address many of the same themes and concerns that people have today. What's more, story listeners can imagine that they are living in a different place, a different time, or in a different culture. This "walking in another's shoes" experience can create empathy among groups of people who feel they have nothing in common (Sima and Cordi, 2003).

- **Storytelling helps to build bridges between people and the natural world.** Just as stories can help people empathize with humans who are different from themselves, stories can also help listeners develop empathy for the animals and plants that share our world. I began looking at deer in a whole new way when I learned a story about how the deer got its antlers. The more animal stories I have learned, the more I have begun thinking of animals and plants less as objects and more as community members and neighbors.

- **Storytelling gives storytellers control over an important part of their world.** More and more school programs are creating storytelling clubs and using storytelling in their speech competitions. For children, the ability to learn and perform a story can be a powerful confidence builder. It can also give children control over a part of their lives. At a time when parents and teachers have a great deal of control over a child's life, storytelling gives children a way to face their fears and live out their fantasies in a safe imaginative environment (Sima and Cordi, 2003).

  Telling stories also gives children a chance to practice public speaking skills and develop confidence in their ability to communicate with others.

# A History of Environmental Storytelling

Over the past 20 years, environmental educators and storytellers have used a variety of stories in their environmental education programs at schools, nature centers, and libraries. But because there was no accepted definition of "environmental storytelling," there were also no clear guidelines about what makes an effective story for environmental education programs. This led some people to conclude that a story was an "environmental story" if it had an animal in it, even if that story didn't teach anything factual about the animal or its role in the natural environment. The more recent story collections that focus on "environmental stories" seem to define "environmental stories" as "animal stories" or more narrowly as "Native American stories." The problem with equating "environmental stories" with "Native American stories" is that it gives people the impression that the only cultures that value and care for the natural world are Native American. In reality, all cultures have stories about caring for the natural world. Environmental stewardship is a human value, not just a Native American value.

In practice, naturalist storytellers often chose stories that included animals from their own region, like bears, foxes, or blue jays. Not surprisingly, many of these animal stories came form the native peoples of the Americas—the Lakota, Ojibwa, Cherokee, and other nations. Although these stories often teach lessons about the bears, wolves, deer, and other animals of North America, they sometimes also include cultural lessons about the tribe whose storytellers first told the tales. Those cultural lessons may or may not have had any pertinence to the environmental education lessons at hand.

What is more, ongoing debate about the appropriateness of non-native storytellers telling Native American stories, and in some cases, native cultural taboos against telling some native tales during the summertime (as is the tradition among some groups of Ojibwa), have led some teachers and naturalists to search for other stories to use in their programs.

Today I see a new wave of "environmental storytellers" on the horizon. Some are naturalists who want to use the power of spoken word stories to teach their students about the natural wonders of our world. Others are storytellers who would like to add environmental conservation messages to their programs. This book is for both groups and others. I always like to tell people that "storytelling does a world of good." But I have come to realize that it is also true that "storytelling does the world good," for reasons that will become clear as you read this book.

# Kinds of Environmental Stories

> *Science, by its own definition, doesn't give us meaning. It just provides us with facts. . . . Our lives gain meaning only when we tell our story. What the various religious traditions have done over the millennia is to tell the (universe's) story.*
> —David Steindl-Rast

As I began telling stories in environmental education programs, I started by telling "animal stories" because I wanted to get my students interested in learning about the animals that shared our world. But I soon realized that environmental education is much more than just teaching about animals. Soon I was looking for stories that would demonstrate larger ecological concepts as well. Some weren't animal stories but rather involved human characters and human interactions with the environment.

As discussed above, an "environmental story" is one that either teaches listeners something about the animals, plants, and natural wonders of our world or teaches an ecological education concept like diversity, sustainability, food chains, or adaptations.

## Nature Explanation Stories

Nature explanation stories teach listeners something about the animals, plants, and natural wonders of our world. "Why" or "pourquoi" stories tell how an animal or plant got to be the way it is, like "Why Bear Has a Stumpy Tail" (Chapter 6). Some creation myths and natural history stories also fit in this category.

An effective aspect of nature stories is that since they are memorable, they act as a "hook" in the memories of listeners. Once a storyteller has hooked a listener, it is easier to share biology or ecology information that a listener can hang on that story memory "hook" and remember later. Once a student has heard a folktale about how bear got a stumpy tail, that story creates a "file folder" in his memory about bears. Now when he hears bear biology facts, he can put the facts into his "bear file" and remember them more easily because they are linked to an enjoyable bear folktale.

## Ecological Concept Stories

Ecological concept stories teach an environmental education concept like diversity, sustainability, food chains, or adaptations (see Chapter 2). This also includes historical "fact tales" and lesson stories about greed, cruelty, wastefulness, and laziness. "Fact tales" describe how humans have affected the environment in the past and how that affects us today.

### What Doesn't Fit as an Environmental Story?

Folktales that primarily focus on humans interacting with humans often aren't environmental stories. Overwhelmingly anthropomorphic animal stories like "The Three Bears" and "The Three Little Pigs," often aren't environmental stories either because they are really about humans "dressed up like animals." Most ghost or horror stories, King Arthur stories, Robin Hood stories, and myths that focus on human foibles like lust, rage, and revenge also don't fit as environmental stories.

# Finding Environmental Stories

## Finding Nature Explanation Stories

Animal and plant stories appear in written collections and the oral traditions of storytellers from cultures around the world.

1.  Look for story anthologies with sections titled "animal stories." Northern Europe has many animals and plants similar to those in North America.

2.  Look at stories from cultures that were among the last to be Christianized or in places where the Christian church never gained a foothold (like Finland, Nigeria, Thailand, India, Korea, China, and Polynesia). Religious leaders in Christianized European nations sometimes destroyed "pagan" animal stories because they saw them as competition for Christian explanations about the world. As a result, many European nations have lost their environmental stories over time.

3.  Look for collections of animal trickster stories from West Africa (Anansi the spider) and African American stories from the American south (Brer Rabbit). These stories involve animal characters, and in the case of "Brer Rabbit" stories, involve animals from North America. Although some of these stories are anthropomorphic, you can adapt them (Chapter 5) into engaging and biologically accurate animal tales.

## Finding Ecological Concept Stories

Finding ecological concept stories is a little more complicated, because a good background in both environmental education and folklore is required to identify and understand the subtext in these stories. Looking for lesson stories with themes of greed, cruelty, wastefulness, and laziness can get you started. In addition to the concept stories that I have listed in this book, some recently published story anthologies include sections of "environmental stories." Check the bibliography or Chapter 14 for more information.

# Adapting Stories

It is in the nature of storytelling that each individual storyteller adapts a story with his or her own twist or curl. We also see widespread historical examples of storytellers adapting stories that originated in other lands to suit where the storyteller lives now. Storytellers have taken folktales from Ghana, Saudi Arabia, or Great Britain and transformed them into African American Brer Rabbit tales or Appalachian folktales. This is part of the storytelling tradition, and I have followed that tradition with this collection of stories.

I believe that, if done with care and respect, adapting a story can make it more accessible to today's listeners. In retelling the stories in this book, I have adapted them in some ways. In some cases, I have recorded my own versions of these tales without major changes to the animal or plant species or geographic location in my source material. In other cases I changed the animal or plant species in the story to align it with those found in North America. If I made changes to the source material, I describe the tale as "adapted" in the cultural description. When performing these stories, I often tell its country of origin and say "the story changed a bit as it came to this country."

Like any artistic act, adapting stories can be controversial. Although I limit my adapting of stories to secular (nonreligious) stories out of respect for religious traditions around the world, I feel that it is part of our human storytelling tradition to adapt stories for new lands and for a new world of listeners.

# References

Brand, Susan Trostle, and Jeanne M. Donato. 2001. *Storytelling in Emergent Literacy: Fostering Multiple Intelligences.* Albany, NY: Delmar. 354pp. $33.95pa. ISBN 0-7668-1480-7pa.

Haven, Kendall. 2000. *Super Simple Storytelling.* Englewood, CO: Teacher Ideas Press. 229pp. $25.00pa. $25.00. ISBN 1-56308-681-6pa.

Sima, Judy, and Kevin Cordi. 2003. *Raising Voices: Creating Youth Storytelling Groups and Troupes.* Teacher Ideas Press. 239pp. $32.50pa. ISBN 1-56308-919-xpa.

Weaver, Mary, ed. 1994. *Tales as Tools.* Jonesborough, TN: National Storytelling Press. 213pp. $19.95pa. ISBN 1-879991-15-2pa.

# Environmental Collage Activity

**Grade Level:** 3–6

**Environmental Themes:** habitat, diversity

**Curriculum Areas:** science, social studies, visual arts

**Student Skills:** inferring, comparison, creativity

**Materials:** old magazines, scissors, glue, paper

## Instructions:

1. Give students the definition of "environment" (the place where an organism lives, like a forest or wetland). An animal's habitat is a portion of that environment. You can think of it as an animal's "home range," the smaller area that provides an animal with food, water, shelter, and space. By comparison, a student's "environment" could be his town and a student's "habitat" would be the neighborhood he lives in.

   Ask students to make a collage of their environment by cutting out pictures from magazines and pasting them on a piece of paper.

2. Ask students to choose a wild animal that lives near their home. Have them make a second collage of that animal's environment on a separate piece of paper. Use an encyclopedia, the Internet, or library resources if students aren't sure where the animal lives or how it does so.

3. Ask the students to compare and contrast the two collages. What similarities do they see between where wild animals live and where people live? Would the animals they chose be able to survive if people built more houses in their environment, or would they have to move elsewhere?

4. Have students pair up and compare their human environment collages. How are they similar? Why are they different?

## Evaluation:

Have students either write a short essay or give a short verbal report about how human environments are different from and similar to the environment of a particular wild animal. Is "the environment" limited to the natural world of forests and prairies and mountains, or does it include human-made buildings and communities as well?

From Kevin Strauss, *Tales with Tails: Storytelling the Wonders of the Natural World.* Westport, CT: Libraries Unlimited, 2006.
Copyright © 2006 by Kevin Strauss.

# Animals Everywhere Activity

**Grade Level:** 1–6

**Environmental Themes:** adaptation, habitat

**Curriculum Areas:** science, physical education

**Student Skills:** inferring, comparison

**Materials:** a safe outdoor area to explore (preferably with bushes and trees), clipboards, paper and pencils, magnifying glasses (optional), binoculars (optional)

## Instructions:

1. Tell students that you are all going on a "Neighborhood Safari." Their job is to find as many animals and signs of animals as possible. Make a list of animals you expect to see outdoors. Make another list of the "animal signs" that animals might leave behind: nests, chewed leaves, fur, feathers, tracks, trails, smells, holes in trees or bark (woodpeckers or insects), droppings (white droppings from birds). The job of students is to record what they find. They can record their findings either as a written list or as a map of the neighborhood, with animals and animal sign locations listed on the map. Instruct students not to chase or disturb wildlife. Their job is just to make observations.

2. Spend at least 30 minutes exploring. Then go back inside and discuss what the students found. Where did you see the most animals or animal signs? Where you surprised by what you found? What sort of habitats are most likely to have a lot of wildlife, a lawn or woods area? Why do you think this is true? If students don't see animals outdoors, does that mean that the animals are not there? (No, animals are generally shy around humans and look for places to hide when they see, hear, or smell us coming.)

3. Choose some stories that involve the animals that the students found signs of. Tell or read those stories to the children. Do the animals in the stories remind them of the animals they saw outdoors?

## Evaluation:

Review student "Neighborhood Safari" lists. Have students answer some of the discussion questions above as an essay, and after they hand their answers in, discuss the answers as a class.

From Kevin Strauss, *Tales with Tails: Storytelling the Wonders of the Natural World.* Westport, CT: Libraries Unlimited, 2006.
Copyright © 2006 by Kevin Strauss.

# Chapter 2

## A Crash Course in Environmental Education Concepts and Values

Our natural environment is both beautiful and complex. We know and understand some things about the natural world and are just beginning to understand others. The goal of environmental education programs is to help us appreciate the natural wonders of our world and realize the effects we are having on the environment. Part 1 gives you a sense of the concepts used in environmental education programs, so that you can more effectively identify and use environmental stories in your programs. In Part 2, the environmental stories section, you will find animal facts sections that give you a clearer understanding of the biology and ecology of specific animals and plants common to North America.

## The History of Environmental Education

Environmental education programs in the United States have their roots in the early twentieth century with programs like nature study, conservation education, and later outdoor education, but this field really hit its stride in the 1970s when environmental education became part of many school programs. Inspired by books like Rachel Carson's *Silent Spring*, Earth Day celebrations, and the political ecology movement for cleaner air, cleaner water, and the protection of forests and wildlife species, many educators added environmental education or ecology topics to their science and social studies curriculums. The goal was to help students understand the biology and ecology (habitat, food chains, sustainability) of organisms in our world and how humans affect the natural systems on which all life depends.

Today, many schools have environmental education programs either as a separate week at an environmental education center or as a subject area taught by classroom teachers.

## Environmental Education Basics

Environmental education seeks to teach students about the life systems and interconnections in the natural world. While we sometimes think of the "natural environment" as just the wild forests, mountains, and waterways in our world, the term also applies to the "built" environments of cities and farms, since human actions in these communities have a huge impact on other parts of the environment. Another term used for this area of study is "ecology." That term, from the Greek *oikos,* for "home," is literally the study of homes, whether they are the forest habitat of the gray wolf or the home and neighborhood of a fifth grader and her family.

## Concepts

Many environmental education programs organize their curriculum around environmental education "concepts." A concept is an important idea or lesson. There are many ways to teach a lesson like "Everything is Connected." An instructor could lecture about the idea, have students play a simulation game that demonstrated the interconnections in nature, have students observe examples of natural connections in the outdoors, or take students on the "virtual fieldtrip" of a story. Generally speaking, the more hands-on and interactive a teaching technique is, the more engaging and effective it is in teaching a concept. Unfortunately, the more hands-on an activity is, the fewer students can participate at the same time. Storytelling can help bridge the gap between teaching effectiveness and efficiency (reaching a large group of students at the same time) by engaging students to use their imaginations to explore and think about a new environmental education concept.

## The Four Laws of Ecology

In his 1971 book, *The Closing Circle: Nature, Man, and Technology,* environmental scientist and social activist Barry Commoner defined the central rules of how the natural world works as the "Four Laws of Ecology." These laws describe ecological principles and put the sometimes-complicated scientific laws into a more accessible format. These laws still underlie much of the basis for environmental education programs and concepts.

### *Everything Is Connected (Interdependence)*

Ecologists often describe the natural world as a series of interconnected natural cycles. Plants, animals, and habitats are interconnected through cycles like the food chain, air cycle, and water cycle, as well as other systems. For example, the food chain demonstrates the connections between predators and prey. Grass grows, a mouse eats the grass, a snake eats the mouse, and a hawk eats the snake. Sometime later, the hawk dies and decomposes into the soil. Those soil nutrients feed a new generation of grass, and the cycle begins again.

Scientists once thought that changes in one population of animals or plants wouldn't significantly affect other plants or animals, but ecologists now cite numerous examples of these interconnections in the natural world. Many natural history stories describe how some human actions have "unintended consequences" because of these (often invisible) environmental interconnections.

---

### Bald Eagles and DDT

Few people could have predicted that when farmers and health department officials in the United States sprayed the chemical known as DDT to kill mosquitoes and other pest insects, the impact of the spraying would go far beyond insect control. Mosquitoes and other pest insects spread diseases and ate agricultural crops, so it seemed logical that we would want to get rid of them. We didn't know that these chemical pesticides would have impacts on birds like the bald eagle. But that appears to be what happened in the decades before stricter pesticide application laws and the protection of the 1973 Endangered Species Act (ESA).

As a long-lasting pesticide, DDT washed into waterways where aquatic insects and fish ingested it. Bald eagles eat fish as a large part of their summer diets. At about the same time that people began spraying DDT across North America, female eagles began producing eggs with thinner shells. Many of these thinner eggs broke when the female eagle incubated them, killing the undeveloped eaglet inside. The result was a steep drop in eagle populations. Scientists studying the decline in eagle populations determined that DDT was the cause of the thinner eggshells. Because of this research and the publicity from books like *Silent Spring,* the U.S. government banned the use of DDT in the United States in 1972. Since then, DDT levels have dropped in North America.

That, in conjunction with the habitat protections of the ESA, has helped the bald eagle population to recover in North America over the past 30 years. In 1963, there were just 417 known breeding pairs of bald eagles in the lower 48 United States. In 2004, there were an estimated 7,678 breeding pairs in the same region. The U.S. Fish and Wildlife Service currently lists the bald eagle as a "threatened" (rather than an "endangered") species and has proposed delisting the species entirely in the next few years. Developing nations in tropical regions still use DDT for the control of malaria-carrying mosquitoes. Some biologists argue that in our interconnected environment, this "foreign DDT" could still find its way back to our shores and affect our wildlife.

### *Everything Goes Somewhere (There Is No Such Place as "Away")*

The natural world has no real example of "garbage." When a tree dies, funguses digest the wood and turn it into soil. When a deer dies, wolves, foxes, ravens, and eagles eat the animal's meat, organs, fur, and bones. Insects clean up the last bits of meat. Mice and chipmunks chew on the bones. Funguses and other decomposers digest any bits of meat and bone not eaten by animals. In the end, what's left of that deer decomposes into soil nutrients.

Before the advent of the Industrial Revolution, most things that humans made decomposed. But after the petrochemical revolution of the mid-twentieth century, humans began producing products such as plastics, insulating foam, and other substances that do not decompose or that decompose so slowly that they last decades or centuries in the soil. Humans think they get rid of garbage by sending it to the dump (now the "sanitary landfill") , but even when buried in a landfill, garbage doesn't really go "away." Over the last few decades, researchers have documented cases of poorly constructed landfills leaking and contaminating nearby drinking water wells as well as rivers, lakes, and streams.

Human examples of this law go back even further. At the start of the Industrial Revolution in the late 1700s, air pollution from new coal-fired factories in England caused health problems for workers and families living nearby. The solution was to build taller smokestacks to send the smoke and dust higher into the atmosphere. For a while, the plan seemed to work. It sent the pollution so high into the atmosphere that people thought it really had gone "away." In the 1800s and 1900s, industries in the United States built the same kind of large smokestacks, thinking that was the way to send the air pollution "away." But in the 1960s, researchers began seeing frogs, fish, and other aquatic organisms disappearing from lakes in the northeastern United States.

Scientists determined that acid compounds from faraway factories and power plants were raining down in these lakes as "acid rain." This acidity changed the habitat conditions in lakes just enough that some species couldn't survive there any more. While the change in lakes wouldn't harm people who drink the water or swim in the lakes, it killed small algae organisms that feed small insects that feed fish and frogs. In some cases, frog and salamander eggs would die if left in the acidic lakes. This was an example of how "everything goes somewhere." Since that time, tighter pollution controls from the U.S. Environmental Protection Agency appear to have reduced the amount of acid compounds power plants are releasing into the air.

Of course, cleaning the air costs money. Some industries are pressuring politicians to weaken environmental regulations, claiming that the regulations are too expensive. In some cases, they have succeeded. Frogs, fish, and salamanders don't vote and can't lobby Congress. Acidity seems to be holding steady or returning to a more balanced (neutral) acid level in some affected Eastern lakes, but this could change if the U.S. government weakens its clean air laws.

### *There Is No Such Thing as a "Free Lunch" (Everything Costs Something)*

This concept seems obvious but sometimes is overlooked. We have all heard the adage "if it sounds too good to be true, it probably is." The same applies in the natural world. There is a cost—although not necessarily a financial cost—for everything we do. Every action requires some type of resource consumption. More important, the person who benefits from an action may not be the person paying the "bill" in the end. One example of this is the impact of some clear-cut logging practices on trout streams in the Pacific Northwest in the 1960s and 1970s, long before loggers had developed "best management practices" to protect soil and water resources during logging operations. Clear-cutting is a low-cost method of harvesting trees, but it has a big impact on the environment. When it rains, soil no longer secured to the hillside by living tree roots washes into nearby trout streams, clouding the stream and suffocating the native trout. In this case, the trout, trout anglers, and the U.S. Fish and Wildlife Service (i.e., taxpayers) paid the "cost" of this form of clear-cut tree harvesting. The logging companies benefited, as did the people and industries using wood products. In effect, because of how government regulates resource use, taxpayers often end up subsidizing an industry.

In our society, we often treat our natural resources, such as clean air, clean water, public land, wildlife, and other public resources as "free" resources that anyone can use. Unfortunately, some people take advantage of this situation, leaving the federal government—and the American taxpayers—to pay the bills for expensive environmental cleanups.

### Nature Knows Best

This law is a statement of faith in the natural processes of the world. While some humans aspire to "improve" on the natural world by "getting rid" of mosquitoes, wolves, dandelions, or other "pest" species, such projects seldom truly improve the environment, and such eradication programs often end up with unintended consequences (see "Everything Is Connected") . This law also points out that animals and plants are adapted to a specific habitat. Polar bears, with their thick fur and insulating fat layer, would not be able to survive in the heat of a desert or rainforest.

Our modern industrial farming practices are an example of our attempts to "improve" on nature by controlling insect pests with chemical pesticides. In the last 60 years, pesticide use in the United States has increased tenfold. At the same time, we have lost more crops to pests than ever before. Before the widespread use of chemical pesticides in the 1940s, farmers lost about 7 percent of their crops to pest insects. Today farmers lose about 13 percent to insect pests. What's more, insects quickly develop "resistance" to pesticides, requiring the production of new and possibly more toxic pesticides to "keep up" with the bugs.

Not every country has decided to stay on the pesticide treadmill. Many European nations have reduced or eliminated their pesticide use. Even some developing nations, like Indonesia, are looking for nonchemical solutions to the problem of agricultural pests.

---

### Insect Control in Indonesia

In the 1970s, farmers sprayed chemical pesticides on their rice fields to control a species of leafhopper that feeds on rice. At first the spray did a good job killing the pest species. But that wasn't all that it killed. The spray also killed spiders and bees that preyed on the leafhoppers. Over time, the leafhoppers evolved immunity to some pesticides. As these pesticide-immune leafhoppers began to reproduce, they had no natural enemies in the rice fields, and their population exploded. Soon the leafhoppers were consuming more rice plants than they had before farmers began using pesticides. In 1986, the Indonesian government banned many pesticides and helped farmers manage their farms to encourage colonization by bees, spiders, and other leafhopper enemies. By 1995, Indonesia was able to grow and export an additional 4.5 million tons of rice per year (Scott, 1995).

---

## Other Environmental Education Concepts

### Habitat

**To survive, animals and plants need to live in an appropriate habitat.** A "habitat" is an animal or plant's home. Animals and plants all need the same four things from their habitats: food, water, shelter, and space. In a forest habitat, oak trees provide squirrels with food (acorns) and shelter (leafy nests or trunk hole). Watery tree sap, nearby fruit, or ponds provide the squirrel with water, and an acre of forest provides a squirrel with plenty of space. While some animals need to live in a specific habitat, like beavers in rivers and lakes, other animals, like crows, can live in a variety of habitats, from forests to meadows to farms to cities. Generally speaking, animals and plants have specific "adaptations" (see below) to help them survive well in their habitat.

### *Adaptations*

**Animals and plants have physical and behavioral adaptations (or "tools") that help them survive in a particular habitat.** Adaptations are physical or behavioral attributes used by an animal or plant that help the species to acquire its basic needs. Physical adaptations include a beaver's chisel-like teeth and a rose bush's thorns. A beaver uses its teeth to cut down trees for food and building materials. A rose's thorns help protect it from grazing plant-eaters like deer.

Behavioral adaptations include the way that a spider spins a web or how a beaver builds a dam. If a spider didn't spin a web, it would be more difficult for it to catch food. By building a dam, beavers create a pond deep enough to protect their lodge from predators. Often an organism has adaptations that work best in one or a few habitats, although some animals, like mice and dandelions, are "generalists" whose adaptations allow them to survive in a wide range of habitats. These generalists often survive well living near humans in our cities or farmlands, and because of their flexibility, many of these species have expanding populations and become "pests."

### *Diversity*

**Diversity is the key to stability.** Most people agree that cultural, gender, and artistic diversity enriches our culture in the United States and other countries. Immigrants to this nation bring new ideas and perspectives that help us build a stronger economy and a richer artistic tradition. Diversity is important in the natural world as well.

Generally speaking, a forest with many different species and ages of trees is more stable and enduring than a monoculture (single-species) forest with just one species of tree, or a forest with trees that are all the same age. If a forest consisted of just 20-year-old aspen trees, and an aspen disease struck the forest, many, if not all, of the trees would sicken and die. Soon it wouldn't be a forest any longer. On the other hand, if the forest consisted of aspen, birch, and pine trees and the aspen disease struck the forest, the disease might still kill all of the aspen trees in the forest, but the forest would remain because of the diversity of other trees that still live there.

An example of what happens when disease strikes a nondiverse forest occurred with elm trees in the twentieth century. A fungal disease later labeled "Dutch elm disease" killed thousands of elm trees in the cities of the eastern United States. When urban foresters replanted in cities, they planted a wider variety of species of trees to avoid a repeat of this disaster.

What's more, everything has a role to play in nature, even if we don't know what that role is. Many species contribute to the survival of other species. For instance, many wild orchids need to grow in a symbiotic relationship with certain kinds of soil funguses. When these flowers are pulled out of their native ground and replanted in potting soil, they often die.

### *Stewardship*

**Every person can make a difference.** Once people learn about their connection to the natural world, the next step is for them to change their behavior and begin to take better care of the environment. Caring for the environment is known as " environmental stewardship," and people can do it in many different ways. Environmental education programs have used several strategies to change human behaviors, but one of the most effective is to demonstrate how environmental changes like air or water pollution affect people directly. When conservationists can show people how a recycling program would save taxpayers money, citizens are often much more willing to recycle paper, plastic, and aluminum, rather than putting those items in the garbage.

# Environmental Education Terms

Like any field, environmental education uses some terms that may seem confusing to outsiders. Here is the inside track on environmental education terms:

- **Adaptation:** A physical attribute or behavior that helps an animal or plant survive in its environment.

- **Biodiversity:** Different kinds of plants or animals all living in the same place. One concern that environmental scientists have had is that as species become extinct, we are reducing the number of diverse living natural resources on the planet (we are wasting our "natural capital"), which disrupts food chains and alters the balance of nature.

- **Carnivore:** An organism that primarily eats meat for food. Wolves, hawks, and weasels are examples of carnivore **predators**.

- **Decomposer:** An organism that primarily eats dead things and helps recycle them into soil again. Funguses, vultures, worms, and bacteria are examples of decomposers.

- **Diversity:** Different kinds of things all in the same place. We can see artistic diversity in any art museum and political diversity in the newspaper during an election season. We see cultural diversity among people whose ancestors or parents came to the United States from virtually every corner of the globe. Many people cite these examples of diversity as a sign of strength in our country, since it provides us with a wealth of ideas on how to solve problems and create art. We also see biological diversity in our old-growth forests, prairies, and wetlands. The more different kinds of habitats we have, and the more different kinds of plants we see in an area, the more different kinds of animals we will see there as well. Diverse habitats are also more resilient to disturbance.

- **Food chain, food cycle:** A simplified description of who eats and is eaten by whom in an environment. For instance, grass grows in a meadow, the grass is eaten by a grasshopper, the grasshopper is eaten by a songbird, and the songbird gets eaten by a hawk. Sometime later, the hawk dies and its body decomposes and turns into soil, which grows more grass.

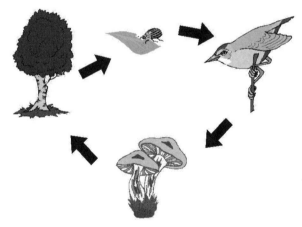

Simple Food Chain

- **Food web:** A much more complicated description of who eats and is eaten by whom in an environment. Rather than describing just one linear sequence of connections, a food web describes several interconnecting food chains.

- **Habitat:** An animal or plant's home or home territory. A habitat contains the food, water, shelter, or space that the species needs to survive.

- **Herbivore:** An organism that primarily eats plants for food. Deer, beavers, and rabbits are examples of herbivores. Herbivores are often **prey** species in an ecosystem and are eaten by carnivore **predators**.

- **Interdependence:** The idea that many plants and animals are dependent on each other for food, homes, and other needs. For instance, when a landowner cuts down an old oak tree, that action will affect the squirrels and birds that have nests in the tree and the deer, turkeys, and blue jays that feed on the tree's acorns.

- **Niche:** A plant or animal's role or "job" in nature.

- **Omnivore:** An organism that eats both plants and meat for food. Bears, opossums, raccoons, and humans are examples of omnivores. Omnivores are sometimes "mid-level" **predators**, feeding on herbivores but also being eaten by larger **predators**.

- **Predator:** An organism that feeds on another living thing. Hunting animals are examples of predators.

- **Prey:** An organism that is fed upon by another living thing. Most organisms in the natural world are prey for something else.

- **Recycling:** The process of breaking something down and using it again. Humans recycle glass, metal, and paper resources. Funguses and bacteria recycle dead plant and animal material and turn it into soil.

- **Sustainability:** The idea that humans can harvest resources from the environment perpetually, as long as they don't take too much of any one resource. A common definition of "sustainability" is to "meet the needs of the current generation without compromising the ability of future generations to meet their needs." One example of sustainable logging is selective tree harvesting in a forest. In this process, loggers cut only certain trees in a forest, leaving younger trees to grow and reproduce so future loggers can return to cut more trees, which in the intervening years have become mature.

- **Trophic levels:** A graphic representation of roles in an ecosystem. Naturalists often represent trophic levels as a kind of biological "food pyramid," with "producers" in the largest section on the bottom, **herbivore** "consumers" like rabbits and deer in the middle section, and **carnivore** "consumers" like wolves and hawks making up the smallest section at the top.

  Producers are green plants, including trees, bushes, herbs (flowers), ferns, algae, and other green plants. Producers make their own food from sunlight, soil minerals, water, and air. Consumers don't make their own food. Instead, they feed either on producers (plants) or on other consumers. Animals are the most common form of consumers, but funguses and bacteria also fit into this category because they feed on other organisms as well.

  A category's size in the food pyramid is a representation of its biomass (weight) in the natural world. There are more plants in the world than there are herbivores (plant eaters), and there are more herbivores in the world than there are carnivores (meat eaters).

- **Water cycle:** A natural cycle in which water evaporates from plants, oceans, or rivers and rises into the air. There it condenses to form clouds. When the clouds get too heavy with water, raindrops form and fall to the earth. Plants and soil absorb some of the water; the rest runs into streams, rivers, lakes, and eventually the ocean. Then the water cycle starts all over again with evaporation. The earth continually recycles the same water molecules over and over again through this process of evaporation, condensation, and precipitation.

# References

Scott, Michael. 1995. *The Young Oxford Book of Ecology.* New York: Oxford University Press. 160pp. $30.00. ISBN 0-19-521166-9.

# Reviewing the "Four Laws of Ecology" Activity

**Grade Level:** 4–9

**Environmental Themes:** interdependence, Commoner's Four Laws of Ecology

**Curriculum Areas:** science, social studies, language arts

**Student Skills:** comprehension, problem solving, inferring, comparison

**Materials:** poster of Commoner's Four Laws of Ecology, paper, pencils

## Instructions:

1.  Put up a poster of all four of Barry Commoner's "Four Laws of Ecology." Ask students to provide examples from their own lives that demonstrate those laws. Are there times when those laws don't seem to apply?

2.  Ask students to write down examples of a time when they noticed one of the "laws" in action. What happened? How did it make them feel?

3.  Have students share examples with a partner or a small group. At this point students will be sharing short personal stories.

## Evaluation:

Have students write down their "Laws of Ecology" stories in essay form. Did the examples that students gave make sense? Were the students able to translate the theoretical "Laws of Ecology" into their own words so they made sense in their own experiences?

From Kevin Strauss, *Tales with Tails: Storytelling the Wonders of the Natural World.* Westport, CT: Libraries Unlimited, 2006. Copyright © 2006 by Kevin Strauss.

# Ecology Tales Activity

**Grade Level:** 4–9

**Environmental Themes:** adaptation, habitat

**Curriculum Areas:** science, social studies

**Student Skills:** comprehension, problem solving, inferring, comparison

**Materials:** copies of folktales, paper, pencils

**Instructions:**

1. Starting with Commoner's "Four Laws of Ecology," reword the laws in terms that students develop.

2. Look for stories that either demonstrate or refute those laws. Compare and contrast those two kinds of stories. Are they really opposites of each other? Why do you think people would tell both kinds of stories? Discuss this as a class or in small groups.

3. Retell the "Four Laws of Ecology" stories either individually or in a play at an Earth Day or Arbor Day event for your school or library.

**Evaluation:**

Were students able to find stories that either supported or refuted the "Four Laws of Ecology?" Did students take part in class or small group discussions of why people would tell both kinds of stories?

From Kevin Strauss, *Tales with Tails: Storytelling the Wonders of the Natural World.* Westport, CT: Libraries Unlimited, 2006. Copyright © 2006 by Kevin Strauss.

# Chapter 3

## A Crash Course in Storytelling (for Educators and Students)

*Three apples fell from heaven. One for the teller, one for the listener and one for the person who took the story to heart.*

—Armenian proverb

## Kinds of Stories

Now that you are plunging into the world of storytelling and know some of the definitions, you should become familiar with the kinds of stories you will find here. This section acts as your map through the landscape of storytelling.

- **Fable or anecdote:** A short story that contains a clear moral or message. While some versions of "Aesop's Fables" end with the phrase, "The moral of the story is . . . " modern storytellers seldom pound the moral into their listeners' ears. If a story is a good story, you don't need to say the moral for listeners to "get it." "The Tortoise and the Hare" is one example of a fable.

- **Fairy tale:** A longer story that involves supernatural intervention by fairies, witches, or other magical folk. Common collections include "Grimm's Fairy Tales." "Cinderella" is an example of a fairy tale.

- **Folktale:** Sometimes a catchall term for traditional stories told by "the people" (or folk). More specifically, folktales are similar to fairy tales in that they are longer stories. But these stories don't involve supernatural intervention. "Little Red Riding Hood" and the "Three Billy Goats Gruff" are examples of folktales.

- **"Why," "pourquoi," or explanation stories:** Stories that explain how things got to be the way they are, such as how bear got a short tail or why rabbits have long ears.

- **Myths:** Stories that demonstrate the worldview of a particular group of people during a particular period of time. Most religious stories fall into this category. "Myth" acquired its secondary meaning of "things that aren't true" when members of one religious group tried to discredit the beliefs of another religious group. Creation stories are an example of mythic tales.

21

- **Legends:** Stories that may have begun as historical tales but grew and developed fictional or "mythic" aspects over time. The legends of King Arthur and the Knights of the Round Table are an example of this kind of story.

- **Tall tales:** Stories that include unbelievable or exaggerated events. The stories of Paul Bunyan and Pecos Bill are examples. The characters are often giants or have giant-sized abilities, like the ability to cut down a forest of trees with one swing of an ax, the way Paul Bunyan does.

- **Personal stories:** Stories of something that happened to you or your family. While these stories are based on factual events, a storyteller might "improve upon" facts to make a narrative flow better. This doesn't make it a fictional story; it is merely "creative nonfiction." Remember that a story can be "true" even if every element isn't perfectly "factual."

- **Histories**: Personal stories that happened to someone that we don't know. While some high school history teachers will teach history as if it is an endless series of dates and rulers, my favorite history teacher just told us stories about the people who made up European history. Historians sometimes get nervous when someone takes history and turns it into a narrative. Storytellers have to make some assumptions when telling a story, but by putting the "story" back in "history" we can help listeners care about what happened in England in 1066 or why our government invented the Social Security system.

# How to Become a Storyteller

You probably already tell stories. You may not think of the narratives you tell as "stories," but that is exactly what they are. Everyone is born with the tools to tell stories. Some people decide that they want to tell stories as a job, or as part of their "day job" at a school, library, office, clinic, or consulting service. Others share stories with their families and friends. Whether you decide to pursue storytelling as a profession or to tell as an inspired amateur, the way to be a good storyteller is to practice and tell stories as much as possible. Like any other skill or art form, the more you do it, the better you get. But the most important thing is that you give yourself license to tell stories. Remember that while it seems like it is a great leap to go from being a story listener to a storyteller, it is really only a distance of about three inches: the distance from your ear to your mouth. Once you hear a good story, all you have to do is retell it in your own way and suddenly, you are a storyteller. What's more, a good story will carry you over that short distance with ease.

## Finding a Story

There are many good resources for environmental stories. Start with the stories that you already know. How can those stories help you to teach about nature?

This book includes more than 60 stories for you to use. Also check out the book and Internet listings in the bibliography. Visit your library. Section 398.2 under the Dewey Decimal system, and the children's section, J398.2, have great story resources. If after searching you just can't find a story that fits your needs, then you may need to adapt a story or create an original story. Learn about that in Chapter 5.

## Learning a Story

There are many ways to learn and tell a story, but I have found that the steps below work well for both beginning and experienced storytellers.

### *Begin with a Short Tale That You Love*

It is difficult to tell any story that doesn't appeal to you. To tell a story well, you have to be invested in the story. The story should connect with you on an emotional level. That way, you will spend the time to craft the story and to tell it well. If you feel that you "must" tell a particular story whether you like it or not, it will probably come out with as much energy as the Shakespeare poem that you had to memorize and perform in sixth grade. While it is possible to tell a story that you don't like, I wouldn't recommend it, for you or your listeners. Storytelling should be an avocation, something you like to do; otherwise it will be very difficult to do it well.

When I started telling stories as a naturalist, I would flip through folktale books looking for a story about a particular species like a deer or a bear. I would read the story a couple times and then try it out with students. It only took a couple of times for me to realize that something wasn't working right. I noticed that partway through the story, I wasn't enjoying telling it, and that was coming through in my performance. My listeners' eyes glazed over and they began fidgeting or looking away.

Especially when you are starting out in storytelling, choose stories that are only one to three pages long and can be told in three to five minutes. After you have learned a few shorter tales you will be ready to move on to longer stories.

### Read the Story Four Times

Read the story once to make sure that you like it. Read it again for the plot line. Read it a third time for the dialogue, and read it once more to put it all together. Then put the book away for a while. After reading a story four times, it should be stuck in your brain.

### Think about the Setting of the Story

All stories are related to a place, and the storyteller must bring that sense of place to life for listeners. Close your eyes and imagine the surroundings in a story. Try to describe them with all five senses. You don't want to "tell" people about the story setting; you want to "take" them to that place, using vivid descriptions and strong verbs to carry the action.

### Make a Story Outline

Think of the story as if it were a series of pictures in your head (not just words on a page). While some storytellers do well writing out a text outline of the story, I prefer to use a "Story Scene Outline" (see sidebar).

---

**The Story Scene Outline**

Draw four boxes on a piece of paper. Draw a picture of the opening scene of the story in the first box. Draw a picture of the closing scene of the story in the last box. Then draw pictures in the second and third boxes to get listeners from the beginning to the end of the story. Now you have four pictures that carry you from the beginning to the end of the story. It is these images that you will be remembering when you tell the story. When telling your story, move from describing one picture to describing the next, fleshing out the story as you go. By connecting these picture events in a narrative, you will complete the story.

Think about a story as something that you tell "scene by scene," not "word by word." The idea is that tellers should not try to memorize the text of a story. Tellers often use the words from a text, or words that they hear from another storyteller, to create story images in their heads. But when they retell the story, they retell it by describing those pictures in their own words.

As you become more familiar with the story scene outline, making story pictures in your head will become second nature. Soon you won't even need to write it down; you will just automatically make it in your head.

---

### Practice, Practice, Practice

Tell your story into a tape recorder, in front of a mirror, in the shower, in the car, and with your friends and family. You will notice that the more often you tell a particular story, the more it grows and changes into your own unique version of that tale. The more a story grows, the better it gets and the easier it will be for you to tell. I am a big fan of digital tape recorders for story practice. These recorders let you record hours of story practice without leaving you with dozens of unlabeled practice cassette tapes to clutter up your desk.

### Know How to Start a Story and How to End It

Always know how you will start your story (like "Once upon a time . . ." or "Long, long ago . . . ") and how you will end it (like "they lived happily ever after" or "and that's the end of the story") . Knowing the first line and the last line of your story will give you "bookends" or "boarders" to the story. Those boarders help me feel more comfortable when telling a new tale. A pause before the last line of a story can add to its power.

### Tell the Story to Strangers

You can read about storytelling and practice storytelling all you want, but until you tell a story to another person, you aren't a storyteller. This is one of the scariest parts of the process, but it is also the most rewarding. If you are a teacher, librarian, or naturalist, then your job gives you a built-in audience. If you don't have an audience already, volunteer to tell stories at a school library or at an open mic performance, so you can "get your feet wet" in the world of storytelling.

### Get Involved with Some Local, Regional, or National Storytelling Organizations

Joining a storytelling group will help you learn new storytelling techniques, hone the skills you already have, and practice the art of storytelling in a supportive environment. The National Storytelling Network (NSN) is the national storytelling organization in the United States. Its Web site (www.storynet.org) has links to other regional and local storytelling organizations across the country. It also has a storyteller directory, a calendar of events, and links to story Web sites. NSN holds a conference in mid-July each year.

## Telling a Story

Storytelling is a lot like learning to ride a bike. We start on tricycles and then get a bike with training wheels. Once we have our balance, the training wheels come off and we sail down the street on our two-wheel bike. Soon it is second nature to balance on two skinny wheels. In my mind, learning a story is the "tricycle stage"; telling a story to a tape recorder, mirror, or pet is the "training wheel stage"; and telling a story to another person is riding the bike.

At some point you have to take the training wheels off and tell a story. This can be a scary thing. You are going on a quest. But the dragon you face isn't a 50-foot, fire-breathing reptile, it is your own fear of public speaking and embarrassment. In a recent survey people reported having a greater fear of public speaking than any other fear, including fear of death. So if you're nervous, it's normal.

Something that I like to keep in mind is that when I am telling stories, I am not what the audience is there to see. I am just the conduit for the story. It is the story that people want to hear. It is the story that is important. That idea makes me less nervous and reminds me of my real role in the act of storytelling.

### What About Performance Techniques?

The best storytellers I know don't focus much on "performance techniques" like stage voice, body language, or theatrical movement. They just tell their stories, putting them on and inhabiting them like a well-worn shirt. The "techniques" they use arise naturally out of the stories that they tell. Don't worry about "performance techniques" until you have told stories for at least a year. Just learn and tell good stories that you love. The rest will take care of itself.

When it is time to tell a story, take a breath, pause, look into the eyes of your listeners, start your story, and let the magic happen.

# Putting Together a Story Program

When I took the step from telling individual stories as part of environmental education lessons to crafting 45-minute storytelling school performances, I realized that story programs are a whole different animal compared to telling one lone story. In some ways a story "concert" or performance has some parallels with a music concert. When I am putting together a story performance, I use the following structure:

1. An opener story—this is often a short, funny story that sets the stage for the rest of the performance. Sometimes I open a program with "The Talkative Turtle" or "The Wide Mouth Frog" (both in Chapter 9).

2. A longer second story, like "Why Bear Has a Stumpy Tail" (Chapter 6) or "Wolf and Mouse as Farmers" (Chapter 7).

3. A short third story, like "Why Wolf Lives in the Woods" or "Deer's Antlers" (both in Chapter 6).

4. Alternating longer and shorter stories.

5. A closing or "Amen" story that has a punch and leaves them with a strong, memorable message that wraps up the program into a package so listeners can take it home. Closing stories include "The World's First Wolf" and "It's in Your Hands" (Chapter 13).

Since I often perform nature story programs, I want students to hear the language of science as well as the language of story. So between stories, I use props like puppets, animal pelts, and animal skulls to talk about the biology of the animals in the stories. My goal is to show listeners that story and science are not in opposition to each other. Rather, stories and science are two different and equally important tools for helping us to understand our world.

## Of Storytelling and Butterflies

In *Sea of Cortez,* John Steinbeck describes the difference between a "field biologist" and a "lab biologist." He contends that a field biologist is the "real" biologist because he is studying the real animals, not dead creatures pickled in formaldehyde.

That got me thinking about the similarities between storytelling and butterfly biologists. From my perspective, spoken word stories are like butterflies skimming across the meadow from flower to flower. They are beautiful, but they move so quickly that they are difficult to study. That is why some biologists catch butterflies in a net, kill them, and pin their wings to a board. That process of capturing and preserving a butterfly seems analogous to recording and preserving a story by writing it down in a book or recording it on a tape or CD. That preserved butterfly will never change, grow, or reproduce, but we can learn a great deal from it. Those written or recorded stories also will never change or adapt. In some artistic ways, they are dead, but we can learn a great deal from them, now and in the future.

But just as both kinds of butterflies (alive and preserved) are important in biology, we need both kinds of stories as well. We can measure and study the preserved butterfly. In the same way, we can compare, study, and preserve stories in books and recordings.

Just as a preserved butterfly is different from a living one, a written story is different from a spoken one. I believe that a story only lives on the tongue of its teller. It is the job of a storyteller to take the written version of a story out of a book and breathe new life into it on a stage or at the kitchen table. Unlike biologists with their butterflies, storytellers can bring preserved stories back to life. Metaphorically, it is our job to take those dead, preserved story butterflies off the foam boards and breathe life into them so they can skim, dance, and live in the meadow of our lives once again.

# Storytelling Ethics

While storytelling is an art form, for some tellers it is also a business and for some a cultural tradition. Just as legal codes help people get along in civil society, an ethical code helps us get along in this artistic society.

When I was first learning about storytelling, "storytelling ethics" was a scary topic. I, like most people, didn't want to commit any unethical (or illegal) storytelling behavior. The problem was that there didn't seem to be any hard and fast rules for how to be an ethical storyteller. What was worse, during these ethics discussions, I sometimes felt like only "certain people" had the ethical right to tell certain stories. This made me nervous. I wasn't sure which stories I was "allowed" to tell and which I wasn't. I think all storytellers struggle with these issues. What follows are some guidelines, more of a map really, to help new and experienced tellers cross the dangerous and sometimes intractable sea of "storytelling ethics."

## Copyright Law

When dealing with ethics, start with the law. Our society developed copyright laws to protect authors and help them receive payment for their artistic work. When an author writes an original work, it is automatically copyright protected. That means that someone else can't take that work, put his name on it, and publish it or sell it. While original work is copyright protected as soon as an author creates it, to get maximum protection under the law, it is a good idea to register a work with the United States Copyright Office (www.copyright.gov/).

Under the law, you can only copyright original work, like a fictional story or a "word for word" adaptation of "public domain" stories like "Little Red Riding Hood." A story is considered in the public domain and usable by anyone if it is a traditional folktale (having been told for hundreds of years already) or its copyright has lapsed. Although the length of copyright does change, it is now set at the life of the author plus 70 years. A good guideline is to consider any written work that is older than 100 years in the public domain.

### Original Material Ethics

Original literary work and poetry as well as personal stories, family stories, and original tales, even if they sound like "traditional" folktales, are the copyright-protected property of the work's creator. To perform this kind of material, you must secure permission from either the author (or storyteller) or the publisher. Teachers and librarians can perform copyrighted work at their own school or library under the "fair use" clause of the copyright law. But once you are traveling to other schools and libraries as a paid professional storyteller, you need to get permission to perform copyrighted work. You should always credit the author when performing that person's work. Many storytellers do this in their introduction with a statement like "This is *Why Owl Has Big Eyes* by Jane Doe, told with permission."

### The Golden Rule Approach

I believe that stories live on the tongues of storytellers. I also believe that stories are one of the gifts we can share with each other. It is our job as people to give and to receive these gifts. Many tellers advocate the "Golden Rule" in storytelling: "Do unto others (and their stories) as you would have them do unto you (and your stories)."

Respect the tellers and the cultures that gave us the stories that we tell. Cite your sources (Mooney and Holt, 1996). Phrases like "this is a story from the Ashanti people of Ghana" or "Long ago in the land of Finland, people say . . . " can effectively credit a culture and set the scene for a tale. Also, learn about the cultures that created your stories. Were the stories told only at a certain time of year? Were the stories told for a particular reason? This knowledge will help you tell those stories more effectively by helping you understand the setting and the context of a story.

## Folktale Ethics

Traditional folktales like Aesop's fables and Grimm's fairy tales are "public domain" stories according to the law, meaning that a storyteller can't legally forbid other tellers from telling traditional folktales, such as "Little Red Riding Hood." Where this can get sticky is when a storyteller copyrights a particular version of Little Red. In that case, that "word for word" version of the story belongs to the author. To avoid problems with this, look for several versions of a story you would like to tell. Read them over, close the books, make a story scene outline, and start telling your own version of the story. The more that you tell a story "scene by scene," the more you will craft your own unique version of the tale.

## Performance Imitation

In many art forms, apprentices learn by copying the work of a master. The same is true in storytelling. Beginning storytellers often learn the craft by "copying" and retelling versions of a story that they heard from another storyteller. It is important to remember that this is only a learning technique. Once you are performing at schools or on a stage as a professional storyteller, it is part of your job to find your own stories and craft them into your own unique version of that tale. In my mind, a professional storyteller should either be finding and telling folktales that other storytellers aren't performing or recrafting well-known stories in new and interesting ways.

If you hear someone else's version of a traditional story and would like to retell it, talk with the teller and find out where he or she found it (Geisler, 1997). If you intend to perform the story, do some research and develop your own recrafted version of that story. Often by reading two or three versions of a particular story, making a story scene outline, and retelling a story a few times, you will have recrafted your own version of a story.

## Telling Religious Stories

Often questions of who is "allowed" to tell a certain story arise when telling religious stories. While the Christian Bible, Jewish Torah, and Muslim Koran are some of the most identifiable religious texts, every culture in the world has stories that represent its cultural worldview. In this context, the oral creation tales of the Lakota are just as "religious" as written scriptures from other cultures. These religious stories help people explain how the world works and define our place in it. Because religious or "mythic" stories play such an important role in many cultures, it isn't surprising that some groups are nervous about "outsiders" telling that group's religious stories.

Storyteller Dan Keding deals with these issues by not telling the religious stories of other existing cultures. He does retell the myths of the ancient Greeks and ancient Egyptians, since those cultures no longer exist. But he doesn't retell tales from the Muslim Koran or the creation tales of the Lakota. While this approach may not work for everyone, it does allow Keding to avoid the concerns some people have about telling religious stories. Many storytellers restrict their telling of religious stories to those of their own culture. I feel comfortable retelling stories from the Christian tradition since I was raised in that tradition.

Here it is also important to point out the difference between "mythic" religious stories and lesson stories. Mythic religious stories, like the creation story in the Jewish Torah or the crucifixion of Jesus in the Christian Bible's book of Matthew describe the worldview of a people. These are the kinds of stories that people are most protective of. If a religious or cultural group allows "outsiders" to tell their stories too often, those outsiders could conceivably redefine that group and its stories.

But there are other stories with religious content that are more historical or educational in nature. Catholic stories about St. Francis of Assisi, stories about the Muslim wise fool known as Nasrudin, and the many Jewish wisdom tales told by religious teachers like Rabbi Jacob Kranz (the Maggid of Dubno, Poland) are lesson stories that all cultures can benefit from. In my experience, no one has questioned my use of these kinds of stories in my programs. These lesson stories are different from "mythic" stories in that they don't explain how the world was created or who God is. They simply teach lessons on universal themes like kindness, creativity, or generosity.

## Can Just Anyone Tell Native American Stories?

At environmental storytelling workshops, this is one of the most common questions that I hear. Like me, many naturalists cut their storytelling teeth on books like *Keepers of the Earth* by Michael Caduto and Joseph Bruchac. This series of books combines traditional Native American stories with environmental education activities. But now there is some debate in the storytelling world about whether it is appropriate for non-native storytellers to tell native stories. My best answer to "Can anyone tell Native American stories?" is "maybe."

The answer really depends on the story and the Native American nation that first told it. Each of the more than 400 native cultures in North America has its own traditions for when, where, and how to tell certain stories. There is even debate within some native nations about when their stories should be told. As a German American storyteller, I am no expert on the Ojibwa people who live in my region, to say nothing of the other native cultures. But as a naturalist storyteller, I have wrestled with this question and come to the following conclusions:

1. **You don't need to tell Native American stories to tell environmental stories.** Every culture around the world has environmental stories. It is just a matter of finding them. This book and others listed in the bibliography have done that.

2. **Some Native American stories may not be appropriate for environmental education programs.** Native American stories, like all stories, are artifacts of their home culture. As an environmental storyteller, I want to tell stories about animals and plants, not about the cultural beliefs of the Ojibwa or Lakota. Some Native American stories contain cultural lessons that fit well in that nation's cultural context but aren't very useful for some environmental education or library programs. Remember, just because a story comes from a Native American culture doesn't mean that it is an environmental story.

3. **White people often don't understand other cultures.** In my experience, many European Americans seem to think about stories differently than do many Ojibwa or Lakota people. Even well-meaning white people are used to defining "religious" stories as stories in the Christian Bible or the Jewish Torah. We call everything else "secular stories." This view can get us into trouble when we tell stories from other cultures that don't share this view. It might lead us to assume that the oral stories of the Ojibwa aren't religious and that they shouldn't receive the same respect we accord to Christian Bible stories. In the majority white culture, we are also used to taking what we want. We should always remember the Golden Rule.

4. **Ethnic restrictions will hurt this art form.** As a storytelling community, we need to realize that if we begin restricting the telling of certain stories to certain racial or cultural groups, we will be opening a Pandora's box of issues: Does it matter if you were raised in the culture that first told the story? What percentage of blood relation "qualifies" you to tell certain stories? Does my German heritage qualify me to tell only German stories, or can I tell stories from all across Europe? Are Grimm's fairytales "fair game" for anyone to tell, or do you have to be German to tell "Little Red Riding Hood"? Do storytelling restrictions apply only to native or minority cultures, or to all cultures?

Does all this mean that non-natives shouldn't tell Native American Stories? No. But it does mean that we should be careful about the stories we tell from minority cultures and how we tell them.

### *Guidelines for Non-Natives Telling Native American Stories*

1. Learn about the native nation that first told the story you want to tell. Find out that culture's storytelling traditions and guidelines.

2. Ideally, learn stories from a native teller. An Ojibwa storyteller is more likely to know the cultural context of his or her culture's stories than a non-native teacher (Bruchac, 1996).

3. If you can't find a native teacher, use book resources that were written by native authors and storytellers as your source material.

4. Be very careful about using stories that seem to be creation stories or religious tales. Just as I wouldn't presume to tell a religious story from the Koran without doing a lot of research, I would be uncomfortable about telling an Ojibwa creation myth without knowing a lot about the Ojibwa people and their storytelling traditions. This is one of those "fuzzy" areas in storytelling. As a storyteller, I believe that it is my job to take care of the stories that I know and pass them on in a respectful manner. This is hard to do if I know nothing about a group's storytelling and religious traditions.

### *Alternatives to Telling Native American Stories*

If you decide in the end that the Native American stories that you can find don't fit your storytelling needs, there are several alternatives to telling Native American stories in environmental education programs.

#### Nature Explanation Stories

- Europe has animals and animal stories similar to some in North America.

- African American stories often focus on animals like the trickster rabbit and trouble-making fox.

- Adapt stories from other nations and settings to fit here in North America with North American animals (Chapter 4).

- Create original animal and plant stories (Chapter 4).

#### Ecological Lesson Stories

- Find stories from non-native cultures that contain the themes you are looking for. Many "values stories" from the Jewish, Islamic, Hindu, and Christian traditions highlight ecological values like generosity, responsibility, and kindness. Remember, ecological values are human values.

## Responding to Critics

Although it is unlikely that anyone will ever criticize you for telling a particular story, especially if you follow the guidelines above, it may happen. Sometimes people are critical for legitimate cultural or ethical reasons. Sometimes they are critical to prove that they are "right" or that they know more than you do. Sometimes they are critical to stake out their own storytelling "territory" and protect it from competitors.

Regardless of the reason behind the criticism, resist your first impulse to be defensive and explain why you tell the stories that you do. This is one of those situations where your ears will get you farther than your mouth. Ask the person to explain his or her concerns. Ask for resources you could go to for more information about those concerns. Thank the person for his or her perspective, and then *walk away*.

Don't make any rash decisions based on the criticism. Give yourself a week or more to think about the criticism. Did it make sense to you? Did the critic have the story's (or the culture's) best interests in mind, or could his or her motivations have been more self-serving? Talk about your concerns with your peers. After a week, decide to either make changes in how you operate or dismiss the criticism. Realize that no matter what you do, 10 percent of people in the world will find fault with it. It simply isn't possible to please all of the people all of the time.

## The Man, the Boy, and Their Donkey (Aesop)

Once a man and his son were leading their donkey to market. They passed a group of people on the road and the people began to murmur, "They are foolish. Why aren't they riding their donkey?" So the man and his son climbed up on the donkey's back. They passed another crowd and heard those people say, "Look at what they are doing to that poor beast. They are riding it to death." Not wanting to insult those people or ride their donkey to death, the man and son got off the donkey and lifted it up on their shoulders. As they were crossing a bridge over a river, the donkey, nervous at being carried, began to kick. The man and son dropped the squirming donkey into the river, where it drowned. A crowd walked by and told the man and his son how foolish they were for carrying the donkey. When they heard why the man and his son were carrying the donkey, they just shook their heads. One old man said, "Sometimes you have to choose who you listen to."

# When to Use Stories in Education

While teachers, naturalists, and environmental educators could present an entire educational program using environmental stories, most likely you will use individual stories to make a point in an education lesson that may also contain lecture, hands-on activities, and outdoor explorations. There are three points in any educational lesson at which a story could be used effectively: the opening, transitions, and the closing.

- **Opener:** Use a story to lead off a lesson. When I am teaching a lesson on forest diversity, I might start with a diversity-themed story like "The Tinker and the Clock" (Chapter 13). Then I would return to the story at the end of the class and ask students what that story had to do with the lesson they just completed. Stories like "Why the Sky Is up So High" and "The Frog Hunt" (both in Chapter 13) are good for these situations.

- **Closer:** Use a story at the end of a lesson as the "pow!" that will inspire students to take a lesson to heart. Stories like "It's in Your Hands" (Chapter 13) are good for these situations.

- **Transition times and rest times:** Outdoor environmental education programs often involve hiking. Rest times on a hike or transition times between topics can be great opportunities to introduce a story. Stories used at these times can get students to think about a topic in a new way and help them give their "logical/mathematical" brains a rest while they use their "auditory" and creative intelligences. Short tales like Aesop's fables can fit well as transitions. I tell "Deer's Antlers" (Chapter 6) as a way to talk about the various adaptations or "tools" that deer have to help them survive in the forest. As students sit in the forest, looking at all those low-hanging branches, the story takes on a new dimension for them.

# References

Bruchac, Joseph. 1996. *Roots of Survival: Native American Storytelling and the Sacred.* Golden, CO: Fulcrum Publishing. 206pp. $24.95. ISBN 1-55591-145-5.

Geisler, Harlynne. 1997. *Storytelling Professionally: The Nuts and Bolts of a Working Performer.* Englewood, CO: Libraries Unlimited. 151pp. $25.00pa. ISBN 1-56308-370-1pa.

Mooney, Bill, and David Holt. 1996. *The Storytellers Guide: Storytellers Share Advice for the Classroom, boardroom, Showroom, Podium, Pulpit and Center Stage.* Little Rock, AR: August House. 208pp. $23.95pa. ISBN 0-87483-482-1pa.

# Taking the Plunge
# (into Storytelling) Activity

**Grade Level:** 6–12

**Environmental Themes:** none

**Curriculum Areas:** language arts, social studies

**Student Skills:** comprehension, sequencing, public speaking

**Materials:** copies of Aesop's fables from Chapters 6–13, paper, pencils, lots of courage

## Instructions:

1. Ask students to choose an Aesop's fable or another short story from Chapters 6–13. Have them go through the steps for learning a new story (Chapter 3).

2. Then have the students pair up and tell their story to their partners in one minute. They can use their "story scene outline" if they need it. Ask students how they feel about the story that they just told. Is that the way you would normally tell a story to someone?

3. Have students retell their stories in three minutes. What was different about this retelling? Was it a better story this way? What did they have to add to the story to make it last three minutes?

4. Have students retell their stories in five minutes. What was different about this retelling? Was it a better story this way? What did they have to add to the story to make it last five minutes? What length story was the easiest to tell? What length story was the most fun to listen to? Why do they think this is the case?

## Evaluation:

Have students form groups of four and retell their five-minute stories again. Ask volunteers to share their stories with the entire class. Have students write down their versions of that story. How are their versions different from the original? How are their versions the same? Which version do they like better?

From Kevin Strauss, *Tales with Tails: Storytelling the Wonders of the Natural World.* Westport, CT: Libraries Unlimited, 2006. Copyright © 2006 by Kevin Strauss.

# Jabbertalk Activity

**Grade Level:** 6–12

**Environmental Themes:** adaptation

**Curriculum Areas:** language arts, social studies

**Student Skills:** creativity, comprehension, problem solving, inferring, visual communication

**Materials:** copies of Aesop's fables from Chapters 6–13

## Instructions:

There are many ways to communicate a story. Through this activity, students will get a chance to use body language and facial expressions to tell a story.

1. Using the same story that they learned in the "Taking the Plunge" activity, have students get new partners and attempt to tell the story to that partner using nothing but nonsense words and body language. The goal is to get students to realize how much body language they use in their storytelling. Although participants will at first be reluctant to try this activity, after the teacher demonstrates how to "Jabbertalk" a well-known story like "Little Red Riding Hood" they will jump right in. Allow each partner a chance to jabbertalk a story for a minute or so.

2. Ask volunteers to demonstrate their jabbertalk story and then have students guess what story it is (partners can't guess since they already know what the story is).

## Evaluation:

Did this activity get easier the more you did it? What did you learn from this activity?

From Kevin Strauss, *Tales with Tails: Storytelling the Wonders of the Natural World.* Westport, CT: Libraries Unlimited, 2006. Copyright © 2006 by Kevin Strauss.

# Clothing Stories Activity

**Grade Level:** 1–12

**Environmental Themes:** adaptation

**Curriculum Areas:** social studies, history, language arts

**Student Skills:** interpersonal communication, listening, inferring

**Materials:** none

**Instructions:**

1. Have students pair up. Then ask them to spend one minute telling their partners about an item of clothing or jewelry they are wearing.

2. Switch and have the other partners tell a clothing story.

3. If you have older students and a small class, ask volunteers to retell the clothing story that they heard from their partners.

**Evaluation:**

- What happened to the noise level in the room while people were telling "Clothing Stories?"

- What emotion did you notice in the room? (Usually it is joy or excitement.)

- How did students know if their partners were listening to their stories?

- Which was more fun, telling or listening? Why?

This is a good "icebreaker" activity to get people to meet each other, learn about each other, and realize the power of storytelling.

From Kevin Strauss, *Tales with Tails: Storytelling the Wonders of the Natural World.* Westport, CT: Libraries Unlimited, 2006.
Copyright © 2006 by Kevin Strauss.

# Chapter 4

## Adapting or Developing New Environmental Stories

### Prometheus and the Animals

Long ago the gods were lazy. They made the land and the seas, but couldn't be bothered to make all of the animals that would live in the world. Zeus passed that job over to Prometheus, a titan. Now some would balk at such a difficult job, but not a titan named "forethought." He was a natural-born planner, and he loved to make things.

"If there is nothing there, then I will have to make it," he said as he set to work. He began deciding what kinds of animals the world would need. Gathering clay and mud, leaves and sticks, and some of the magic from Mount Olympus, Prometheus made animals like deer and rabbits to trim the plants, so they wouldn't grow across the forest paths. He made animals like wolves and foxes to feed on the deer and rabbits so they didn't eat all of the plants in the world.

For centuries, the titan toiled at his work. One day, Prometheus looked at the list of jobs that Zeus had given him. It was still very long. He began to think that he would never complete this task, and that made him angry. Why should he work so hard as the gods lazed around in the shade?

In a moment of anger, Prometheus lifted the huge half-finished creature he was making and smashed it on the ground. The creature broke into a thousand, thousand pieces. But those pieces were no longer just clay and wood. They had touched the hands of a god. Those tiny pieces sprouted wings and tiny legs. They scurried or flew or hopped into the world. They were the first insects and spiders, and to this day they do the thousands of jobs that other creatures cannot do: pollinating flowers, consuming the dead, and feeding the smallest birds and bats. That's the way it was and that's the way that it is and that's the end of the story (a tale inspired by Greek mythology).

We all have times when we are looking for a story and we just can't find it. Either the story doesn't exist or it isn't easy to find. If you can't find appropriate environmental stories to tell, you may have to adapt or create a new story to fill a story need. Just as Prometheus used mud and sticks to make the first animals, you can draw pieces from the existing story and natural resources in the world to create new stories. This is a lot more work than simply finding and learning a story. But if you take the time to adapt a traditional story or create an original story, it will be much better suited to the environmental lesson you are teaching.

# Adapting Existing Stories

When seeking new environmental stories, the first place to look is the treasure trove of existing traditional stories found in our hearts, memories, and books. For thousands of years, storytellers who immigrated to new lands took their stories with them, adapted them to new environments, and shared them far and wide. For example, many African American folktales told for generations have echoes of tales from Ghana and Kenya, but the newer American versions include animal species found in North America, not in Africa, such as the blue jay or the black bear.

In Chapter 1, I briefly discussed adapting folktales. As a general rule, it is fine to change the setting of a story and the animal characters. Those changes have been part of the storytelling tradition for thousands of years. But to retain the essence, or the "heart," of the story, don't change essential events of the story like the plot or the ending. When I change the animal characters in a story, I look for similar animals in North America. The story "Turtle Wins at Tug-of-War" (Chapter 9) is found in both the African American tradition and the traditions of the nation of Nigeria. When I adapted the Nigerian story, I changed the main character, the elephant, into a bear because they are both big land animals. I changed the hippopotamus into a moose because they are both big animals that spend a lot of time in the water. Turtle stayed the same because turtles are found here. I later realized that I wasn't the first one to adapt this Nigerian folktale; African American storytellers did the same thing in the 1700s and 1800s. Their version of the story also involves Bear and Turtle.

When adapting stories, it is important to be respectful. It may be inappropriate to adapt another culture's religious stories. Likewise, to take a traditional story from one country and adapt it so it sounds like a traditional story from another country (e.g., taking a traditional Russian story with a witch character and turning it into a traditional-sounding Irish story with a leprechaun character) seems dishonest. Generally speaking, animal stories are less likely to have religious connotations in most cultures.

I believe that as long as storytellers are respectful of the stories that they adapt and are honest about what they are doing, they are operating within the long tradition of adaptive storytelling.

# Creating New Stories

If you can't find a good story to adapt, you may have to start from scratch and create your own original environmental tale. Why develop new environmental stories? You may want to develop an original environmental story if the stories that you find

- reinforce negative animal stereotypes,

- are set in too "foreign" an environment, or

- are too anthropomorphic

—or you simply can't find any.

But before you can create a new story, you need to know what makes a story effective, what makes it "work." Start by reading other environmental stories. That will give you a sense of what stories already exist and help you understand the ingredients of a good story. Once you know the elements of a good story and have a sense of the patterns storytellers have used before, it will be easier for you to develop original tales.

# The Anatomy of an Effective Story

Think about the folktales, novels, and movies that you really like. What do they all have in common? They probably have story structure (a beginning, a middle, and an end), compelling characters, a conflict, a resolution, and an important message (either implicit or explicit in the story). Think of these as the ingredients for making a great story soup. Without effective use of all these story ingredients, the story will taste flat.

- **Story structure:** Many good stories have a clear beginning that introduces the characters, a middle in which characters face increasingly difficult challenges, and an ending in which characters resolve the big crisis of the story.

- **Characters:** Characters really drive a good story. If listeners can relate to and sympathize with the characters, they will care about the characters and are more likely to enjoy the story. People need to develop an emotional connection with story characters; otherwise even the best storyline can fall flat. Compelling characters are often underdogs. They have faults, face problems, and often succeed against great odds. Realize that the longer you tell stories, the more likely it is that the characters in your stories may take on some of your personality traits as well. That is just one of those things that happens in storytelling.

- **Challenge or crisis:** All good stories have some kind of crisis or challenge in them. It can be a person versus person challenge, a person versus nature challenge, or a person versus herself challenge. In a person versus person challenge, the main character (or hero) faces a villain. In a person versus nature challenge, the hero faces some natural phenomenon like a flood, a mountain, or a storm. In a person versus herself challenge, the hero needs to battle her own weaknesses or "inner demons."

    While we may prefer a world in which we don't have to face these kinds of challenges, our stories absolutely require a challenge or crisis. Without that element, the story becomes boring and falls flat.

- **Resolution:** Many stories have overt resolutions in which the hero defeats the villain. But other stories have internal resolutions, in which a hero learns something new about himself or finds a way to get what he wants without defeating the villain. All stories need some kind of outcome that gives listeners a sense of closure at the end of the tale.

- **Important message:** One of the great benefits of telling stories is the opportunity to pass on the timeless lessons that stories contain. Traditional stories already contain important lessons. But when you develop an original story, you may have to make sure it is teaching the lessons you want it to teach. Look at what happens to the characters in your story. Is kindness rewarded in the story? Do greedy or rude characters lose in the end? Does the story give a reason why an animal is the way it is today? Does the story give us a new perspective on an animal we normally fear or dislike? Answering these questions will give you a sense for some of the many lessons that a story can teach. Starting a story with a proverb or quote can help you keep a lesson in a new story.

    Lessons can't be overly didactic, though. Many listeners will turn off if it seems that a storyteller is preaching to them. A lesson can be explicit and manifested by the characters in the story, as is typical in Aesop's fables, or it can be implicit and require listeners to think about the story a bit before they understand it. The "Tinker and the Clock" (Chapter 13) is the latter kind of story. Don't worry if your listeners wonder what the story means after they hear it. Stories stick in our minds, and listeners may figure them out upon further reflection.

    Even when telling Aesop's fables, I don't announce "the moral of the story" at the end. In my experience, if the tale itself doesn't teach the lesson, that one line at the end won't be much help. In addition, many listeners stop listening if they are being told how to understand a story. In this way, listeners can develop their own meanings from a story. I also believe that a story may have more than just one lesson or moral. When I ask listeners in a school program what lesson they hear in a particular story, I often get a half dozen different answers.

These discussions illuminate the diversity of people's ideas. It lets them know that there are many "right" answers to the question, "What does this story mean?" I believe that listeners hear the lesson that they most need to hear when they listen to a story.

## Creating Original Explanation Stories

There may be times when you just can't find a useful story to illustrate the concept of, for example, "adaptation" for a nature program. These stories, also known as "pourquoi" or "why" stories, explain how an animal or plant got to be the way it is today. Stories like "Why Bear Has a Stumpy Tail" (Chapter 6) and "How Birds Got Their Colors" (Chapter 8) fall into this category. Remember that these stories can explain a physical feature, like a wolf's sharp teeth, or a behavior, like why the sun lives in the sky.

If you can't find the right kind of explanation story to suit your purposes, take the opportunity to create an original one. The creation of new stories can be daunting, but with a few simple steps and practice, you can develop explanation stories that are as compelling as traditional tales. After all, sometime in the past, a storyteller created "Why Bear Has a Stumpy Tail" and told it to someone else.

### *The Adaptation Story-Builder*

Sometimes it is easier to work backward to create stories that explain things like a beaver's flat tail or a bear's hibernation. Start by drawing four large boxes on a piece of paper. These are your "story boards."

1. Decide what you want your story to teach. Put that at the top of your page. (Do you want a story about how wolves got sharp teeth or why beavers build dams?)

2. Decide on the ending for your story. Draw a picture of this ending in the last box on your paper (e.g., now beaver has a flat, scaly tail).

3. Decide how the animal looked (or acted) when the story started. Draw a picture of this "beginning" in the first box on the paper (e.g., "Once beaver had a round, furry tail like fox and squirrel . . .") .

4. Decide why the animal's body or behavior changes in the story. Did its tail get burned? Or frozen in the ice? Try to make this step logical or at least imaginatively possible. Whatever happened to the animal should be both unexpected and appropriate.

5. Go to the beginning of the story and write the beginning and middle so they meet up with your ending.

Look at stories like "How Snake Lost Her Legs" (Chapter 9) or "How Birds Got Their Colors" (Chapter 8) to see examples of original adaptation stories that I have developed using this technique.

## Turning Proverbs and Quotes into Stories

Using proverbs and quotes can be a great way to trigger new story ideas. The right proverb could also provide you with a strong lesson for a story. When I taught a class in beaver ecology, I wanted to develop a new story about the importance of diversity. I remembered the Aldo Leopold quote "The first law of intelligent tinkering is to save all the parts." From that I began crafting a story about a "Tinker," a traveling repairman, and a clock. I chose the clock because it has several different kinds of gears and springs and other parts. That story became "The Tinker and the Clock" (Chapter 13), and I use it in my environmental story programs today.

Page though a book of proverbs from different countries or use the quotes below to craft an original story:

> *That land is "a community" is the basic concept of ecology, but that land is to be "loved and respected" is an extension of ethics. . . . All ethics . . . rest upon a single premise: the individual is a member of a community of individual parts. . . . The first rule of ecology is: keep all the parts.*
> (Aldo Leopold)

*The Four Laws of Ecology: (1) Everything is connected to everything else; (2) Everything must go somewhere; (3) Nature knows best; and (4) There is no such thing as a free lunch.* (Barry Commoner)

*In wildness is the preservation of the world.* (Henry David Thoreau)

*The politics of growth in America is the politics of denial. We're denying that there's any limit to our ability to continue getting more and more prosperous and using more and more natural resources.* (John Elder)

*Only mature people might utter the two words our civilization most desperately needs to hear: That's enough.* (Bill McKibben)

*No action is without its side effects.* (Barry Commoner)

*When the well is dry, we know the worth of water.* (Ben Franklin)

*The earth speaks to us if we listen, but it doesn't shout above the roar.* (Arleigh Jorgenson)

*When one tugs on a single thing in nature, he finds it attached to the rest of the world.* (John Muir)

*Anyone who questions the ability of an individual to make a difference has never been stuck in a tent with a mosquito.* (Anonymous)

*In the end we will conserve only what we love. We will love only what we understand. And we will understand only what we are taught.* (Baba Dioum, Senegalese conservationist)

*Kindness is remembered, meanness is felt.* (Yiddish)

*Where there is greed, what love can be there?* (Sikh)

*He who grabs for much grasps little.* (Mexico)

*He who has no care for the distant future, will have sorrows in the near future.* (Korea

*The highest wisdom is kindness.* (Yiddish)

*The earth was not given to you by your parents, it was loaned to you by your children.* (Kenya)

*Nothing is to be feared; it is to be understood.* (Marie Curie)

*Use what talent you possess. The woods would be very silent if no bird sang except those who sang the best.* (Henry Van Dyke)

*Start by doing what is necessary. Then what is possible and suddenly, you will be doing the impossible.* (St. Francis of Assisi, the Patron Saint of Ecology)

*It is better to prevent than to regret.* (Brazil)

*An ounce of prevention is worth a pound of cure.* (England)

*We will be known forever by the tracks that we leave.* (Dakota [Native American])

*Rain does not fall on one roof alone.* (Cameroon)

*What goes up must come down. What goes around comes around.* (England and Ojibwa [Native American])

## Turning Natural History into Stories

### *Beware of "Environmental Urban Legends"*

History provides great examples for environmental stories. Talking about how past human choices affect us now can make it easier to illuminate the importance of conservation and pollution control today. Often magazines like *Audubon* or *International Wildlife* or the Giraffe Heroes Web site (www.giraffe. org) can give you ideas for natural history stories and stories about how ordinary people have worked to make a difference in the world.

But be careful about taking some of these "natural histories" at face value. In her research for environmental "fact tales," storyteller Fran Stallings found a great deal of fake environmental history stories. One example is "Parachuting Cats into Borneo." You can find unattributed versions of this story all over the Internet, and that should be your first clue that a story probably isn't true.

# Parachuting Cats into Borneo

In the early 1950s, the Dayak people of Borneo suffered a malarial outbreak. . . .

The World Health Organization (WHO) sprayed the pesticide DDT to kill the mosquitoes that carried the malaria. The mosquitoes died, but so did other insects and lizards and cats. The rat population exploded, and soon WHO had to parachute 14,000 live cats onto Borneo to control the rats.

"Operation Cat Drop," now almost forgotten at the WHO, is a graphic illustration of the interconnectedness of life, and of the fact that the root of problems often stems from their purported solutions.

This is a wonderful story. Unfortunately it isn't true. Stories like "Parachuting Cats into Borneo" are a kind of environmental urban legend. Some of these stories are so good that they spread like wildfire in the environmental education community, often being recorded in nature center lesson plans and even textbooks from the 1980s. The only problem is that like the urban legends of "Spiders in the Hairdo" or "The Choking Doberman" that we all heard as teenagers, these environmental urban legends aren't true either, even though they are often presented as factual natural history.

I first ran into the story "Parachuting Cats into Borneo" when I read it in a lesson plan at a Minnesota nature center. Being a young naturalist, I took it at face value. Later, when I was researching the source of the story, I couldn't find evidence that it actually happened. I did find evidence of parts of the story, but much of it seemed to be fiction. Like all good urban legends, it seems possible and contains a grain of truth.

When searching on the Internet, I found dozens of references to parachuting cats in speeches and Web sites that warned about the dangers of "messing with nature." But I found little factual evidence of the story. When I searched documents from the World Heath Organization I hit pay dirt. In the WHO archives I found a document that confirms that during the 1950s, WHO did sanction the use of DDT in Borneo to control disease-spreading mosquitoes. The spray did kill the malaria-spreading mosquitoes, and malaria rates did go down. The spray also killed wasps that parasitized a hut thatch caterpillar. But that is where the official record ends. There is no report of poisoned lizards, dying cats, or parachuting cats.

### The Danger of Using Environmental Urban Legends

It is perfectly normal for storytellers to tell fables and pourquoi stories as part of our jobs, but we need to be honest about what we are doing. To some extent, when we tell historical stories we are stepping into the role of the historian, and that role has a stricter standard for facts than folklore does. Just as it would be inappropriate for a high school history teacher to teach fake history like "slavery never occurred in the United States," it is inappropriate for storytellers to tell fake natural history, no matter how well-meaning they may be.

Spreading fake natural history stories may seem like a way to build support for environmental stewardship, but doing that builds a house of cards. Once listeners discover that a particular "natural history story" is really just a fairy tale, they will begin to doubt everything else that you told them. Do yourself a favor and maintain your credibility by researching your natural history stories. Besides, with so many documented examples of how humans really are affecting their environment, there are plenty of real natural history stories to tell. It is important that natural histories be history and not another kind of urban legend.

**How to Avoid Environmental Urban Legends**

To avoid perpetuating environmental urban legends, look for a reference on any supposed "natural history story." Most wildlife, science, and nature magazines provide well-researched information.

Factual natural history stories should have references to a doctorate-level researcher and a university or scientific journal article to back them up. Also, ask yourself if this story seems "too good to be true." If it does, perhaps the story isn't true. You can also look for frauds and urban legends using "urban legend" Web sites on the Internet.

Two of my favorite Web resources for natural history stories are from *Science News* magazine:

www.sciencenews.org/

www.sciencenewsforkids.org

While the main Web site provides research-based articles on a wide range of science topics, the "Science News For Kids" section arranges articles by topics. Go to the "environment" section.

Magazines like *Science News, National Geographic, Nature,* and *Discover* provide good research-based information for accurate natural history stories. Many of these magazines also have Web sites.

### *Developing Natural History Stories*

To develop your own natural history stories, follow these steps:

1. Choose an animal or plant to be the center of the story.

2. Research your organism. Find out what it eats, how it lives, and how it protects itself.

3. Then use one of the two options below:

   a. Develop a story based on an encounter your organism has with an enemy or danger. If you choose to tell your story from the organism's perspective, try to do so without being anthropomorphic (e.g., The Three Little Pigs).

   b. Research a real natural history event, such as the extirpation (local extinction) and recovery of beavers in North America or the impact of Dutch elm disease on elm trees and forests in the United States ("Dutch Nightmare on Elmwood Street," Chapter 13).

## Addressing Environmental Issues with Storytelling

Turn on the news any day and you will hear stories about "environmental issues." Problems like global warming, acid rain, species extinctions, air pollution, water pollution, and deforestation seem to be with us to stay. Both sides of the environmental debate use aspects of storytelling in their work. Environmental activists tell stories about the last passenger pigeon or the grandmother who couldn't go for walks in her neighborhood because of the smog. Opponents of environmental programs like the Clean Air Act or the Endangered Species Act tell stories about the "huge" impact that higher fuel efficiency standards and other environmental laws will have on our corporations and, by extension, our jobs.

In many cases, as with any political discussion, the two sides seem to polarize the issue, making it seem that if the conservationists win, our economy will crash and we will all lose our jobs, and if the corporations win, we will be left with poisoned air and drinking water. The truth, of course, lies somewhere in between. The important thing to remember is that we will pay for our actions one way or the other. (There is no such thing as a "free lunch.") Some people argue that it is cheaper and easier to prevent pollution than to clean it up later.

### *An Environmental Issues Primer*

Over 30 years after the first Earth Day celebration, most scientists now agree that solutions to environmental problems are not scientific or technological. Environmental solutions are social and political in nature. We have mountains of scientific evidence describing the reasons for environmental problems like air pollution and species extinction. It has become clear over the past three decades that we possess sufficient knowledge to solve or prevent environmental problems, but as a society our political and corporate leaders lack the will to make the changes needed to protect and preserve our natural environment. In some cases, leaders even question whether air pollution, wildlife extinctions, and other environmental problems are even important in our society. Somewhere there is a disconnect between knowledge of the problems and actions that contribute to solutions.

That's where the public has to get involved. Politicians and business leaders sometimes listen when their constituents or customers vote or spend money in ways that show that we care about protecting the environment in commonsense ways.

Since there are so many environmental issues, and since corporations are now getting more and more savvy about hiring scientists to question the scientific findings of more independent environmental researchers at universities and government institutions, it can sometimes be difficult to know whom to believe. I follow the "democratic approach" to science. By that standard, when 51 percent of Ph.D. scientists in a given field come to a particular conclusion, I figure that should be good enough evidence to have us follow their recommendations. There always seems to be at least one fringe scientist who will claim that global warming doesn't exist, just as there always seems to be at least one historian who argues that the Holocaust never happened. The important thing is to listen to mainstream scientists, not the fringe researchers.

In some cases, corporate and political leaders may call for "more research" on an issue in order to determine the nature or extent of an environmental problem. Some critics contend that calls for "more research" are just another stalling tactic to keep government and businesses from taking action to address environmental problems.

The following environmental problem descriptions come from environmental science textbooks and other scientific literature and provide a "middle of the road" consensus view of some of our most prevalent environmental problems. Keep in mind that because the natural world is interconnected, these problems have many causes and many effects.

### Global Warming (Global Climate Change)

*Problem:* As humans pump huge amounts of carbon dioxide into the air through power plant emissions and car exhaust, that gas is building up in the atmosphere. It seems that the carbon dioxide gas in the air allows sunlight to reach the earth, but then traps heat in our atmosphere. Since this warming is the same thing that happens in a greenhouse, some call this the "greenhouse effect."

Higher air temperatures warm the earth's waters and melt the glaciers and polar ice caps, which in turn raises ocean levels. Warmer air and water could even change worldwide weather patterns, making some places colder, others wetter; some places drier, others more susceptible to catastrophic storms. We are already seeing the effects of global warming in the environment. Meteorologists who track long-term weather data report that the 15 hottest years on record have all happened since 1980. The year 1998 was the hottest year in the past 1,000 years. The glaciers in Montana's Glacier National Park are now half the size they were 100 years ago and are on track to disappear completely by 2030. Air temperatures in Alaska have risen by 5 to 10 degrees in the last 100 years. Already we see animal species like raccoons and opossums moving north to areas that used to be too cold for them. Northern species like caribou seem to be moving farther north as well.

*Possible Group Solutions:*

- Tighter pollution regulations like the Kyoto Protocols, which require a cut in worldwide carbon dioxide production

- A nationwide shift to renewable and non-greenhouse gas–producing energy sources

- Requirements for more energy-efficient vehicles and power plants

- A "carbon credit" system for industry through which the government will regulate how much carbon dioxide industries can produce. Industries that can reduce their output of carbon dioxide can sell their "carbon credits" to more polluting industries. These kinds of programs use the free market to drive environmental cleanup programs.

*Possible Individual Solutions:*

- Conserving energy
- Driving efficient cars
- Walking or biking rather than driving
- Encouraging political leaders to strengthen and enforce environmental protection legislation

**Air Pollution (Acid Rain, Mercury Pollution, Smog)**

*Problem:* Burning coal in electric power plants and gasoline in cars releases acid compounds and other toxic chemicals, such as mercury and sulfur dioxide, into the atmosphere. Those acidic pollutants travel in the clouds and then rain down on lakes and forests, damaging trees and changing the chemical composition of some lakes to the extent that frogs and fish can no longer survive there. Polluted air in cities can be dangerous to children and the elderly as well as those with breathing problems.

*Possible Group Solutions:*

- More stringent pollution regulations and enforcement
- A nationwide shift to renewable and alternative energy production like solar energy, wind energy, and hydroelectric energy
- Requirements for more energy-efficient vehicles

*Possible Individual Solutions:*

- Conserving energy
- Driving efficient cars
- Trying to walk or bike rather than driving
- Pushing political leaders to strengthen and enforce environmental protection legislation

**Water Pollution**

*Problem:* The waterways that support aquatic species and provide humans with life-sustaining water are inundated with pollutants from a variety of sources. When we can identify the specific source of pollution, such as a wastewater treatment plant or chemical spill, it is called "point-source" pollution. If the source of a pollutant cannot be pinpointed, it is called "non-point source" pollution, and can include silt from erosion, automobile emissions, and chemical runoff from farm fields and yards. Some pollution from fertilizers or leaking septic systems might seem benign because it provides nutrients for plants to grow. However, if the aquatic algae get too much natural or chemical fertilizer, they will "bloom" or grow rapidly. When these huge algae colonies die, they decompose and use up much of the oxygen from the water. This can suffocate fish and other aquatic organisms that can't escape the aquatic "dead zone" that results. Water pollutants can also introduce foreign chemicals that also upset the balance of nature. Extreme erosion can wash so much silt into rivers and lakes that it chokes all aquatic life in the area. Because of water pollution, the mouth of the Mississippi River in southern Louisiana now produces a "dead zone" in which no aquatic life exists. That zone can extend up to 7,800 square miles out from the Louisiana shores into the Gulf of Mexico (an area larger than New Jersey). The dead zone often lasts from May through September each year.

*Possible Group Solutions:*

- Tighter regulations on the use of lawn and agricultural fertilizers
- Tighter regulations on the creation of industrial livestock operations and the management of animal waste that these operations produce
- Creation of new wetlands to replace the millions of acres of drained wetlands that once filtered and cleaned runoff water before it ran to rivers and lakes

*Possible Individual Solutions:*

- Limiting the use of fertilizers on lawns or gardens, especially if you live near waterways or on a hillside
- Making sure that your septic system is up to date and not leaking into ground water or surface water
- Conserving water in your household; the less water we use, the less water we have to clean at wastewater treatment plants
- Encouraging politicians to create and strengthen clean water laws
- Testing your well water to make sure it isn't contaminated by agricultural chemicals or other pollutants
- Filtering polluted water sources before using them for drinking or cooking

### Extinction of Species (Loss of Biodiversity)

*Problem:* Worldwide, many species are declining at an alarming rate. By conservative estimates, on average one known animal species and almost two known plant species have become extinct every year since 1600. But this only counts the animals and plants we know about. Scientists estimate that thousands of species have not yet been categorized, especially in the species-rich tropics. Pulitzer Prize–winning Harvard biologist Dr. E.O. Wilson estimates that extinction rates hover at about 10 species extinctions per year, a thousand times faster than estimated rates before the appearance of humans in the geologic record (Wilson, 2002).

Although extinctions did occur prior to the presence of humans in the geologic record—especially after violent environmental changes like the meteorite strike that may have ended the age of dinosaurs 65 million years ago—extinctions today happen at a faster rate than at any time since the great dinosaur extinction.

Some people may say that it isn't a problem to lose species that we don't know anything about, but this misses the point. Humans do not live in isolation; we are part of the earth's ecosystem. When we lose species, we waste the "natural capital," or wealth, of the world. Many species provide free environmental services like pollination, pest control, and seed dispersal. If these creatures disappear, we will have to create and pay for alternative technological methods to fill the same need. Many recently discovered plants contain compounds that can cure illnesses like cancer.

Statistically, about 40 percent of species extinctions are related to the impact of alien species or diseases that decimate local populations. Wild pigs on the Hawaiian Islands have damaged forest areas. Imported mongooses in Hawaii are decimating the local bird populations.

Another 36 percent of extinctions are due to habitat destruction like filling swamps for development or cutting down forests for development and logging. Kirtland's warblers depend on large patches of second-growth jack pine for nesting sites. Because forest managers have eliminated jack pine to grow more commercially valuable stands of red pine and aspen, these warblers are becoming homeless. Many prairie plant species became endangered or extinct as farmers converted over 90 percent of the tall grass prairie ecosystem into highly productive farmland.

About 23 percent of extinctions have come from over-hunting or over-fishing. Before the hunting laws in the United States were enacted in the mid-1900s, many animal species were easily hunted to extinction. The passenger pigeon is the most well-known species to fall victim to over-hunting. Writers report that there were flocks of millions of birds. But their large flocks made them easy targets for hunters. The last member of this species, Martha, died in the Cincinnati Zoological Garden in 1914. The American bison nearly suffered a similar fate, but conservationists salvaged enough members to breed them in captivity and return them to small areas of their original range.

*Possible Community Solutions:*

- Strengthening laws like the Endangered Species Act. This law helps large, charismatic species like the gray wolf and bald eagle.

- Passing new "endangered habitat" protection laws that are more likely to help protect a wider variety of species

- Developing and enhancing sustainable development programs in the world's poorest countries that will provide poor nations with jobs that don't require them to cut down their forests or mine their fisheries for export

- "Green Space" legislation and "anti-sprawl" development regulations to help preserve wildlife habitat

*Possible Individual Solutions:*

- Asking politicians to pass and enforce laws that protect species

- Managing your land to increase habitat for native species

- Working to remove alien species from your land

- Reducing or eliminating your use of chemical pesticides that harm wildlife

**For More Information**

There are always many sides to any issue, so be sure to educate yourself about environmental issues. Visit the Web sites below to learn more about these issues. The following organizations provide research-based environmental information:

The United States Environmental Protection Agency—www.epa.gov

United Nations Environment Programme—www.unep.org

Earthjustice—www.earthjustice.org

National Wildlife Federation—www.nwf.org

Natural Resources Defense Council—www.nrdc.org

## Turning Environmental Issues into Environmental Stories: Environmental Issues Storytelling

### *Method 1, the "Natural History Story"*

1. Choose an issue.

2. Research at least two sides of the issue with book resources or on the Internet. Look for scientific evidence of what will happen in the future if human actions don't change.

3. Choose a character and location for your story. Tell your story through the character's eyes, whenever possible. The character may be a human, animal, or plant.

4. Choose a concrete problem or crisis that you could discuss in a story. Create a turning point or tipping point at which we see the effect of this environmental problem.

5. Decide on an ending. It could be a solution to the problem or a "cliffhanger" in which you stop the story and let listeners discuss solutions to the environmental problem.

# The Last Birch

She didn't know what was happening. She held her white branches in the air and dropped her yellow seeds every winter. Humans called her a "paper birch," but that didn't matter to her. Each year she grew taller on the hillside, watching the sun rise and fall. But as the years went by, she noticed fewer and fewer of her sisters growing in the valley to the south. The summers grew warmer and warmer every year. Soon her seeds wouldn't sprout in the too-warm soil. New bugs and diseases began to take her sisters one by one, until she was the only birch on the hillside. She could still see a few sisters on a hill far to the north. The trees that grew up around her looked different than she did, with their thick brown bark and acorns. Tall grasses sprouted up at her roots as the north woods faded and the savannah spread across the hill.

This is an example of a story that "could be true" in about 50 years. Already more oak trees are sprouting in parts of northern Minnesota that used to be the exclusive home of more northerly species like paper birch and white pine.

### *Method 2, the "Human History Story"*

When I am developing a story about a particular environmental issue, I first take a close look at what reputable scientists are saying about it. Then I look at what our history and natural history tell us about similar events in the past. Finally, I put together a story that draws a comparison between history and what is happening now.

An example of this kind of story is what happened to the Sumerian Empire in what is now Iraq and the Roman Empire in Italy. Some historians now believe that soil erosion and food shortages led to the weakening and collapse of these empires.

### *Method 3, the "Hope Story"*

Environmental stories should motivate people to care for our natural world. I try to tell stories that show how humans have successfully solved an environmental problem that they caused. Stories about the reintroduction and recovery of endangered species like the gray wolf and bald eagle are great examples of humans protecting and restoring the natural world. These are the stories that we must tell if we want people to care for the natural world. People need to see that it is possible to fix the problems we are causing in the environment. They need to know that things can get better, and they can help. People should feel empowered by stories and believe that they have the capacity and opportunity to effect change in our world.

## Turning Personal Events into Environmental Stories

Our lives and personal histories are a goldmine for environmental stories. You can use a childhood nature encounter or real-life animal encounter to explain environmental education concepts. You can tell a story about a special outdoor place from your childhood, or a memory of what happened to a favorite forest or wetland when developers turned it into a strip mall or housing development.

Be careful when developing these stories that you do not create an "us versus them" image in which conservationists are always "good" and developers or corporations are "bad." This simplistic interpretation of the world ignores the complexity of environmental problems and will likely either make people feel guilty or push people away from conservation messages. Instead, focus on the emotional impact of changes that you see in the environment. How did those changes affect you personally? How have you changed your own lifestyle to conserve our resources? Remember, developers build houses for us and farmers grow food for us. We are part of the problem *and* part of the solution. It will cost all of us more time and money to take better care of the environment. The question is, do we make that investment now, or in 10, 20, or 30 years, when the problems will be worse and probably cost more to fix?

### The Danger of "Doom and Gloom" Environmental Stories

As a naturalist and a storyteller, I dislike how some environmental activists use "gloom and doom" stories to frighten people into recycling, conserving water, or banning a particular pesticide. Those scary stories often leave listeners feeling helpless about the current state of our world. When telling natural history or personal nature stories, I avoid creating "doom and gloom" stories with themes like "If we don't conserve energy, all of our lakes will turn to acid (from acid rain)," or "If we don't recycle, we will soon be buried in garbage."

These catastrophic storylines can often leave listeners feelings overwhelmed and powerless. While fear can be a useful motivator in some cases, it only works if a listener can do something personally to alleviate the crisis. Environmental problems by their very nature are too big for any single person to solve. We need to work together to find and implement solutions.

When I am telling environmental stories, I want to help people connect with and care about the natural world. I also want to encourage people to change their behavior to take better care of our planet. Stories that make people throw up their hands and give up won't succeed at either of these goals. For examples of more effective environmental stories, check out Chapters 6–13.

# References

Wilson, Edward O. 2002. *The Future of Life.* New York: Alfred A. Knopf. 229pp. $26.00. ISBN 0-67-945078-5.

# Adaptales Activity

**Grade Level:** 4–9

**Environmental Themes:** adaptation, habitat

**Curriculum Areas:** science, language arts, social studies

**Student Skills:** comprehension, creative expression, inferring, comparison

**Materials:** copies of several short adaptation stories, paper, pencils

## Instructions:

1. In this activity, students will develop their own original animal adaptation stories. Start by reading or telling examples of this genre of folktale. Describe the steps for developing an original adaptation story and some of the reasons that people have developed and told these stories.

2. Hand out the "Adaptation Story List" (below) and ask students to choose a topic and follow the steps listed above to create an original story.

3. Ask students to share their stories as a written tale, and for older students, as a told tale. Have students edit their stories again after they have told them.

## Adaptation Story List

"How Birds Got Their Colors"

"How Bear Lost His Tail"

"How Birds Got Their Feathers"

"Why the Sun Rises and Sets Every Day"

"Why Foxes Are So Clever"

"How Snake Lost Her Legs"

"Why Mosquitoes Buzz"

"Where Insects Come From"

"Why Ants Are Everywhere"

"Why Sun and Moon Live in the Sky"

"How Deer Lost Her Tail"

"How Rabbit Got Her Long Ears"

"Why Roosters Crow in the Morning"

## Evaluation:

Was it easier to edit a story after telling it a few times? (It usually is.) What value do adaptation stories have in society today?

From Kevin Strauss, *Tales with Tails: Storytelling the Wonders of the Natural World.* Westport, CT: Libraries Unlimited, 2006.
Copyright © 2006 by Kevin Strauss.

# Nature Memory
# Story/Pictures Activity

**Grade Level:** 3–8

**Environmental Themes:** adaptation, habitat

**Curriculum Areas:** science, language arts, visual arts

**Student Skills:** comprehension, comparison, narration, creative expression

**Materials:** paper and pencil

**Instructions:**

1. Tell students that they are going to use their imaginations to visit an outdoor place that they have been to before. Ask students to close their eyes and imagine a trip to a forest, park, or lake. What smells did they smell? What sounds did they hear? What did they see when they were there? What happened on the trip?

2. Give students about five minutes, then have them write a story or draw a picture of the event.

3. From that record of the event, have students tell a short (one- to two-minute) version of the story to a partner.

**Evaluation:**

How did drawing a picture or writing a story about an event affect their memory of the event? Do they think it was it easier to go though the imagination and writing/drawing stage than it would have been to just try to tell a story about an event? Why? If students aren't sure about the answer to this one, have them tell a personal story just from memory.

From Kevin Strauss, *Tales with Tails: Storytelling the Wonders of the Natural World.* Westport, CT: Libraries Unlimited, 2006. Copyright © 2006 by Kevin Strauss.

# Nature Poetry Activity
# (Five Forms)

**Grade Level:** 5–9

**Environmental Themes:** adaptation, habitat

**Curriculum Areas:** science, language arts

**Student Skills:** comprehension, problem solving, comparison

**Materials:** paper, pencils, a few short demonstration poems in the forms below

## Instructions:

1. Poems, with their focus on rich language, rhyme, and sensory imagery, can often help students see the natural world in a new way. Writing poems can also help students use more evocative language in their stories. For younger students, start with the shorter "formula" poems like the acrostic and dreamspark. For older students, move on to the more challenging forms of the cinquain and free verse. As the workshop leader, write some of your own versions of these forms. Share your poems with your class or group. Ask for volunteers to read their poems in front of the group. You may have few volunteers to read their own poetry, and that's fine. Students may be more comfortable having a teacher or adult leader read their poems for them.

2. Poetic forms:

*Acrostic:* a poem in which the first letter in each line spells a word vertically.

> Example:
> > **E**very day
> > **A**ll I can imagine is
> > **G**liding, flying
> > **L**ooping and climbing like an
> > **E**agle up in the sky

*Haiku:* a three-line poem with the first line of the poem having five syllables, the second line having seven syllables, and the third line having five syllables.

> Example:
> > the wind shakes the trees
> > as the rain washes over
> > the grass and flowers

*Dreamspark:* a five-line poem in which the first line starts with "I dreamed that," the second line starts with "I was . . . (an animal, plant or natural feature)," the third line describes where things were happening in the dream, the fourth line describes an action that you did in the dream, and the fifth line describes how you did it.

> Example:
> > I dreamed that
> > I was a bald eagle
> > In the mountains
> > Soaring high on the winds
> > Free and happy

From Kevin Strauss, *Tales with Tails: Storytelling the Wonders of the Natural World.* Westport, CT: Libraries Unlimited, 2006. Copyright © 2006 by Kevin Strauss.

# Nature Poetry Activity (Five Forms), *continued*

*Cinquain:* a five-line poem in which the first line has two syllables and is the title, the second line has four syllables and describes the title, the third line has six syllables and describes action (often with "ing" words), the fourth line has eight syllables and is a description of a feeling, and the fifth line has two syllables and is another word for the title.

Example:

eagle
dark wings, white head
soaring, watching, hunting
a joyous return to the sky
raptor

*Free verse:* a poetic form without rules or conventions. It is one of the more popular forms with today's poets, but the freedom of the form often makes these poems more difficult to write.

Example:

the oak stands in the forest
silent, like a guardian
watching, always watching
as birds set their nests
and snow cloaks her branches,
and she smiles every day
as the sun sets fire to the sky.
stretching arms up to the sky
she has lived here for centuries
she knows that many things change in the world
but the forest lives on

3.  Be sure that you don't evaluate or give suggestions on the poems. Criticism comes later, when students are older and can self-evaluate their work. This is the "creative" stage, designed to help students get comfortable creating poems and other artwork. Harsh criticism at this stage could make students think they are "no good at poetry." Modeling how adults write poetry can help students feel comfortable writing poems as well.

**Evaluation:**

Which kind of poem was the easiest to write? Which kind of poem did they enjoy reading the most?

From Kevin Strauss, *Tales with Tails: Storytelling the Wonders of the Natural World.* Westport, CT: Libraries Unlimited, 2006.
Copyright © 2006 by Kevin Strauss.

# Proverbially Speaking Activity

**Grade Level:** 8–12

**Environmental Themes:** everything is connected, there is no such things as a free lunch

**Curriculum Areas:** social studies, language arts

**Student Skills:** comprehension, inferring, comparison

**Materials:** list of proverbs (see above)

**Instructions:**

1. In this activity, students will choose a proverb and develop a short (one-minute) story about it. First, give students a list of environmental proverbs (see pages 38–39) and ask them to choose a proverb that appeals to them. Then, individually or in small groups, have the students develop a four-sentence story that explains or demonstrates that proverb.

2. In the first sentence, students will set the scene and introduce the story characters. In the second sentence, the students will introduce a problem or crisis. In the third sentence, characters will develop a solution to the problem, and in the fourth sentence, students will state their proverbs in their own words (paraphrase).

3. Once students have developed a four-line story about a proverb, have each tell it to a neighbor as a one-minute story. Then ask them to tell it as a three-minute story. Ask volunteers to tell their stories in front of the group.

**Evaluation:**

How did the students' stories grow and develop in the one-minute and three-minute versions? Were they surprised by the story they ended up with?

From Kevin Strauss, *Tales with Tails: Storytelling the Wonders of the Natural World.* Westport, CT: Libraries Unlimited, 2006.
Copyright © 2006 by Kevin Strauss.

# Chapter 5

## Advanced Environmental Storytelling Techniques

# Common Challenges for Beginning Storytellers

Just like riding a bike, storytelling is all about balance. Finding balance is part of a storyteller's job. Once you have been telling stories for a while, you might want to take a closer look at what you are doing in performances. All professional storytellers work on technique throughout their careers.

One good way to look at your performance technique is to videotape yourself at a performance or to have a friend or "storytelling coach" evaluate you. Common storytelling performance challenges include

- standing or sitting too stiffly,
- gesturing wildly or constant pacing,
- talking too quickly,
- talking too slowly or pausing too often, and
- being worried about telling the story the "right" way.

That last one needs some explanation. In our literate, printed-word society, we often make the mistake of thinking that the version of a story in a book is the "right" version of that story. We forget that for thousands of years, these same stories traveled from the mouths of tellers to the ears of listeners and never graced a printed page.

A written story is like a snapshot of a particular story at a particular time in history. Think of it as a snapshot of you when you were a teenager. That snapshot will never change, even though you will grow and change over time. A printed story is no more artistically "alive" than that photo.

When thinking about the difference between a printed story and a spoken story, I think of the Chinese proverb: "A closed mind is like a closed book—just a block of wood." While we can preserve stories in our libraries, it takes a human being to read or tell those stories and bring them to life in our minds.

So the short answer to the question "What is the 'right' version of a story?" is that there is no "right" version of any story. There are many versions, and your own version will be different from everyone else's. Your version will even change and develop a bit each time you tell it. That's what makes storytelling interesting.

Just as there is no one "right" version of a story to tell, there is also no one "right" way to tell a story. Some storytellers are very theatrical and use a lot of body language to tell a story. Others stand very still. The most important thing is to find a style that works best for you. Experiment.

# Developing Effective Animal Characters

I learned early on that telling stories about animal characters is different from telling stories about humans. So I developed techniques to help create more effective animal characters. I did this for three reasons:

1. Using effective animal characterizations will make an animal story more fun for the teller and the listeners.

2. Developing well-rounded animal characters gives you a chance to portray an animal to an audience using a variety of storytelling skills (body language, voice tone, voice rate, and verbalized thoughts).

3. Using "animal storytelling" character techniques will help a teller create characters that are more educational and more true to science.

## How Animal Characters Are Different from Human Characters

Animal characters are different from human characters because animals are different from humans. Although we can't know exactly what animals are thinking, we can assume animal characters think differently from human characters. Animals are usually focused on survival-level issues like finding food and avoiding predators. Animals don't have the luxury of esoteric ideas like "justice" or "beauty." Because animals are focused on survival, animal characters are often much more "down to earth" than human characters. Bodily functions like defecation, snot, or devouring live prey aren't a big deal to them. Animal characters don't tend to be all that reflective about the world. They do what they need to do and then move on. You won't see a wolf sulking over missing a deer on a hunt. In addition, animal characters see, smell, and hear the world very differently from humans, so their perspectives on the world are very different from our own.

## The Five Facets of Effective Animal Characters

### *A Good Animal Character Moves Like an Animal*

As I am developing an animal character, I first try to visualize how it moves. How an animal moves tells us a lot about what it is thinking and doing. Although humans are far more isolated from the natural world now than at any time in our history, there are still some easy ways to watch live animals. Visit a zoo, park, nature preserve, or pet store and have a look at the animals there. If you can't see the species in person, watch a video. Ideally, watch the same animal species that you have in your stories. If you can't do that, look for one that is related. If you can't find a lion at the zoo, look for a tiger, a leopard, or a bobcat. As you are watching the animal, try to "get inside its head," to figure out what it is thinking. If you are feeling especially playful, imagine an interview with the animal. What would it tell you about itself?

When portraying animal characters, use body language and facial expressions to convey your characters. Crouching a bit for smaller characters and standing tall and straight for big animals can convey character in a nonverbal way. I get the most mileage out of facial expressions. Beavers are easy; I just take on an overbite. For owls I stoop and puff out my cheeks. Play around with animal charades to get a feel for what works for you.

Remember that you can also convey a character by using only part of your body. Using an arm for a snake or a hand for a swimming fish can show movement and character all at once.

### *A Good Animal Character Sounds Like an Animal (or Its Cartoon Likeness)*

Real animals don't speak English, but they do communicate, often with some kind of vocalization. Work on developing a unique voice for the one or two main animal characters in a story. Watch animal cartoons and animal puppet programs to get a sense of how cartoon writers and puppeteers convey character though voice.

Generally speaking, big animals have deep voices and small animals have high voices. You can also vary the pace at which you speak. Big animals come to life with slower voices and smaller animals speak more quickly. Biologically this makes sense since a mouse has a much faster heart rate and breathes much more quickly than a bear. In other cases, choose a speaking pace that fits the animal's movement (see above); rabbits talk fast because they run fast. Turtles talk slowly because they move more slowly.

In addition to using vocal tone and pace, you may also want to insert some animal vocalizations in an animal character's speech. When I am talking like a crow, I might insert an occasional "caw" into its speech. That way, without using changes in tone or pace, listeners get the signal that the crow is still talking.

### *A Good Animal Character Uses Its Senses the Same Way the Real Animal Does*

This step takes some research, but it is well worth the effort. Knowing how an animal senses its world will give you a real feel for how it thinks and how it reacts to problems. Most animals have at least one sense that is far superior to human senses. In many cases, animals can smell, hear, or see us in the forest long before we ever see them. That's why most people don't see very many animals during a stroll in the woods. Make sure that your animal characters reflect this ability.

Wolves, like many mammals, have an excellent sense of smell. Canines (wolves, dogs, foxes) "see" the world through their noses. A wolf can track a moose by smell up to a mile away. So when telling a story involving a wolf, rather than just saying "Wolf saw the Deer," I say "Wolf smelled the air and caught the whiff of something good to eat. 'Mmmmm, deer, I love deer for dinner!' "

The animal facts sections in Part 2 and this animal traits table include information about how many animals use their senses. Check out the wildlife books listed in the bibliography. Naturalists, zookeepers, and the Internet can also help with information on a specific animal and its senses.

### *A Good Animal Character Has Reasons for Doing What It Does*

Find out why your animal character acts the way it does in a story. This knowledge will help you develop your animal characters from the inside out. Is your animal character acting the way it does because of biology? (Predators are often portrayed as "evil" characters in stories.) Or is the animal acting a certain way because of a human-created archetype? Are your story owls always wise? Discover your animal character's motivation.

In workshops, I have storytellers pair up to conduct an "Animal Analysis" role-play, in which one teller acts as a psychologist and the other is the animal character. The "psychologist" asks the "animal" why it acts the way it does. You can do the same thing with your imagination, "interviewing" an animal in your head. Otherwise rent or check out a wildlife video about your animal, or at the very least, find a picture of your animal. Sit down with paper and pencil and analyze your character.

### *A Good Animal Character Will Grow and Mature over Time*

You can work on and develop animal characters now, but also realize that your animal characters, like other characters in stories, will develop over time. The more you tell stories with animal characters, the more your animal characters will develop distinctive voices and movements all on their own. Don't be surprised when this happens.

## Animal Characteristics

| Animal | Physical Traits | Ecological Relationships | Symbolism |
|---|---|---|---|
| OMNIVORES (eat plants and meat) | | | |
| Black Bear | poor eyesight, keen sense of smell, gorges on food to prepare for up to 6 months of winter sleep (not a true hibernator), climbs trees | eats mostly plants (berries, catkins, seeds), also eats ants, wasp nests, fawns and honey | big bully, often portrayed as slow or stupid, some cultures see bear as a healer and wise creature |
| Crow/Raven | can see in color, very intelligent, adaptable, tool user, over 100 vocalizations | eats just about anything from fruit to carrion (dead animals), often 'clean up' dead animals, known to follow wolves to a kill | often portrayed as a trickster, other times portrayed as a symbol of death or evil |
| Mouse/Rat | good senses of smell and hearing, can chew through just about anything, only sees in black and white | eaten by hawks, owls, snakes, foxes, and other predators, consumes crops, reproduces very quickly | 'underdog' character, quick-witted, adaptable, social, sly |
| Turtle | shell is modified ribs, sleeps through cold winters buried in lake mud, moves slowly | well-protected animal, some live on land, others in water | protection, endurance, longevity, patience, strength, stability, slowness |
| HERBIVORES (eat plants) | | | |
| Rabbit/Hare | poor eyesight, keen hearing and sense of smell, fast runner, snowshoe hares change from brown to white in winter | reproduces very quickly (up to 18 young per year), prey for wolves, hawks, and other large predators | trickster, fickle, clever, swift, lucky, fertility symbol |
| Butterfly/Moth | tastes with feet, color vision, powerful sense of smell, short-lived (2 weeks in some cases) | nectar drinker, pollinates flowers, moths fly at night, butterflies during the day, moth larvae (caterpillars) can be destructive to plants and clothing | resurrection and transformation, spring, lightmindedness |
| Deer | good sense of smell and hearing, fast runner (over 35 m.p.h.), can defend self with hooves, antlers fall off every winter | prey for wolves and cougars, can damage forest trees if population is too high | beauty, purity, grace, vanity, speed |
| CARNIVORES (eat meat) | | | |
| Wolf | good senses of smell, hearing, and sight, hunts in family (pack) groups, sharp teeth, strong jaws | predator, kills deer, moose, farm animals, pets; kills easiest prey (often old, young, or sick) | portrayed as evil, helpful, foolish, or wise by different cultures; symbol of ferocity, cruelty, courage, family |
| Owl | excellent senses of night sight and hearing, can detect prey in total darkness, no sense of smell, sharp talons (claws), and beak, wings are designed for silent flight | predator, kills mice, and other rodents, reduces prey populations | death, night, cold, evil, wisdom, powerful sight |
| Snake | smells with its tongue, can't hear airborne sounds, decent eye-sight, some snakes can use a kind of 'heat vision' to detect prey, needs to warm up on cold days before it can move, some are venomous | predator, eats mice, rats, birds, worms, insects, hibernates underground during cold winters | healing, protection, evil, death, immortality, intelligence, elegance |

# Anthropomorphism in Environmental Stories

As a naturalist, I have always been attracted to animal stories as a way to teach people about the mammals, birds, insects, and other creatures who share our world. Animal stories seem to take us back to a time when people were closer to the natural world—both physically and spiritually—than we are today.

The problem is that some animal stories, including Aesop's fables and well-known folktales like "The Three Little Pigs," don't teach us much about real animals. Instead, they give us anthropomorphic animals—creatures that look like animals but act like people. While telling these stories in a regular storytelling program isn't a problem, overly anthropomorphic stories may not be a good fit for environmental education story programs. But as a narrative technique, some aspects of anthropomorphism provide both useful metaphors and misleading pitfalls for environmental education storytellers and their listeners.

## Connecting with Animals Through Story

Anthropomorphism in a story can help listeners personally identify with and care about animals both in a story and in the natural world. In a society that is increasingly suburbanized and in which people seem to have less and less contact with nature, animal tales can help us connect with wildlife on an emotional level. Animal stories also allow us to imagine that animals might think and feel in some of the same ways that we do.

Anthropomorphic animal characters also provide us with an opportunity to teach important lessons about human behavior in an indirect, disarming way. In one of my favorite wolf tales, Aesop's " Why Wolf Lives in the Forest" (Chapter 6), a hungry wolf asks a dog where he gets so much food. When the wolf later learns that the price of a full belly is being tied up for much of the day, he decides that he'd rather live in the forest and be hungry than be tied up on the farm and be full.

All listeners have aspects of wolf and dog in their personalities, and by thinking about these metaphorical, allegorical animals, we can help determine our own course in the world. We may think about this story when changing jobs or seeing our current job change into something we don't like. At those times we may ask ourselves which is more important: the freedom of the hungry wolf or the security of the tethered dog.

## Potential Problems with Anthropomorphism

One of the problems in telling anthropomorphic animal tales is that we may forget that animals don't really think, feel, or act exactly the way humans do. In some folktales wolves are negatively stereotyped as "villainous" and "cruel" for killing other animals. But ecologically speaking, wolves eat meat so they can survive.

As a naturalist, my approach to anthropomorphism is to put as much knowledge of animal biology and ecology into my stories as possible. I encourage the audience to realize that the wolf isn't being "cruel" as it makes his way through the world; it is merely doing what it needs to do to survive.

When I am performing an entire program of wolf stories, I tell several different kinds. Some tales feature wolves that are perceived as dangerous, but other stories have wolves that are kind, foolish, or clever. I am always careful to present at least one story in which a wolf is dangerous in my programs. Just as it is a problem to view of wolves as strictly "cruel," it is equally problematic to view them as "kind and cuddly," like a pet puppy.

In society today, possibly because of unscientific folktale and media images of wildlife and our lack of experience with real wild animals, children and adults seem to be less cautious around wild animals than they were in the past. There have been cases in recent years in which people have approached grizzly bears in national parks so they could photograph the bears. In other cases, park visitors have tried to hand-feed black bears and deer. In some cases, these wild animals began to expect handouts. They approached and even injured park visitors who did not feed them. In the end, park officials have often had to kill "habituated" animals to protect park visitors. We must be careful not to confuse metaphorical story animals with the real animals in the woods.

In addition, storytellers should remember that many folktales were written down in the 1800s, when people categorized animals as "good" (benefiting humans) and "evil" (competing with human society). This act of writing down stories preserved the stories and the historical cultural biases they contained. Thanks to scientific research and ecological theories, many societies are now coming to a new understanding of the animals and plants that share our world. This understanding views animals and plants as integral parts of the "web of life," not as manifestations of good or evil in the world. Each animal and plant has its role in nature, even if humans don't currently understand or value that role.

## Utilizing Anthropomorphism

You can take several steps to utilize anthropomorphism effectively and responsibly in your stories:

1. **Learn more about the biology of the animals in a story.** The more you know about the physical and behavioral characteristics and ecology of the animals in your stories, the more effectively you can present the animal characters (see "Developing Effective Animal Characters"). If you are telling a story about a wolf, find out where wolves live, what they eat, and how they find their food. Find out how a wolf uses its senses (many animals use their senses of smell and hearing much more than humans do). Although you may not immediately use those biological facts in your telling, the information will help you understand how to "think" like a wolf and flesh out the wolf characters in the stories you tell. It will also allow you to present a more biologically accurate and educational wolf character in your telling. By adding more biology to a story, you can turn an overly anthropomorphic story into a useful environmental story and at the same time create an exciting new version of a traditional story.

2. **Learn more about the "psychology" of animals in a story.** Scientifically speaking, animals act the way they do for a reason. Usually animals act in a particular way to help them find food, find a mate, or escape an enemy. By considering why an animal acts a certain way, you can give a more well-rounded view of your animal characters. By approaching animal characters this way, you will give your audience a chance to understand that wolves, bats, and other animals act as they do because of environmental and biological circumstances, not because they are cruel or kind.

3. **Learn more about the "archetype" that humans have assigned to particular animals.** In Jungian theory, an archetype is the primal character and predisposition to behavior assigned to a particular group. It is important to remember that these archetypes are culturally based. In Germany, wolves in stories are often portrayed as cruel; in Finland, wolf characters are often portrayed as foolish; and in Russia and North America, wolves are often portrayed as helpful. One way to oppose a negative archetype of a particular animal is to tell stories that show multiple sides of that animal character.

4. **Point out "unscientific" aspects in a story.** If your goal is to teach about animals, you will want to choose your stories carefully. "Little Red Riding Hood" may not fit well in a program about wolf biology, but it may fit very well into a program about cultural views of wolves. After telling a story, you may want to point out the unscientific aspects of that story. When I tell the traditional German version of "Little Red riding Hood," in which the wolf eats the grandmother, I always remind my audience that this story comes from a long time ago in Europe. Now in North America you are more likely to be struck by lightning than be hurt by a wolf. Even though wolves are predators and are capable of killing deer or moose, they don't seem to hunt humans. In a program I may also mention that every year, domestic dogs kill over a dozen people in the United States. The take-home message: Fido is probably more dangerous than a wolf.

5. **Understand and discuss the "lessons" in a story.** Sometimes when I tell animal stories, I talk with my listeners about the "lessons" in that story. I give the audience 30 seconds to talk with a partner about the lessons they heard in the tale. Then I call on three audience members to share what they discussed with their neighbors. Listeners often realize that story animals are metaphors for human behavior.

## Responsible Storytelling

It is important to be mindful of what you are teaching with a story. By evaluating the animal stories that we tell, we can focus on the lessons we want to teach and avoid the unintended consequences of negative animal stereotypes. By highlighting the positive aspects of anthropomorphism and mitigating its negative aspects, storytellers can continue to use animal stories to teach about, and connect their listeners to, the real and metaphorical animals of our world.

# Lineup by Animal Height Activity

**Grade Level:** 3–12

**Environmental Themes:** adaptation, interdependence

**Curriculum Areas:** science, social studies

**Student Skills:** problem solving, inferring, comparison, comprehension

**Materials:** none

## Instructions

1. This activity is geared to helping students think about how animals move and communicate. Have students line up by height, without talking.

2. Once they are lined up, ask them to think of an animal, any animal. Now ask them to line up by animal height. They cannot speak during this activity. They can only communicate using the vocalizations and body language that their animals would normally make.

3. Once students have lined up by their animals' heights, go down the line and ask them which animals they chose.

## Evaluation:

Discuss how well the group did at lining up by animal height. Was it hard to determine which animal was larger? How did students communicate what animals they were? How might the gestures/movements and vocalizations used in this activity help students as storytellers as they are presenting animal characters?

From Kevin Strauss, *Tales with Tails: Storytelling the Wonders of the Natural World.* Westport, CT: Libraries Unlimited, 2006.
Copyright © 2006 by Kevin Strauss.

# Putting Science into a Story Activity

**Grade Level:** 3–12

**Environmental Themes:** adaptation, interdependence

**Curriculum Areas:** science, social studies

**Student Skills:** inferring, comparison, comprehension, creative expression

**Materials:** examples of traditional Aesop's fables (Don't use the ones in Chapters 6–13, since they are already adapted for environmental education programs.) You can find them online if you use an Internet search engine to search for "Aesop's Fables."

## Instructions:

1. This activity is dedicated to the idea that "animal fables+ science facts = good environmental education stories." Most fables were designed to teach human lessons and not animal biology, but storytellers can remedy that fact with a careful choice of stories and the inclusion of biological and ecological information in the story. Give students six examples of short Aesop's fables that involve animal characters.

2. Ask students to choose a story that they like and research the biology of the animals in the story using naturalist guidebooks, the encyclopedia, the Internet, or the biology information in this book (Chapters 6–13). Have students add one biological fact (e.g., "Wolf smelled the air and knew that a goat was nearby . . ." or "Turtle knew that his short legs were slow, but he figured that Hare wanted to race . . .") to their stories and write the story out in a "Story Scene Outline" (Chapter 3). Have the students tell their stories in a one-minute version to a partner.

3. Once both partners have told their stories, have students add one more biological fact and retell their stories in a two-minute version.

4. Once both partners have told their stories, have students add one more biological fact and retell their stories in a three-minute version.

## Evaluation:

Which version of the story (of the one-, two-, or three-minute versions) was easiest to tell? Which version was the most interesting to listen to? How did adding biology information affect their telling of the story?

From Kevin Strauss, *Tales with Tails: Storytelling the Wonders of the Natural World.* Westport, CT: Libraries Unlimited, 2006.
Copyright © 2006 by Kevin Strauss.

# Fairy Tale Facts Activity

**Grade Level:** 4–8

**Environmental Themes:** adaptation

**Curriculum Areas:** science, social studies

**Student Skills:** comprehension, problem solving, inferring, comparison

**Materials:** copies of four short fairy tales that involve animal characters (like "Little Red Riding Hood," the "Three Bears," the "Three Little Pigs," or "Puss in Boots"), picture books of the same stories, paper, pencils, wildlife books

## Instructions:

1. Choose a fairy tale that involves animal characters. Read (or better yet, tell) the stories to the students (or have older students read the stories to the group). Ask students to make a list of:

   A. Realistic parts in the story (a clever crow, etc.)

   B. Fantasy parts of the story (talking animals, etc.)

   Appearance:

   Actions:

   Food:

   Method of travel:

   Overall characterization (e.g., villain, kind, helpful, silly)

   Other:

2. Ask students: Do these stories really teach us very much about the animals? What impression do you have of the animals? Do you think the stories gave an accurate portrayal of what animals are really like? Are the overall characterizations of the animal characters consistent across several fairy tales (e.g., are wolves always villains in the stories)? What does that tell us about the cultures that first told these stories?

3. Advanced activity: Have older students choose an animal from one of the stories and research its biology. Have them rewrite a story by inserting more biology information into it. Use biology to explain why animal characters acted the way that they did in the story. (Maybe there was a drought in the forest and all of the deer and beavers disappeared, and Wolf was forced by hunger to search for wayward pigs for dinner.) Have students retell their new versions of traditional stories to members of their own class or a younger class.

## Evaluation:

Why might it be important to be able to differentiate between parts of a story that are realistic and parts that are fantasy? How might stories like "Little Red Riding Hood" affect how humans interact with wildlife like wolves? Do students display an understanding of which parts of a story are realistic and which parts are fantasy?

From Kevin Strauss, *Tales with Tails: Storytelling the Wonders of the Natural World.* Westport, CT: Libraries Unlimited, 2006. Copyright © 2006 by Kevin Strauss.

# Part 2

## Environmental Stories

# Chapter 6

## Animal Stories: Large Mammals

Mammals are warm-blooded animals that have hair or fur on their bodies, give birth to live young (i.e., don't lay eggs) and produce milk for their babies. Of the 1.2 million known animal species in the world, 4,200 of them are mammals. On average, mammals have larger and more "advanced" brains than other animal groups. Humans are members of this group.

## Wolf

*Themes:* adaptation—wolves living in the woods, decision making, habitat

### Why Wolf Lives in the Forest (Aesop)

Long, long ago, in a deep, dark forest, Wolf was hungry. Now this wasn't unusual. Wolves always seem to be hungry. In fact, wolves spend most of their time chasing deer and other animals for food. But just because Wolf chases food, doesn't mean he catches it. And when Wolf can't find any animals, he goes hungry.

On this particular day, Wolf hadn't eaten for weeks. You could see the shape of his ribs sticking out on his sides. It was almost as if all the deer and rabbits in the forest had evaporated like the mist on a hot, sunny morning. Wolf thought and thought about where to find food. Then it hit him.

"There is always food near where people live, maybe I should go there," thought Wolf.

Now Wolf knew it was dangerous to hunt near humans. Some of the wolves that went there never came back. But Wolf had never been this hungry before. So as the sun dipped red behind the western hills, Wolf walked through the forest to the edge of a farmer's field.

Wolf sniffed the air and scanned the field, looking for a calf or lamb that was off by itself. A small animal like that would make a good meal and quiet Wolf's grumbling belly.

It was then that he heard a strange barking sound. He hadn't heard that sound before. As he looked across the field, Wolf saw that the sound was coming from a creature that looked a lot like him, and it was running right at him.

"I wonder if we're related, maybe on my mother's side," thought Wolf.

"Woof!" said the creature.

"Cousin, why are you speaking so strangely? We wolves never bark like that," said Wolf.

The creature stood up straight and glared at Wolf.

"I'm not your cousin. I'm a dog and we bark when we see wild animals near the farm. And you're a wild animal. Woof! Woof! Woof!" said Dog.

Then Wolf noticed how fat Dog was. That got Wolf thinking.

"Say cousin, how is it that I am starving in this forest while you seem to have plenty of food to eat?" said Wolf.

Dog stood up even taller, smiled a toothy smile, and said proudly, "I work for my meals. I chase wild animals and robbers away from the farm, and for that work I am well paid. Every evening, my master scrapes his table scraps into a bowl and feeds me until I can't eat another bite."

"You mean you don't have to hunt for your food and catch it in the forest?" said Wolf.

"Of course not, why would I do that? The only hunting I do is for fun," said Dog.

That gave Wolf an amazing idea.

"Say cousin," said Wolf, "do you think that your master could use another worker? I could chase wild animals away from the farm. I'm very good at that; I chase wild animals every day. Besides, since we are related and all, do you think you could get me a job, cousin?"

"Well, I guess so. There is always plenty of work to do. Let's go ask my master," said Dog.

So as darkness settled on the fields, Wolf and Dog walked up to the farmhouse. As they got closer to the house, the light from the windows shown on them, and for the first time, Wolf noticed that Dog had no fur around his neck.

"Cousin, why don't you have any fur on your neck?" asked Wolf.

"Oh that, it's nothing, you'll get used to it."

"Get used to what, Dog? What are you talking about?"

"Well it's nothing, really. My master doesn't want me running off during the day, so he ties me up near the house. Sometimes when I see a rabbit during the day, I forget that I'm tied up and I run after it. Then the rope pulls and wears away at the fur on my neck. It's fine though; all I do is sleep during the day. You'll get used to it," said Dog.

Wolf stopped. He looked at the dark forest, then back at Dog and the lighted house and then back at the forest, again.

Wolf turned back to Dog, shaking his head and said, "No cousin, I don't think I can get used to that."

Wolf turned and ran back to the darkness of the woods. Ever since that day, wolves have lived in the forest and dogs have lived with people, and they have never spoken to each other, since.

**Teller notes:** This story provides a folktale reason for why wolves and dogs (genetically similar creatures) live in different places. Scientists believe that over 10,000 years ago, humans took wolf pups out of the wild and began domesticating and selectively breeding them the same way that they domesticated horses, cows, and sheep. After thousands of years of selective breeding, humans have developed all the different breeds of dog, from the Great Dane to the dachshund. The big difference between wolves and dogs is that dogs are bred to listen to and respond to humans, while wolves aren't.

*Themes:* food chain, problem solving

# A Foolish Wolf Learns from His Mistakes (Adapted from Finland)

Once a long time ago, Wolf was hungry. He hadn't eaten for days and his stomach grumbled like far-off thunder. He knew he couldn't just wait for food to drop out of the sky. He had to work to find the food he needed. He sniffed the air as he walked. And then he smelled it, the scent of beavers.

"Beavers! I love eating beavers for dinner. They're my favorite food."

He crept closer and closer to the smell. He could hear some splashing at the edge of the river. Then he burst from the forest to find a mother beaver and six beaver kits (babies) next to the shore.

"All right beaver, time for dinner, and you're the dinner," he growled.

"Oh, ah, Mr. Wolf. Well you've caught us here and we can't get away from you, as big and as strong as you are," said Mother Beaver. She paused for a moment. "But you know, my children and I are very muddy right now, and I never let my children come to dinner unless they are clean. Would you mind if we washed up a little more in the river, and then we'll be right there. What do you think?" she asked.

It was true that the Wolf didn't like eating too much dirt. When he looked at the muddy beavers, he said, "Uh, OK, but hurry it up."

Then he curled up on shore for a short nap. Wolf loved napping once he knew that dinner was on the way. Meanwhile, Mother Beaver led her kits down a little deeper into the water and they splashed water on each other. And as they washed they moved farther and farther into the river. They looked at Wolf, and then moved into deeper water. Until suddenly, "splash," they dove into the water and started swimming as fast as they could with their webbed beaver feet. They were almost across the river when Wolf realized what was happening. By then the beavers were already too far ahead. When they reached the opposite shore, Mother Beaver called back to the wolf.

"I'm terribly sorry, Mr. Wolf, but we won't be able to make it for dinner today. Maybe next time."

"Grrrr, all right, well I won't make that mistake again. There are other animals that I can eat in this forest," said Wolf as he set off into the woods.

It wasn't long before the Wolf's sensitive ears heard a sound like a clap of thunder coming from a clearing. He could smell sheep in the air and when he got to the clearing, he saw two rams butting heads.

"I love eating rams for dinner, they're my favorite food," thought Wolf.

He had learned his lesson from the last encounter. He wasn't going to let these rams run off. He ran right up to them.

"OK, rams, time for dinner, and you're the dinner! So get ready."

"Well, Mr. Wolf, I suppose you've got us. But if you eat us both now, we'll continue to fight in your belly, and I'm sure that would give you indigestion. How about you let us finish our fight, and then you can eat the loser?" said the largest Ram, winking at the smaller one.

"OK, but no running off. I'm staying right here in the middle of the field," said Wolf.

The two rams backed up to butt heads again, but this time, instead of ramming into each other, they both rammed Wolf— one from one side and one from the other. They knocked him out cold and ran off into the woods, smiling.

When the wolf awoke, the rams were nowhere to be seen, and every bone in his body hurt.

"Ugh, maybe I was a little too close to my food that time. I won't do that again," he thought.

Now Wolf was even hungrier than before. He decided to hobble into the hills. As he was walking he smelled something. It smelled very tasty. It smelled like deer.

"Ha-ha, I love little fawns for dinner. They're my favorite food," said Wolf.

Wolf followed that smell up a hill that was covered in thick green grass. At the top of that hill, he saw a young spike buck, all by itself, munching happily on the grass.

Wolf had learned from the last two encounters. He ran right up to the buck and grabbed on to its hind legs, so it couldn't run away or butt him with its antlers.

"OK, deer, time for dinner, and you're on the menu."

"Oh, ho, Mr. Wolf, I guess you caught me. There's nothing I can do now. But, Mr. Wolf I have just one request," said Deer.

"What is it? Hurry it up. I'm hungry," said the Wolf.

"Well, Mr. Wolf, I walked through a briar patch earlier today and got a huge thorn in my back foot and I can't seem to get it out. I would be more than willing to let you eat me and put me out of my misery, **if** you could pull that thorn out first."

Wolf let go of Deer's legs.

"Is that all you want me to do? No problem. Where's that thorn?"

"It's right there on my back foot."

Wolf looked closer and closer at Deer's foot. Then Deer reared back and kicked Wolf right in the face, sending him tumbling head over heels down the hill. As Wolf lay in a crumpled heap at the foot of the hill, he forgot all about dinner and began thinking about his life.

"What am I doing? Am I a cook, that I should ask my food to wash before I eat it? Am I a judge, that I should let my food decide an argument before I feed? Am I a doctor that I should pull out a thorn before I dine? No. I am a wolf. And I'd better start acting like one."

From that day on, wolves were a lot harder to trick. But to this day, they still have a hard time getting dinner.

**Teller notes:** Wolves feed on a wide range of wild and domestic prey species. Like most predators, they seem to concentrate on whatever food is easiest to catch. Several studies have shown that wolves often are most successful at catching very young, very old, sick, or injured deer, moose, or caribou. But even when prey is abundant, like most predators, wolves fail to catch their prey much of the time. In some cases, a wolf will succeed in catching prey only 5 percent of the time. That means that a wolf needs to chase deer several times before it catches one.

# Wolf Facts

**Name:** gray wolf (*Canis lupus*)

**Other names:** timber wolf, prairie wolf

**Size and coloration:** Gray wolves are 2½ feet tall at the shoulder, about the size of a German shepherd dog; they weigh about 80–90 pounds; they can be gray, tan, white, or black.

**Senses:** *Smell*—Wolves have an amazing sense of smell. They can track a moose by scent up to a mile away. Scientists estimate that a wolf's sense of smell is 100 times better than a human's sense of smell. In some ways, wolves actuall "see" their world through their noses.

*Hearing*—They also have acute hearing. Scientists estimate that a wolf can hear another wolf howl up to six miles away on the open tundra and up to four miles away in a forest.

**Food:** Wolves are predators. They use their sharp teeth to catch and kill deer, beaver, moose, hares, and other animals for food. They also scavenge dead animals (carrion) for food. A 100-pound wolf can eat up to 20 pounds of meat at one sitting. They will also dig holes and bury meat in "food caches" for later. Wolves sometimes hunt in packs and seem to show some cooperation in catching and killing large prey, like a 1,200-pound moose. Wolves generally kill prey that is very young, very old, sick, or injured. Healthy, adult prey can usually outrun or fight off a wolf pack.

**Travel:** Wolves can sprint up to 35 mph for short periods of time and can jog or "lope" all day at 5 mph. A wolf can easily travel 50 miles a day.

**Ecological niche:** Consumer carnivore; eats "weaker" or unlucky members of prey species

**Habitat:** Wolves are most common in forests today, but they can live in a wide range of habitats, from meadows to mountains.

## Other fun facts:

- Despite what folktales say, wolves are generally shy creatures that avoid human contact. The few times I have seen wolves in the wild, they turned and ran away as soon as they saw me.

- Wild wolf attacks on humans are extremely rare. The handful of wolf attacks that have occurred in the past 200 years in North America usually involved rabid animals or wolves who were fed for so long that they lost their natural fear of people. Wolves don't see humans as food or competition. They generally only kill prey animals like deer and beaver, or competitor animals like coyotes and dogs. This doesn't mean that wolves are harmless, though. Wolves can kill a 1,200-pound moose, so they are certainly capable of killing a 200-pound human.

- In Europe, the story is different. There are historic records of fatal wolf attacks in France, Germany, and other countries. Some scientists contend that this might have been due to an outbreak of rabies in Europe or to wolves learning that humans are edible when they scavenged human bodies that were left on battlefields.

- Wolves live in family units called "packs." A pack consists of a mother and father wolf, often called the "alpha male" and "alpha female." The rest of the pack consists of the offspring from this pair. In Minnesota, wolf packs average five to eight wolves. Pack members hunt together in the winter, defend a territory, and work together to raise the young each year. Wolves that leave a pack or "disperse" to a new area may find a mate and form their own new pack.

- Wolves don't "howl at the moon." They do howl at any time of the day or night. They howl to communicate with other pack members, to find a lost pack member, to get ready for a hunt, or to advertise their territory and frighten off other wolf packs.

### Other wolf stories in this book:

"Wolf and Mouse as Farmers" (adapted from Egypt) (p. 93)

"Why Squirrels Live in Trees" (Finland) (p. 96)

"Robin's Red Breast" (Ireland) (p. 114)

"The First Wolf" (Finland) (p. 202)

### For more information:

Visit the International Wolf Center's Web site www.wolf.org for wolf facts, pictures, and a live Web cam of wolves at the center.

# Bear

*Themes:* adaptation—short tail and hibernation, food chain

## Why Bear Has a Stumpy Tail (Sweden)

One winter's day, Bear was hungry. He sniffed the air and gazed over the snowy woods. Then he smelled it: fish.

"Mmmm, I love fish," said Bear. He could see Fox coming up the hill with three fish on her back. Bear hid behind a bush, hoping to surprise Fox and steal some fish. As Fox climbed the hill, she noticed Bear's long black tail sticking out from behind the bush. Fox knew that she needed a plan.

"I didn't steal these fish from that fisherman just to lose them to Bear," thought Fox.

Then, when Fox was almost to the bush, she called out, "Boy these fish are heavy. I wish I had some help carrying them back to my den. I'd be happy to share them with anyone who helped me."

Just then Bear came out from behind the tree, looking for a free meal.

"Hey Fox, I can help carry your fish," said Bear, "I'm very strong."

"Bear, I was just thinking of you," said Fox. "I was thinking that I have so many fish that I should really share some with my good friend Bear. But then I thought to myself that that wouldn't be a very nice thing to do."

Bear frowned.

"Why wouldn't that be a nice thing to do, Fox?"

"Well Bear, I could give you a fish now, and you would be hungry in a couple hours," said Fox. "Or I could teach you how to fish, and then you would never be hungry again. But I don't have much time, so I can only do one or the other. Which will it be, Bear?"

Bear thought about that for a moment and finally decided that he should learn how to fish.

"Wonderful Bear, wonderful," smiled Fox. "All you have to do is go down to the frozen pond, break a hole in the ice with your paw, and put your long, furry tail into the water. When you feel fish nibbling on your tail, pull it out and you'll have all the fish you want."

Of course, that wasn't how Fox got his fish, but Bear didn't know that. Bear did as he was told, and Fox went home to eat his stolen fish.

After Bear had stuck his tail in the icy water and waited and waited, finally, he tried to pull it out. But it wouldn't move.

"I must have caught a really big fish on my tail!" thought the excited Bear. He pulled and pulled until he heard a snap and fell forward on his nose. When Bear looked behind him, he saw that his tail was no longer attached to his rear end.

After that, Bear decided that he didn't want to eat fish anyway. He went off to his den and went to sleep. From that day on, bears have had stumpy tails, and from that day on, when snow falls and ice forms on the lakes, rather than going ice fishing, bears sleep all winter long.

**Teller notes:** Animals that have long tails like monkeys, squirrels, or red foxes use them for something. Some monkeys use their tails as a fifth arm to grab onto branches. Squirrels use their fluffy tails to help them balance on branches, and foxes use their tails as a blanket to help them stay warm. Since a large tail wouldn't seem to confer any of these benefits on an animal as large as a bear, it seems natural that bears wouldn't evolve to have long tails. Such an appendage might just get in their way.

*Themes:* adaptation—fur color
*Pronunciation:* sauna (SOW-na), a Finnish steam bath

# Why Bear Has a Black Coat (Adapted from Finland)

Long ago, Bear was white. He was white like the snow or white like the clouds on a sunny day. While Bear liked being white in the winter, so he could hide behind snowdrifts, in the summer, he couldn't hide at all.

"I need to get a new color for my fur," said Bear one day.

He began looking around at all of the other animals. He didn't really like the gray of a wolf's fur or the brown of the deer. He didn't like stripes on a chipmunk, but then he saw Fox.

"Red, that's the color that I want for my fur," thought Bear.

Of course, he didn't know how to get that color for his fur. So he had to think about that.

"I know," said Bear, "I'll paint my fur."

So he went out into the forest and gathered all of the raspberries and strawberries and baneberries that he could find. He squished them up in his paws and spread them all over his fur and he turned . . . pink. That wasn't exactly the color he was going for. And what was worse, it wasn't permanent! The first time he went for a swim, the berry colors washed right out of his fur and he was white again.

"Wait a minute, if Fox already has a red coat, maybe he can tell me how I can get one, too!" thought hopeful Bear.

So Bear caught a couple fish, for a gift, and then went looking for Fox. He found Fox napping at the edge of a field.

"Hey Fox, how's it going?" said Bear.

Fox slowly stretched and opened his eyes.

"It's going fine with me, how's it going with you," he said.

"Well Fox, I had a couple extra fish, so I thought I would share them with you, since we are such good friends and all," said Bear.

Fox didn't remember being especially good friends with Bear, but a fish is a fish. So he helped himself to the meal. When they finished eating. Bear looked over at Fox.

"Say Fox, how did you get such a wonderful red coat?"

Fox smiled, because he saw a chance to play a trick on the gullible Bear.

"Well, I can't tell you how we foxes got our red coats, but I can show you how we did it."

"You'd do that for me?" said Bear.

"Sure," said Fox. "Anything for my good friend, Bear. The first thing you need to do is find a big hollow red pine tree. When you find that, come get me again."

"No problem Fox, I know this woods like the back of my paw. I'll find a hollow tree in no time flat," said Bear.

Bear searched on the hills and he searched in the valleys and he searched by the river until he found a big hollow red pine tree lying on its side. When Fox saw the tree he told Bear. "Now the next step is to gather a lot of sticks and grass and brush."

"What for?" said Bear.

"It's part of the plan. Now do you want a red coat or not?" said Fox.

Bear started gathering the sticks and twigs. When they had a pile of sticks and grass and brush, Fox told Bear to climb into the log.

"What do I do in there?" said Bear.

"You can take a nap. I'll take care of the rest from out here," said Fox.

Bear liked to take naps, so he settled into the log and was soon snoring away. In the meantime, Fox covered the log entrance with sticks and brush and lit it all on fire. Bear woke up when he smelled the smoke.

"Hey, hey Fox, what's going on!" shouted Bear.

"It's a sauna, Bear. The heat from the fire will get the log to sweat and then that red pine sweat will drip on you and turn your fur red, like mine," lied Fox.

For a little while, Bear believed what Fox had said. But soon, the smoke filled the log and it burned Bear's eyes and his nose and his throat.

"No red fur coat is worth this," thought Bear.

He put his head down and ran through the flames and out of that log. He felt his fur on fire, so he kept running and jumped into the river.

The water put out the flames, and when Bear climbed back on shore, he realized that his fur had changed color, but not the way he had wanted it to. Now his fur was burned sooty black from the flames, all except for a white patch on his chest, which his chin covered as he ran through the fire.

That is why Bear is black to this day and why Bear no longer trusts Fox.

**Teller notes:** Contrary to their common name, not all "black bears" are black. Most of them are black, but some are brown and some are even white. Scientists believe that the dark color of black bears' fur may have helped them to hide in the forest from natural enemies back in the days of saber-tooth tigers and short-faced bears.

*Themes:* adaptation—hibernation, food chain

# Why Bear Sleeps Through the Winter (African American)

One day, as all the animals were getting ready for winter, Rabbit, Squirrel and Chipmunk were all out gathering seeds and nuts for food. But as they searched, they found little to eat, and then they saw why. There were huge bear paw prints all over in the woods.

"Boy, if this keeps up, Bear is going to eat up everything in the forest," said Rabbit.

Squirrel and Chipmunk agreed.

"But what can we do about that?" said Squirrel. "If I were to say anything, Bear would just eat up my stash of nuts and laugh all the way home."

"Well, if we don't know the answer," said Chipmunk. "Maybe we should find someone who does."

The three went off through the woods. The first animal they ran into was Frog. They told her their problem. She didn't have a solution, but she had a suggestion.

"Let's go ask Mole."

So they went to ask Mole. He didn't have a solution either, but he did have a suggestion.

"Let's go ask Fox."

So they went to go ask Fox, because everyone knows how clever Fox is.

Fox agreed that if they didn't do something, when winter hit and food was hard to find, Bear was likely to gobble up all that was left.

"We need a plan," said Fox. "Now we all know how strong Bear is, so we can't just chase him off. And we know how much Bear loves to eat. But what does Bear love more than eating?"

The animals all thought, and then Mole squeaked, "Sleep! Bear loves to sleep."

"Exactly," smiled Fox.

They thought some more, and by the time the sun went down, they had a plan. The next day, Squirrel went scampering through the trees until he found a big hollow log lying on its side. Then he ran back and led the other animals to the log.

"Yes, this will work perfectly," mused Fox. "Now, you know your jobs."

Frog and Mole gathered mud and dirt, Squirrel gathered up sticks. Rabbit and Chipmunk gathered berries, nuts, and seeds. In the meantime, Fox gathered some raspberries and went in search of Bear.

When Bear saw Fox coming with some raspberries, he greeted Fox the same way he greeted everybody who had food: "Hey, you going to eat that?"

"No, help yourself," said the smiling Fox. "But if you're really hungry, I found a log with lots of food inside it just down that hill."

"Really?" said Bear in mid-bite.

Fox led Bear right to that hollow log. The animals had filled it with nice, warm leaves and tasty food. Bear gobbled up all the food he could, and then he fell fast asleep in the log. That night, all of the animals came back to seal up the log with mud, leaves, and sticks.

"That should keep him out of our fur for a while," said Fox.

And sure enough, it did. Bear woke up the next day, but it was still dark in that sealed-up log.

"Oh, it must still be nighttime," thought Bear, and he went back to sleep.

Since Bear could never see the sun in that log, he never got up, until the spring, when the snow melted and washed away some of that mud on the log. Bear pushed his way out of the log, stretched and yawned.

"Boy, that was a good nap!"

But when he looked around, he realized that the world had changed while he had been asleep. When he had climbed into the log, it was a frosty fall day, and now it was spring, with green leaves sprouting from the trees! Food was plentiful once again.

"Boy, I should do this every year!" thought Bear as he ambled off into the woods in search of some ants or ferns for breakfast.

That is why, to this day, Bear finds a comfy burrow in the fall and sleeps right through the winter, and that is also why, though food is scarce when the snow flies, there is always enough for animals like Rabbit, Squirrel, Chipmunk, and Fox.

**Teller notes:** This story comes from the African American community in Georgia and the Carolinas. Given similarities between this story and some stories of the Cherokee, Creek, and other native peoples of the region, it seems likely that members of these groups shared stories and got story ideas from each other.

Bear "hibernation" seems to be an effective way for bears to survive the food-poor winter season. Researchers tell us that bears don't truly hibernate. It would be more accurate to say they go into a deep winter sleep. Over 95 percent of the bears that enter this deep sleep survive the winter. But bears have to put on a lot of weight to allow them to sleep through the winter. That is why they gorge on berries, seeds, and other foods each fall. Some bears gain 100 pounds of extra weight before going into their burrows.

# Bear Facts

**Name:** American black bear (*Ursus americanus*)

**Size and coloration:** Male black bears are 5–6 feet long and 2–3 feet tall at the shoulder and weigh between 200 and 350 pounds. Females are smaller, weighing 100 to 180 pounds. Despite their common name, black bears can also be brown (or cinnamon) or white.

**Senses:** Black bears are probably nearsighted, but they have color vision equal to ours. Black bears also have a great sense of smell. Scientists estimate that a bear can smell carrion (dead animals) up to a mile away.

**Food:** Black bears are omnivores, meaning that they eat plants and animals, just like humans do. About 75 to 90 percent of a black bear's diet is plant material from acorns to ferns, berries, catkins, and leaves. Black bears have been known to prey on deer or moose calves in the spring. But most of the "meat" that they eat is from smaller creatures like ants, wasps, caterpillars, and other grubs. One bear at a wildlife refuge in northern Minnesota crawled under a mobile home and came out with a paper wasp nest in its mouth. It gobbled down the wasp nest to eat the wasp larvae inside. Bears will also eat carrion (dead animals). In the fall bears go on a feeding frenzy, consuming up to 20,000 calories per day (the average human consumes about 2,000 calories per day). Black bears put on about 100 extra pounds of weight before going into hibernation. They will lose that weight, about 30 to 40 percent of their total body weight, during hibernation.

**Predators:** human hunters

**Travel:** Despite their size, black bears are fast. They can sprint up to 35 mph for short periods of time. Bears have been known to travel up to 100 miles from their home range in search of good fall feeding sites.

**Ecological niche:** consumer omnivore; eats fruit and spreads seeds in its scat

**Habitat:** deciduous and coniferous forests

## Other fun facts:

- There are two other bear species in North America. The brown bear in the Western Rockies, Canada, and Alaska and the polar bear of northern Canada. Both of those species are larger and more carnivorous than black bears. They are also much more aggressive toward humans.

- Black bears have been known to kill humans, but on a statistical basis, wasps, domestic dogs, and lightning pose much greater risks to the public. In many cases, bear attacks happen in places where tourists had hand-fed bears in the past. When the bears lost their fear of humans, they became more aggressive and dangerous to people. As the National Park Service says, "a fed bear is a dead bear," and park officials often have to kill "socialized bears" to protect park visitors.

## Other bear stories in this book:

"How Chipmunk Got Her Stripes" (adapted from Mongolia)

# Deer

*Themes:* adaptation—antlers and legs, self-acceptance

## Deer's Antlers (Aesop)

One day a Deer was walking thought the forest. But every few steps, he would sniff the air to make sure that he was safe. You see, the world is a dangerous place for deer. They fear wolves and dogs and hunters most of all. But this time, Deer didn't smell any of those things, so he walked to a pond to get a drink. The morning air was still and the pond was smooth like a mirror. As Deer gazed at his reflection on the pond's surface, he thought to himself:

"Look at my beautiful antlers! I should be king of all the forest creatures. No animal has a crown as wonderful as mine."

But then Deer's gaze fell to his legs, his skinny, bony deer legs.

"That's why I am not king. You can't be a king if you have spindly, skinny legs like these!"

Just then Deer heard a twig snap. He looked up to see a hunter with his bow drawn. Deer turned and ran into the woods. The arrow flew right past Deer's head and sank into a tree trunk. Deer zigzagged through the trees. But he could hear the hunter and the hunter's dog right behind. Deer came to a huge oak tree and tried to duck under its branches but, plunk, his antlers got stuck in the twigs. Deer pushed forward and he pushed to the right and he pushed to the left, but he couldn't get loose. He could hear the hunter and the dog closing in. Finally, with one last yank, he pulled back and with a snap, his antlers broke through the twigs. Deer ran around the oak tree and out into a meadow. He leapt and he leapt on those long deer legs until that hunter and his dog were just a bad, bad memory.

A few days later, Deer was walking in that same part of the forest. Once again, he sniffed the air to make sure there wasn't any danger. Then he walked to that pond for a drink. But before he drank he looked at his reflection in the water and said to himself, "Look at my beautiful legs."

**Teller notes:** Deer antlers and deer legs are both important physical adaptations for male deer (bucks). Deer use their legs to escape predators. In the fall, after growing their antlers all year long, bucks challenge each other to "antler shoving matches" to see who will get to mate with nearby does. The strongest and most aggressive bucks often win these contests and mate. Contrary to popular belief, antler size is not directly related to the age of a deer. Size is more closely related to the health and nutrition of the deer. A well-fed, four-year-old buck that eats corn in southern Minnesota is likely to have a much larger rack of antlers than a four-year-old buck from the relatively food-poor regions of northern Michigan, where it can feed only on grass and twigs all summer.

*Themes:* adaptation—deer hooves, turtle shells

# Why Deer Has Split Hooves
# (Adapted from the Philippines)

At the beginning of time, Turtle was walking through the forest when she met Deer.

"Hello, my friend," said Turtle.

Deer stuck his nose in the air and walked right by.

Turtle ran to catch up with the long-legged Deer, thinking, "Deer is strong and popular, if I could get him to be my friend he could help me if I got into trouble."

"Hey, Deer, are you feeling hungry? I bet if we worked together we could easily find enough food for both of us to eat. You could search the tree branches and I could search the ground," said Turtle, struggling to keep up with Deer.

Deer snorted.

"Ha! Work with you? Why would a powerful creature like me need the help of such a lowly dust-breather like you? You should stick to your own slow kind where you belong!"

That insult made Turtle's face turn hot. She felt tears welling up when she shouted out in anger, "If you think I am so slow, then I challenge you to a race."

"Race with a Turtle?" scoffed Deer. "That would be a joke! Besides, all the other deer would laugh at me if I agreed to race with the likes of you."

But Turtle wouldn't give up. She was furious now.

"What do you think all the animals will say when I tell them that you were **afraid** to race with a turtle? If you refuse to race, I will tell everyone that you are a coward who can't face a challenge, even from **me!**"

That worried Deer. More than anything else, Deer cared about what people thought of him.

"Well, if you are that serious, then we will race. But don't think for a moment that I will take it easy on you because you're a turtle," said Deer.

They agreed that three days later they would meet at the edge of the forest and race across seven hills to the river. The first one to step in the river would be the winner.

As soon as the two animals parted, Turtle went to visit some turtle friends.

On the morning of the race, Turtle met Deer at the edge of the forest. Deer snickered.

"Are you ready to lose, Turtle?" said Deer.

"We'll see," said Turtle.

Animals had come from all over the forest to watch the race. Some thought it was a joke; others came in hopes of seeing that rude Deer lose at something.

Rabbit shouted "Go" to start the race, and the animals took off, Deer leaping across the grass and Turtle with her slow, plodding steps. As Deer climbed the first hill, he looked back to see Turtle, but she was nowhere to be found. As he crested the first hill, there was Turtle, running ahead of him.

"How did she get ahead of me?" thought Deer as he ran even faster over the hill, passing turtle once again.

The same thing happened at the second hill and every hill after that. Deer started getting nervous. Every time he thought he had beaten Turtle, Turtle kept coming back!

When Deer once again crested the seventh hill, he didn't see Turtle at the top.

"Ha, I've beaten him at last!" shouted Deer, but then he looked at the river below him. There, splashing in the water, was Turtle. Turtle had won the race!

The birds and the rabbits and the frogs all cheered for Turtle. They were glad that a small animal had won the race.

But Deer was not a good loser. He was so angry about the loss that when he reached the river, he leapt up and tried to smash Turtle under his round hooves. But Turtle was ready for that. She pulled her head and legs into her strong shell. When Deer landed on that hard shell, he landed so hard that he split his hooves in two. That is why, to this day, deer have split hooves.

When Deer had limped off into the woods, Turtle climbed the hill to call out, "You can come out now." Then seven turtles came out of the grass along the race trail. Deer never found out that Turtle had tricked him by placing one of her friends on each hill, but from that day to this, you won't find a deer willing to race with a turtle.

**Teller notes:**  Deer actually run on two "toes" of an elongated foot. This long foot helps deer run swiftly through the woods and helps them to escape predators.

You could further adapt this story by discussing how turtle got the cracks in her shell. I have adapted this story from the tale "Why the Carabao's Hoof Is Split," told by the Tagalog people of the Philippines.

# Deer Facts

**Name:** white-tailed deer (*Odocoileus virginianus*)

**Other names:** Other deer species in North America include the smaller mule deer (*Odocoileus hemionus*) and the much smaller Key deer (*Odocoileus virginianus clavium*). The moose (*Alces alces*) and caribou (*Rangifer tarandus*) are other North American members of the deer family.

**Size and coloration:** White-tailed deer are tan with a reddish-brown back in summer and a dull gray-brown back in winter. Male white-tailed deer are 6–7 feet long and 2½–3½ feet tall at the shoulder. They weigh 200 to 300 pounds. Females are smaller and weigh about 120 to 175 pounds.

**Senses:** Deers' most important sense is smell. Their hearing is also acute, with those large ears. But deer are probably nearsighted and colorblind. When a deer hears something that might be dangerous, it will wait until it can see what it is before running away. When it sees something, it will wait to hear it before running away, but if a deer smells danger, it runs right away, not waiting to see or hear the danger.

**Food:** A deer is an herbivore, meaning that it eats plants. Deer are also ruminants, meaning that they chew their food and swallow it, but then later regurgitate it and chew it again before swallowing it again and sending the food back into another part of their four-chambered stomachs. This process helps deer get more nutrition out of their twig and leaf food. This is the same process that cows use to digest their food. Deers' main foods include grass, flowers, clover, tree seedlings (especially white pines and white cedars), aspen leaves, pine needles, and acorns. Deer eat six to nine pounds of "browse" or plant food per day. A deer can lose up to 33 percent of its body weight in harsh northern winters and still survive.

**Predators:** Wolves, coyotes, bears, and humans all hunt deer for food. But deer are not the helpless prey they might appear in cartoons. One kick from an adult deer could kill or seriously injure a wolf.

**Travel:** White-tailed deer can run up to 42 mph, just slightly faster than their main wildlife predator, the gray wolf. Deer can swim at about 4 mph and have been seen several miles out at sea. They can leap up to 29 feet across and can clear a 7-foot fence. In northern regions, where snow might pile up 20 inches or more, deer might migrate up to 90 miles to traditional "deer yards," where they group together in fir, spruce, or cedar stands to seek protection from cold winds and deep snow.

**Ecological niche:** consumer herbivore and prey species

**Habitat:** deciduous (broadleaf) and mixed (broadleaf and evergreen) forests and forest edges

## Other fun facts:

- Only male deer grow antlers. Males use their antlers in their sparring fights with other males during the fall rut. Stronger males chase off smaller or weaker males and are then more likely to mate with females. Male deer grow a new pair each year and lose them each year in December or January. Mice and squirrels chew dropped antlers for the calcium they contain.

- Deer fawns are born with spotted coats and with virtually no scent. That way if they stay still, they will blend in with the sun-dappled forest floor and it will be difficult for predators to find them.

# Fox

*Themes:* adaptation—tail color, food chain

## Why Fox Has a White Tip on His Tail (Germany)

Long ago, when animals could talk like people, an old woman needed a shepherd to help out at lambing time. Most of the people were busy with their own flocks, so the only one to apply for the job was Fox. At first the woman was suspicious, but Fox had such a gentle voice.

"I've got lots of experience watching sheep," said Fox, smiling to himself. Soon those ewes would give birth and he could gobble up a lamb.

Given no other options, the woman hired Fox. Everything seemed to go well until several days later when Fox came running up to the woman's house.

"It was terrible, just terrible!" Fox sobbed.

"What happened?" said the alarmed woman.

"A bear . . . a big bear came into the field and took a lamb during the night. I tried to stop it, but it was so much bigger than me. I'm sorry, I failed you."

"Nonsense," said the woman. "Other shepherds have lost lambs to bears before. You are doing your best and that's all I can ask."

Fox smiled to himself. Soon he would have another lamb dinner.

That night the old woman felt sorry for the Fox and took him some fresh cream to cheer him up. But when she entered the field, there was Fox, eating a lamb.

"Thief! Liar!" she yelled and threw the bucket of cream at him.

Fox ran for cover, but the cream hit his tail, painting it white. Perhaps it was magic cream or perhaps the woman put a spell on Fox, but every fox's tail has been tipped with white ever since. And ever since that day, no one has hired a fox as a shepherd.

**Teller notes:** Given that the fox has such an unusual bright red coat, it seems surprising that there aren't more surviving stories that explain the coloration. The few stories that do remain seem to focus on how foxes got a white tip on their tails. Foxes use their fluffy tails as scarves or blankets to keep warm when they curl up to sleep during the winter.

*Themes:* food chain, adaptation—hunting techniques

# Fox Learns to Hunt (Original)

At the beginning of time, all of the members of the dog family—Wolf, Dog, Coyote, and Fox—lived and hunted together. But when the bigger animals set off after a deer or rabbit, Fox just couldn't keep up.

One day, while in the middle of a hunt, Fox tripped and fell into a bush. He lay there crying and feeling sorry for himself, when Cat walked up.

"What's the problem," purred Cat.

"I'm just no good at being a dog," said Fox. "I'm too small and my legs are too short and I just can't keep up on a hunt."

" 'Keeping up' is overrated," said Cat, stretching out in the sun. "Besides, there are lots of ways to hunt."

"There are?" said Fox, wiping away a tear.

"Sure," said Cat. "Those dogs are always running around barking and chasing things. You would never see a cat doing that."

"How do you hunt?" asked Fox.

"Well we sneak up on things, like any proper hunter would do," said Cat.

"Could you show me how to do that?" said Fox.

"I suppose I could," said Cat. "If you'll help me catch those red mice in my master's fields."

Fox was a fast learner, and soon he could stalk and pounce on mice almost as well as Cat. Between the two of them, they cleaned out all of the red mice in that field. People say that that is why you don't see red mice in our fields today, and why Fox has a red coat. After all, you are what you eat.

**Teller notes:**    Since I couldn't find a folktale that explained why foxes have red coats, I developed this one. Foxes do hunt like cats, stalking and then pouncing on their mouse prey. Pink flamingos get the pink pigment for their feathers from the plankton they eat. But the same doesn't seem to be true for foxes or other mammals.

# Fox Facts

**Name:** red fox (*Vulpes vulpes*)

**Other names:** The "silver fox" and "cross fox" are other, darker color phases of the red fox. Another North American fox is the tree-climbing gray fox (*Urocyon cinereoargenteus*).

**Size and coloration:** Red foxes are 3–4 feet long (including a 1–1½-foot tail) and 14–18 inches tall at the shoulder. They are reddish-orange or reddish-yellow with white bellies and black legs. Their tails are often tipped with white.

**Senses:** A red fox's senses of hearing and smell are the most acute. A fox can reportedly hear a mouse or vole scurrying in tall grass or under up to five inches of snow. It can hear a mouse squeak up to 150 feet away. Red foxes use their sense of smell to detect enemies, to find food "caches," and to find carrion (dead animal) meals.

**Food:** Foxes are technically carnivores and eat mainly meat, but they also consume berries and nuts on occasion. Their primary prey includes mice, voles, rabbits, hares, chipmunks, grasshoppers, beetles, and grouse. Although they are a member of the canine (dog) family, foxes hunt like cats, sneaking up on prey and then pouncing on it. A fox can leap up to 15 feet to land on a mouse or rabbit. Red foxes will hide or cache extra food under leaves or brush piles so they can eat it later. Red foxes eat about a pound of food per day.

**Predators:** Coyotes, bobcats, and lynx can prey on foxes. Humans also trap them for their fur.

**Travel:** A red fox can run up to 30 mph and can leap 15 feet onto prey.

**Ecological niche:** consumer carnivore; may spread seed from berries in their scats (droppings)

**Habitat:** forests, meadows, and farmland

## Other fun facts:

- Red foxes prefer to live in forest edges, meadows, and open woods. As humans have cleared forests in North America for farms and suburbs, we have created perfect red fox habitat.

- The gray fox (*Urocyon cinereoargenteus*), which prefers life in deep forests, can climb trees to escape danger.

- Red foxes are highly adaptable and often find ways to live near humans. They feed on the mice on farms and on garbage, dog food, rabbits, or cats in urban areas.

## Other fox stories in this book:

# Interview a Mammal Activity

**Grade Level:** 3–8

**Environmental Themes:** adaptation, habitat

**Curriculum Areas:** science, social studies, language arts

**Student Skills:** comprehension, inferring, comparison, imagination, public speaking

**Materials:** paper, pencils, animal pictures, animal resource books (see the bibliography)

## Instructions:

1. In this activity, students will take the role of reporters interviewing different mammals. First help students define how mammals are different from other groups of animals like birds, reptiles, and amphibians. As a group, have students come up with a list of questions for the interview.

2. Have students choose an animal to "interview" (research) and then write out their interview as if it were a news story. Remember, in a news story, you put the most important information first and less important information at the end. In this case, you might put information about misconceptions or fears people have about this animal first. Put well-known information about the mammals toward the end of the article, since that might not be as interesting as new information.

3. Have students find a picture of the animal they are interviewing and make a report about their animal to the class.

## Evaluation:

Did students research their animal to answer all of the questions on the class list? Can students describe the new things that they learned about the animal?

From Kevin Strauss, *Tales with Tails: Storytelling the Wonders of the Natural World.* Westport, CT: Libraries Unlimited, 2006. Copyright © 2006 by Kevin Strauss.

# Adaptation Assessment Activity

| | |
|---:|:---|
| **Grade Level:** | 3–8 |
| **Environmental Themes:** | adaptation, habitat |
| **Curriculum Areas:** | science |
| **Student Skills:** | comprehension, inferring, comparison |
| **Materials:** | large pictures of wildlife (from calendars, posters, or magazines), scissors, paper, and pencils |

**Instructions:**

1. Working in small groups, have students look at an animal picture and try to determine what physical adaptations (or "tools") that animal has. Does it have unusually large ears or eyes? Does it have long legs? How could the animal use these physical tools to survive?

2. Have students make a list of their visual conclusions about the animal's adaptations. Then have the students research what the animal eats, how it avoids predators, and how it finds a mate. Now have students look at the picture again and see if they can find additional physical adaptations that would help the animal survive and reproduce.

3. Have students use sticky notes or paper and tape to put captions on their animal pictures identifying their animal's physical adaptations and how animals use them to survive. Post the posters around the classroom and go on an "adaptation poster tour."

**Evaluation:**

Did students complete the project? Did every member of a group contribute to the project? Can students describe the most surprising fact that they learned from this activity?

From Kevin Strauss, *Tales with Tails: Storytelling the Wonders of the Natural World.* Westport, CT: Libraries Unlimited, 2006. Copyright © 2006 by Kevin Strauss.

# Chapter 7

## Animal Stories: Small Mammals

# Rabbit

*Themes:* adaptation—rabbit ears, stumpy tail

## How Rabbit Got His Long Ears (African American)

A long time back, Rabbit loved to eat fish. They were Rabbit's favorite food. He liked eating them baked or fried or even boiled. Now one day, in the middle of winter, Rabbit was walking down the path when he saw Fox coming up the path carrying three big fish on his back. Fox had just stolen those fish from a fisherman, but Rabbit didn't know that.

"Hey there, Fox, it looks like you caught yourself some fish," said Rabbit. "You wouldn't happen to be interested in sharing any of those fish, would you, friend?"

"Well, I'm not interested in sharing fish, but I will share my secret for catching them," said Fox.

Now Rabbit should have been suspicious of that right away. No real fisherman gives away his fishing secrets. But Rabbit didn't know that.

"All you've got to do is go down to the pond, find a place where someone cut a hole in the ice, and take that long, furry rabbit tail of yours and put it in the water. If you jiggle it around, those hairs will look like little worms. When a fish sees all those tasty worms, it will bite your tail. When you feel a fish bite, just pull up that tail and you'll have plenty to eat," said Fox.

Rabbit was excited. He hopped right down to the pond and found a hole in the ice. He took his furry white rabbit tail and stuck it into the water, and he waited. He waited and he waited until the sun set and the moon climbed high into the sky. The winter wind began to blow so Rabbit decided it was time to go home, except when he tried to get up, he couldn't move. He looked down and saw that his hole in the ice had frozen solid. He was stuck. Now if Rabbit was a big animal like Bear or Moose, he might have tried to pull his tail loose. But Rabbit wasn't that kind of animal. Instead he yelled for help.

"Help, help, someone help me, I'm stuck in the ice, help, help, help!"

Now most of the animals were asleep. But Owl, with her sharp ears, heard Rabbit's plea for help. Owl swooped down and landed next to Rabbit.

"What seems to be the problem, Rabbit?" said Owl.

"Well, I was sitting here trying to fish with my tail, the way Fox taught me, and the water froze and now I'm stuck!" said Rabbit.

Owl just shook her head.

"Rabbit, you should know better than to listen to anything that Fox tells you. But now that you're stuck, maybe I can help you out."

Owl flapped her wings and flew up over Rabbit's head. She reached down with her feet and grabbed on to Rabbit's short, stubby little ears and she began pulling and pulling and pulling and pulling and pulling until . . . "snap," Rabbit was loose! Owl flew Rabbit to a nearby snowdrift and set him down.

"Now you be careful, the next time you go fishing," said Owl before she turned and flew silently off into the night.

Rabbit was just thinking that he didn't really like fish that much, anymore, anyway. But just then, the moon came out from behind a cloud and shown down on Rabbit. Rabbit looked at his shadow on the snow, but he didn't recognize himself. He reached up to his ears and realized that when Owl pulled him out of the ice, she stretched his ears, making them long and thin. But that wasn't the half of it. When he reached around behind him, he realized that he couldn't find his tail. He looked back and saw most of his long, furry white tail still frozen in the pond.

That was the last day that Rabbit ate fish. But they do say that those long ears came in handy for Rabbit, helping him hear when troublemakers like Fox or Wolf are coming his way.

*Theme:* adaptation—stumpy tail

# How Rabbit Lost Her Tail (China)

Long ago there were three rabbit sisters. They loved to hop in the meadow and nibble on clover. And when they weren't nibbling on clover, they were combing their beautiful, long, furry rabbit tails. One day, once they had eaten all of the tasty clover on their side of the wide, wide river, they looked across the river and saw what looked like a beautiful field of tasty green clover on the other side. They could see that clover. They could smell that cover. They could almost taste the clover. Oh how they would love to eat that clover. But then their gazes fell to the wide river that separated them from that field.

"Let's put our ears together," said Older Sister. "I'm sure we can figure out a way across."

Soon they had an idea. Older Sister went to the edge of the river.

"Hey, Snapping Turtle. Hey, Snapping Turtle," she called.

When a large turtle rose from the mud, Older Sister hopped back. The turtle was larger than she imagined and its sharp beak could easily bite off her ears.

"Um, hi, Turtle. How are you today?"

"I am always happier when people leave me alone," growled Turtle.

"Well my sisters and I have been having an argument and I was hoping that you could settle it for us."

"Maybe . . . what's in it for me?"

"Well, we were discussing if there are more rabbits in the world or turtles," said Older Sister. "I was thinking that it must be turtles, but my sisters think it must be rabbits."

"Of course there are more turtles, I have hundreds of children," said Turtle.

"Well I would like to take your word for it, but unfortunately, my sisters need more proof. Is there any way that you could bring your children to this part of the river so we could count them?"

Turtle raised her head. Now this was a contest, and Turtle wanted to make sure that her family won.

"Of course, I'll show you rabbits who has more children. It might take a week, but I will get my children here."

A week later, the rabbit sisters met the turtle family in the river. They saw hundreds of turtles swimming in all directions. There were big turtles and little turtles. There were skinny turtles and chubby turtles. There were slow turtles and there were more slow turtles. But they were all the children of Snapping Turtle.

"Here we are," said Turtle.

"It's very hard to count you with all of your children swimming in all directions," said Older Sister. "Could you all line up from one side of the river to the other? Then we could count you as we hop across your backs."

The turtles lined up across the river. Then the rabbit sisters hopped from one turtle to another counting one, two, three, four as they hopped across the turtles' backs until they reached the other side. When they landed on the grassy shore, the two younger rabbit sisters hopped off to eat clover.

Snapping Turtle called after the rabbits.

"So, who won the argument?"

Older Sister just laughed.

"You may have more children than we have, but we are clearly smarter than you. Thanks for the free ride across the river. We could never have done it without you."

Then she ran off to join her sisters. Snapping Turtle's face turned hot with anger. She knew that she would never be able to catch those rude rabbits, so she bided her time. One day, the rabbit sisters came to a part of the field that had rocks among the clover. They thought nothing of it and started eating their clover. Suddenly they heard a "Snap, snap, snap!" sound. They turned around and realized that three of those "rocks" were really turtles and those three turtles had just bitten off their three tails.

"Who thinks they are clever now," said Snapping Turtle. Then she and her children slowly turned and walked back to the river. That is why to this day, rabbits have short tails and why they steer clear of turtles.

**Teller notes:** Rabbits can actually swim, although most rabbit species don't spend much time in the water. There are rabbit species that live in swamps and marshes and spend much of their time swimming, but they are a minority in the rabbit world. Most rabbits use their strong back legs to hop away from their enemies. A rabbit's poor eyesight probably wouldn't allow it to see clover on a far off field, but it could probably smell its way to a new feeding field. Biologists tell us that animals that have a tail generally use that tail for something. Foxes use their tails to keep them warm when they curl up; squirrels use their tails to help them balance as they run on branches. If an animal species doesn't have a tail, it probably doesn't need one. Besides, if rabbits had long tails, it might be easier for predators to catch them.

# Rabbit Facts

**Name:** eastern cottontail rabbit (*Sylvilagus floridanus*)

**Rabbit basics:** The eastern cottontail rabbit is one of the most widespread rabbit species in North America. Other rabbit family species in North America include the snowshoe hare (*Lepus americanus*) in northern regions and the jackrabbit (*Lepus* species) in the West. They all have long ears and use speed and camouflage to escape their many enemies.

**Size and coloration:** 14–18 inches long; 2–4 pounds; grizzled coats of gray, brown, and white

**Senses:** Hearing is rabbits' most important sense; they also have a good sense of taste. Rabbits are probably nearsighted and colorblind; their wide-angle vision is good at detecting movement.

**Food:** Rabbits are herbivores, feeding on plants like dandelions, clover, alfalfa, and berries in the summer and on tree bark, twigs, and shrubs in the winter.

**Predators:** Virtually every large predator feeds on rabbits and hares, if the hunter can catch them. Wolves, foxes, coyotes, lynx, bobcats, owls, hawks, and eagles are the most common predators. Because they are a prey species, rabbits reproduce very quickly. Cottontail rabbits can have litters of four to eight and produce three to four litters per year. Young rabbits are independent after five weeks.

**Travel:** Cottontail rabbits can sprint up to 30 mph Since this is slower than some predators over open ground, rabbits tend to avoid large, open areas. Instead they stick to shrubby thickets where they can run in a zigzag pattern to throw a fox or bobcat off course and find a brush pile or bush for cover. Rabbits seem to have a good memory about where they can hide in their small territories. They freeze and stay still when they first spot or hear a predator, only running when the predator heads right for them.

**Ecological niche:** Cottontail rabbits are herbivore consumers and a prey species. They are food for many other species. They also spread berry seeds in their scat (droppings).

**Habitat:** Cottontails prefer forest edges and thickets with ample cover, but they are also common in backyards.

## Other fun facts:

- A snowshoe hare's wide back feet help it to walk on top of the snow so it can outrun wolves and lynx. This hare is gray-brown in the summer but changes to white as winter approaches. This white coloration helps it blend in with its snowy winter habitat.

- A snowshoe hare can leap 13 feet horizontally and over 6 feet vertically.

- You can tell if a deer or rabbit (or hare) has eaten a twig by looking at it. Rabbits snip the twig at a clean 45-degree angle with their scissor-sharp front teeth. Deer usually tear twigs off, leaving a ragged bite mark behind.

# Chipmunk

*Themes:* adaptation—stripes, food chain

## How Chipmunk Got Her Stripes (Adapted from Mongolia)

After a long winter, Bear came out of his cave, and he was hungry. It was too early for leaves on the trees or berries on the bushes, and that made Bear angry. You see, Bear isn't all that different from the rest of us in that when he's really hungry, he gets grouchy.

As he stumbled through the woods, Bear met Chipmunk. Bear grabbed Chipmunk with his big paw and was just about to gulp her down when she squeaked, "Wait!".

That surprised Bear, so he stopped. Chipmunk thought fast.

"You look hungry. Would you like some food?"

"Yeah, I want some food. You got some?" growled Bear.

"Of course I do," said Chipmunk. "I store it up all summer so I have it all winter and spring. If you let me go, I'll go down my hole and get you some food."

That sounded like a good idea to Bear, at first.

"Wait a minute, if I let you go, you might just run down your hole and never come up. I'm not letting you go."

Then Chipmunk had an idea.

"I could take off my fur coat and leave it here," she said. "That way you know I will have to come back out to get my fur coat."

So Chipmunk took off her coat and gave it to Bear. Then she scurried down her hole and brought up bundles and bundles of acorns. Bear swallowed each bundle with a single gulp and growled a terse "More!"

Again and again, Chipmunk brought up her bundles of acorns, until her burrow was bare.

"That's the last," she said, hoping that now Bear was too full to eat her.

She edged closer to her hole, just in case he wasn't. Bear gulped down the acorns and then looked at Chipmunk. But now his eyes were calm, and his belly was full.

"You have been generous, Sister Chipmunk. Let me give you a gift."

Saying that, Bear took his claws and scratched stripes onto Chipmunk's coat.

"Now, whenever you are in danger, just freeze, and these stripes will help you hide in the woods."

Since that day, Chipmunks have had black and white stripes on their backs, all because of the day that Chipmunk shared her food with a Bear.

**Teller notes:** Scientists believe that stripes on the backs of animals like chipmunks help to break up their body outline and blend in with their surroundings in much the same way that camouflage clothing helps hunters hide in the woods during bow hunting season.

# Mouse

*Themes:* adaptation—food choices, food chain

## Wolf and Mouse as Farmers (Adapted from Egypt)

Now people change jobs all of the time, but we usually assume that the job that animals do in the world now is the one they have always done. Bees pollinate flowers and bats eat mosquitoes, but it wasn't always that way for the animals. In fact, a long time ago, Wolf was a farmer. Now this may be hard to imagine, but people say that it is a true as the sun in the summer and the breeze in the fall.

Back in those days, every spring Wolf would use his claws to till the soil. Then he would carry seeds in his mouth and spit them all over the ground. But Wolf was not a very good farmer. He would forget to water his crops or he would put off weeding them so he could lounge in the shade a little longer. And when fall came, Wolf's fields gave him very little to eat. It was no one's fault but his own, but Wolf didn't see things that way.

Now most animals, when faced with this situation, would change how they were doing things, but not Wolf. He was stubborn and he didn't like to change what he was doing, no matter how bad the results were. He started thinking about how he could get a good crop out of his fields without putting in any more work. Then it hit him.

"I know what I need. I need a partner," he said. "A partner could do all of the hard work while I just laze around in the sun."

Wolf thought about all of the animals in the valley to decide whom to get for his partner. In those days, all of the animals farmed, and the best farmer in the valley was Mouse, because even though Mouse is small, she is a very hard worker.

Wolf walked up to Mouse's house and knocked on the door. When Mouse answered, she was surprised to see Wolf standing outside. After all, Wolf and Mouse weren't exactly friends. In fact, they were barely on speaking terms.

"Mouse, you and I are going to be partners in farming, see," said Wolf, baring his teeth.

Mouse didn't want to disagree with Wolf, you see, Wolf could swallow Mouse with one gulp.

"Uh, OK, we can be partners. But if we're going to be partners, we need a contract," said Mouse.

"A contract? What's a contract?"

"Everybody knows what a contract is, Wolf," said Mouse. "It is an agreement about what work we will do and how much we will get paid."

"Oh yeah, I know all about that," lied Wolf. "How do we make one?"

"Well, let's see, since you are so good at clearing the land, why don't you do that. Since I am so good at planting seeds, I'll do that part. And we can both water and weed," said Mouse. "As for payment . . . since I live underground, how about I get to harvest everything that grows underground. Since you live above ground, you can have everything that grows there."

"Sounds good to me," said Wolf and they shook paws on it.

The next day, Wolf had rented some land from the bears. He cleared the land and tilled it with his claws. When Mouse got there, she began planting the seeds. But she didn't tell Wolf what sort of seeds she was planting.

The two of them weeded the field and watered the field throughout the summer. Slowly, little dark green leafy stalks rose above the ground. When fall came, Wolf gathered the green stalks, but when he tasted them, "yuck!" They didn't taste very good.

"Maybe they'll taste better later," thought Wolf.

When Wolf was done in the field, Mouse called to all of her friends and relations.

"OK, everybody, dig up those potatoes!"

And as Wolf watched, Mouse and his family dug up basket after basket of tasty potatoes. Later that day as Wolf sat in his cave, chewing on potato stalks, he started thinking to himself, "Wait a minute, Mouse tricked me once, but he won't trick me again."

The next day, Wolf stomped back to Mouse's house.

"OK, Mouse," he growled. "You tricked me once, but we are going to be partners again, see. But this time, I get to have what grows underground and you get left with what grows above ground."

"OK," said Mouse. What else could he say?

Once again, Wolf tilled the land and Mouse planted the seeds. But these seeds looked different from the first ones. Once again, Mouse never bothered to tell Wolf what sort of seed she was planting. As time went by, the seeds grew into tall, green stalks, with ears of corn at the top. When it came time to harvest, Mouse came up to Wolf.

"Say Wolf, under our agreement, I would get everything above ground. But I am feeling generous today, so all I want is the ears of corn. You can have everything else," said Mouse.

"Well, thank you Mouse, that's very generous of you," said Wolf. "And here I thought you would try to trick me again."

Mouse and her family gathered all of the corn from the stalks and went home with baskets and baskets of tasty corn. Wolf gathered the stalks and the skinny corn roots and took them home. But when he tried to eat the corn stalks, they tasted just like straw, because that was what they were. "Yuck!"

Wolf slammed his paw on the ground.

"Mouse tricked me again! Well, I won't let her get away with it this time!" he howled.

Wolf ran up to Mouse's house and pounded on the door. When Mouse opened the door, she was looking right into the moon-white teeth of an angry Wolf.

"Mouse, you tricked me again, so now we are going to have a contest."

"A contest?" squeaked Mouse.

"Yes, a contest. We are going to have a race from the river to the hill. Whoever wins the race will get to have all of the corn and potatoes that you gathered from our field this year," growled Wolf.

"OK, Wolf, whatever you say," said Mouse.

What else could he do? Now Mouse knew that her legs were much shorter than Wolf's legs. She couldn't win with her muscles, so she would have to use her brain. That night, Mouse gathered all of her friends and relations.

"Listen up everybody, I've got a plan."

The next morning, a mouse met Wolf at the river.

"Are you ready to race, Mouse?" laughed Wolf.

"Yeah, I'm ready," said the mouse.

"Get ready, get set, go!" yelled Wolf.

Wolf took off like a shot, running through the tall grass. After running a short ways, he looked back and he couldn't see the mouse.

"Hey Mouse, where are you? I couldn't have left you behind that quickly."

But then, ahead of him, he saw a mouse pop its head up above the grass.

"I'm over here Wolf, you slow-poke," yelled the mouse.

Wolf put his head down and started running as fast as he could. After he had run halfway to the hill he stopped for a rest, sure that Mouse was far behind.

"Hey mouse, where are you?" Wolf yelled.

Then he saw a mouse hopping out of the grass at the base of the hill.

"Hey Wolf, I'm over here. Hurry up you slowpoke!" said the mouse.

Wolf ran faster than he had ever run before, kicking up grass as he ran. When he got to the top of the hill, he was panting and out of breath, but even with his bleary eyes, he could see that he wasn't the first one there. Sleeping in a ball at the top of the hill was Mouse. Mouse opened her eyes and stretched.

"Well, Wolf, it is about time you got here," said Mouse. "I've been here for a while already."

"H-how did you get here so fast?" stammered Wolf.

"We mice are much faster than we look," said Mouse. "Some people say we are faster than the wind. But I like to think that we are just fast enough to get the job done."

Wolf figured then that if Mouse was that fast and that smart, he'd better not try to trick Mouse again. So he walked down the hill and back to his cave, where he began thinking of taking up a new job.

Once Wolf was gone Mouse called out, "OK, everybody, you can come out now." And with that, twenty little mouse heads peeked out of the grass between the river and the hill. You see, Mouse hadn't run the race at all. Wolf just couldn't tell one mouse from another.

After that, Wolf gave up farming. He decided to be a hunter, and he chased what he thought were slower animals, like deer and rabbits. But Mouse decided that she liked being a farmer. It was steady work and there was always plenty to eat. Her children still live on our farms to this day, planting crops and harvesting their share of grain.

**Teller notes:**  Despite what you may have seen in the movie *Never Cry Wolf,* mice are not a major part of the wolf diet. Wolves do sometimes eat mice, but they get more food per calorie of energy expended by catching larger prey like deer.

# Squirrel

*Themes:* adaptation—squirrels climbing trees, habitat

## Why Squirrels Live in Trees (Finland)

Wolf and Dog used to be the best of friends, but one day, they had an argument. Each of them thought that he was strongest. They argued back and forth until Wolf finally said, "OK Dog, if you want to prove you are stronger, I challenge you to a war. You gather the farm animals on your side and I will gather the forest animals on mine."

"Fine! I'll meet you in the forest clearing tomorrow," growled Dog.

Dog recruited Cow, Pig, Sheep, and Cat on his side. At the same time, Wolf recruited Bear, Fox, Wildcat, and Squirrel. Dog and his army got to the forest clearing first. Dog whispered to Cat, "Climb that tree and wait for the forest animals to come. Then jump on the back of the largest animal and grab him by the throat. We may not be the most fierce animals, but maybe we can surprise them and frighten them off."

When the forest animals arrived, Wolf smiled. Cow, Pig, and Sheep aren't much good at fighting.

"Forward, my friends!" called Wolf.

When Bear passed under Cat's tree, Cat leaped down on him and grabbed him by his throat.

"Help, help, someone's got me by the throat!" cried Bear.

Bear flopped over on his back, trying to reach the creature on his back. But Cat held on tight.

When the forest animals saw that the smallest farm animal had the biggest forest animal screaming on his back, they were terrified. Then Dog, Cow, Pig, and Sheep charged forward, and the forest animals ran into the woods. But Squirrel was too small to keep up with all of the larger animals, so he jumped up a tree and climbed high into the branches.

"Wonders have come to pass," said Squirrel. "When a Cat can defeat a Bear, then it is no longer safe to live on the earth."

And to this day, Squirrel has lived in the treetops where he can sit safe from most other animals, although he always keeps an eye out for Cat.

**Teller notes:** As rodents, squirrels have "overbites" like beavers. You might want to use that in your facial expressions for this story.

# Rodent Facts

**Group facts:** The rodent group includes a wide range of creatures, from mice and rats to squirrels, porcupines, and beavers. This is the largest single group of mammals, making up 40 percent of all mammal species. Each member of this group has two top and two bottom incisors (front teeth) that are very sharp, grow throughout the animal's lifetime, and are used for chewing. The name "rodent" means "chewer."

**Food:** Members of the rodent group tend to be herbivores (eating plants) or omnivores (eating plants and animals).

**Predators:** Most carnivores feed on some kind of rodent; owls, hawks, bobcats, foxes, and fishers are all major predators.

**Ecological niche:** Most rodents are prey species, providing food for larger predators.

**Habitat:** Rodents can be found in almost any habitat, from forests to meadows to mountains to cities.

## Other fun facts:

- All rodents have orange incisors (front teeth). These teeth grow constantly, and if the rodent stopped chewing, its teeth would grow so long that it would not be able to close its mouth or chew.

- Rodents survive despite high rates of predation by giving birth to large numbers of young and having multiple litters each year.

## Mouse

**Name:** deer mouse (*Peromyscus maniculatus*)

**Mouse basics:** This is one of the most wide-ranging native mouse species, found over most of North America. Other common mouse species include the introduced house mouse (*Mus domesticus*), which lives in houses and other buildings, and the tan white-footed mouse (*Peromyscus leucopus*), which lives in forests.

**Size and coloration:** 3½ inches long; 3-inch tail; reddish-brown back, white belly, feet, and chin

**Senses:** Mice have wide-angle vision to help them see predators. They also have sensitive hearing (so they can hear predators) and a good sense of smell (for finding food).

**Food:** conifer seeds, maple seeds, nuts, berries, beetles, grasshoppers, snails, carrion, birds, and small mammals

**Predators:** owls, snakes, weasels, foxes, hawks, and most other carnivore (meat-eating) predators

**Travel:** Mice can run up to 8 mph and can jump up to 1 foot high.

**Ecological niche:** omnivore consumer and prey species; also spreads berry seeds and fungus spores in its scat, also spreads seeds that grow in forgotten mouse food caches

**Habitat:** Deer mice prefer mature forests but can be found in most woods, they nest in ground burrows, hollow logs, brush piles, and stumps.

## Other fun facts:

- Although up to 95 percent of deer mice die within one year of birth, primarily due to predation, they can live two to three years in the wild.

- Deer mice have three to six young per litter and can have two to five litters per year.

- Young mice grow to adulthood in six months.

- Deer mice take up to 20 naps per day.

- Deer mice are arboreal (tree climbing) and have been known to take shelter in old bird nests. They also will cache (store) seeds and nuts in hollow logs or other protected areas.

## Chipmunk

| | |
|---|---|
| **Name:** | eastern chipmunk (*Tamias striatus*) |
| **Chipmunk basics:** | Chipmunks are "ground squirrels" that spend much of their time on the forest floor. The stripes on their backs break up their outline and help them blend in with their forest surroundings. |
| **Size and Coloration:** | 3–5 inches long, 3–4-inch tail; gray-brown with black and white stripes down its back |
| **Senses:** | good sense of smell and taste; wide-angle, colorblind vision that is good at noticing movement |
| **Food:** | nuts, berries, buds, mice, frogs, insects, and bird eggs |
| **Predators:** | coyotes, foxes, bobcats, hawks, owls, and snakes |
| **Travel:** | Chipmunks can sprint up to 15 feet per second (about 10 mph). |
| **Ecological niche:** | omnivore consumer and prey species; also distributes berry seeds in its scat (droppings) |
| **Habitat:** | woody or brushy areas |

### Other fun facts:

- Chipmunks are "true hibernators" like bats and turtles. They slow down their breathing and heart rates. Hibernators take a long time to awaken. When a chipmunk gets hungry, it just wakes up, eats some food, and goes back into hibernation.

- A chipmunk can stuff a large number of seeds into each cheek pouch, which can hold as much as its entire mouth, so a chipmunk can gobble up and carry three mouthfuls of food at one time.

- Chipmunks store up a supply of seeds and nuts in their burrows for winter food.

# Squirrel

|  |  |
|---|---|
| **Name:** | gray squirrel (*Sciurus carolinensis*) |
| **Other names:** | Other common species include the much smaller, and more vocal, red squirrel (*Tamiasciurus hudsonicus*) in the evergreen forests of northern regions and the larger, rust-colored fox squirrel in deciduous (broadleaf) woods and savannahs to the south. |
| **Size and coloration:** | 9-inch body; 9-inch tail; gray back and sides with white belly |
| **Senses:** | Squirrels have an excellent sense of smell and keen, color-blind eyesight; gray squirrels use their noses (not their memories) to find buried nuts and can smell a nut buried under a foot of snow and several inches of soil |
| **Food:** | Gray squirrels are herbivores (plant eaters) that eat oak, hickory, walnut, and elm nuts; raspberries; and other berries. Gray squirrels bury seeds and acorns individually, and can hide 25 acorns per hour. By contrast, red squirrels hoard spruce and fir cones in a central "food cache." If the squirrel doesn't return to dig up buried seeds and acorns, they often grow into new trees. Scientists estimate that squirrels planted many of the nut trees now growing in North America. |
| **Predators:** | hawks, owls, fishers, weasels, bobcats, and house cats. |
| **Travel:** | Gray squirrels can run up to 15 mph. When a squirrel climbs a tree, it climbs in a spiral, keeping the tree between itself and any predator. That way, jumping predators can't pull the squirrel off the tree. Gray squirrels can jump up to 8 feet and can fall up to 30 feet without injury. |
| **Ecological niche:** | prey species; also buries acorns and nuts that, if uneaten (about 20 percent of buried nuts), will grow into new trees |
| **Habitat:** | deciduous (broadleaf) forests of maples, oaks, and other broadleaf trees |

## Other fun facts:

- Squirrels use their fluffy tails to balance while climbing and as a "parachute" when jumping from a tree. They also use their tail as a blanket to keep warm and to communicate with other squirrels through body language.

- Squirrels have short attention spans, forgetting about a hunter in the woods after 15 minutes.

- Red squirrels are omnivores (they eat plants and animals), consuming pine nuts, beetles, grubs, bird eggs, hatchlings, and mushrooms. A red squirrel can cache up to 10 bushels of spruce, pine, and fir cones in hollow logs or stumps for the winter. These caches can hold up to 14,000 mushrooms and seed cones, enough to feed the squirrel through two years of seed crop failures. A red squirrel eats the seeds from up to 100 spruce cones per day in the winter. Those seeds give squirrels the fuel they need to survive subzero winter weather.

# Bat

*Themes:* habitat, adaptation—hunting at night

## Bat's Debt (Siberia)

Long ago, when Bat was flying through the forest, he met Hawk.

"Bat, it is time for all of the birds to pay their taxes to King Eagle," said Hawk. "Where are your taxes?"

Thinking fast, Bat dropped to the ground and began running around on all fours.

"Since when is an animal with fur and teeth a bird?" squeaked Bat.

Hawk took another look at Bat. "Perhaps I was wrong. You are not a bird."

Later, while Bat was napping under a tree, Fox walked up.

"Bat, it is time to pay your taxes to King Bear, where is your money?"

Since it worked before, Bat tried a similar ruse. He jumped into the air and flew around Fox's head.

"Since when can mammals fly? Tell King Bear that I am a bird and I don't owe him any taxes."

Fox shrugged her shoulders and walked back to King Bear.

But even though Bat had avoided paying taxes to either the bird king or the mammal king, he was still nervous about it. Even back then, taxes were a thing you might be able to temporarily outrun, but never escape. So from that day on, Bat never again ran on the ground. That way he could avoid running into Fox, and to avoid Hawk, Bat decided that he would stay in a cave during the day and only go out at night for food. It is a good thing that Bear and Eagle sleep during the night. And to this day Bat hasn't paid his taxes.

**Teller notes:** There are many stories that explain why bats fly at night. This story echoes the confusion that people have had with classifying bats. It flies like a bird, but it is a mammal. It looks a bit like a mouse with wings, but it feeds on flying insects, something mice don't generally eat. Once scientists began to classify animals by their exterior features (fur versus feathers), rather than by behavior, it became easier to classify these enigmatic creatures.

You can find a similar tale about Bat in Aesop's fables. In that story, the birds and mammals went to war, and Bat kept switching sides, depending on who was winning. In the end, both the birds and the mammals banished him, so now he must live in a lonely cave and fly only at night.

# Bat Facts

**Name:** little brown bat (*Myotis lucifugus*)

**Basic facts and other names:** The little brown bat is one of the most widespread bat species in North America.
Other common species include the larger big brown bat (*Eptesicus fuscus*) and the silver-haired bat (*Lasionycteris noctivagans*).

**Size and coloration:** Little brown bats are 3–4 inches long and have a wingspan of 9–11 inches; they weigh less than an ounce. These bats have medium brown fur and dark brown wings.

**Senses:** Contrary to the expression "blind as a bat," bats aren't blind. They actually have black and white vision equal to human vision. But since they are active at night, their vision isn't all that important. Little brown bats have excellent hearing and use a sonar-like echolocation to find their flying insect prey.

**Food:** Little brown bats feed primarily on flying insects like moths, mosquitoes, and beetles.

**Predators:** owls, hawks, pine martens, skunks, raccoons, and snakes

**Travel:** Little brown bats can fly up to 22 mph and have been known to migrate up to 480 miles to hibernating caves in the fall.

**Ecological niche:** Little brown bats are insectivores (carnivores), feeding on insects. They are also food to a wide range of predators.

**Habitat:** Little brown bats hunt insects over lakes, streams, wetlands, ponds, and in forest clearings. They roost in caves, abandoned mines, and trees.

## Other fun facts:

- About one-quarter (25 percent) of all mammal species are bats.

- Although bats (like all mammals) can carry rabies, they pose little threat to people. Little brown bats die soon after contracting the disease. Their teeth are also reportedly too small to break human skin, even if they wanted to bite a person. Nonetheless, it is always a good idea to appreciate wildlife from a distance. If you have to handle a bat, always wear thick leather gloves.

- Bats are the only mammals capable of flight. "Flying" squirrels actually only glide from tree to tree.

- Bats don't get tangled in people's hair. Their echolocation sonar lets them know where we are, so they don't run into humans or their hair. If a bat swoops over your head, it is probably diving to catch a mosquito that is about to bite you.

# Animal Scavenger Hunt Activity

**Grade Level:** 2–8

**Environmental Themes:** adaptation, habitat

**Curriculum Areas:** science, social studies

**Student Skills:** observation, comprehension, inferring

**Materials:** copies of Animal Scavenger Hunt card (see below) (laminated if possible), paper, pencils, and clipboards

## Instructions:

1. As a class, discuss the different kinds of "animal signs" that animals leave behind: homes, scat (droppings), tracks and trails, sounds, smells, bite marks, body parts (fur, feathers, bones). Brainstorm what animal signs you are likely to find in the schoolyard or another outdoor area. Discuss how observation is a learned skill. The more that you look for animal signs, even in a city, the more you will find.

2. Divide the group into smaller teams of up to four. Give each team a clipboard, paper and pencil, and a laminated scavenger hunt card. The group's job is to find examples of everything on the scavenger hunt card.

3. Depending on the age of students, have each group make a list of what they find, draw a map of where they find things, or draw examples of what they find.

---

### Animal Scavenger Hunt Card

On a separate piece of paper, make of list of all the animal signs you can find during your search. Look for:

1. Animal Homes: nests, holes in the ground, holes in trees

2. Tracks and Trails: Pathways through grass or in the snow or tracks in mud or sand can show where an animal has traveled. Some animals, like humans and deer walk with a right, left, right, left track. Smaller animals like squirrels and rabbits hop and all for footprints land in the same place.

3. Scats: Animal droppings let us know that animals have been here. Look for white scats from birds, pellet-like scats from rabbits or deer or tube-shaped scats from foxes, coyotes and dogs.

4. Bite Marks: Look for holes in leaves or bites on twigs. Rabbits nip off twigs with a clean cut while deer leave a ragged cut when they nip off twigs.

5. Body Parts: Animal parts could include feathers, fur or bones left from dead wildlife.

---

## Evaluation:

Did students work hard to complete the scavenger hunt? Did students demonstrate "teamwork skills" like respectful communication and cooperation?

From Kevin Strauss, *Tales with Tails: Storytelling the Wonders of the Natural World.* Westport, CT: Libraries Unlimited, 2006. Copyright © 2006 by Kevin Strauss.

# Line up by Mammal Height Activity

**Grade Level:** 2–8

**Environmental Themes:** adaptation, habitat

**Curriculum Areas:** science, social studies, physical education, performing arts

**Student Skills:** acting, observation, comprehension, inferring, humor

**Materials:** none

## Instructions:

1. Mammals come in all shapes and sizes, and the adaptations that an animal has help it to survive in its habitat. To help demonstrate this, have students line up. Then ask them to think of a mammal. For younger children, be sure that they understand what makes an animal a mammal (fur, feeds milk to young, young born live, warm-blooded).

2. Inform participants that from this point on, they can only act and make sounds like their chosen animal (no predation, please). Then ask participants to line up by animal height.

3. After giving participants as much as 10 minutes to line up, go down the line from the "smallest animals" to the largest. Have participants act out their animals and let the group guess what each animal is. Talk briefly about some of the adaptations that the animals use to help them survive (use the "animal facts" sections of this book to gather adaptation information).

## Evaluation:

Did the group accomplish the task? How did they manage to communicate without talking? Did students demonstrate "teamwork skills" like respectful communication and cooperation?

From Kevin Strauss, *Tales with Tails: Storytelling the Wonders of the Natural World.* Westport, CT: Libraries Unlimited, 2006.
Copyright © 2006 by Kevin Strauss.

# Chapter 8

## Animal Stories: Birds

Birds are warm-blooded animals with feathers and beaks. Most birds have hollow bones to make them lighter for flight. Most birds fly. The few species of birds that don't fly (penguins, ostriches, and similar birds) have an alternate form of locomotion. Penguins use their wings as flippers as they swim, and ostriches run on strong legs. Many birds sing songs to attract a mate or to tell rivals that "this territory is taken." Of the 1.2 million known animal species in the world, there are 10,000 species of birds.

Many scientists believe that birds evolved from small, two-legged, meat-eating dinosaurs about 150 million years ago. The clearest link between dinosaurs and birds is a fossil "Archaeopteryx" from that time period found in Germany. Archaeopteryx has feathers and a wishbone (bird features), but it also has teeth, a flexible neck, clawed fingers, and a bony tail (all dinosaur features). Bird feathers are similar in chemical composition to reptile scales. Both birds and reptiles lay waterproof, shelled eggs.

## Birds of Prey

*Themes:* food chain, adaptation—bird feeding behavior

### Hawk's Sewing Needle (Kenya)

At the beginning of the very beginning of time, Hawk and Chicken were best friends. They would go for walks together in the woods; they would fly through the trees or play tag in the meadow. They would even have meals together, and even though Chicken ate seeds and bugs and Hawk at mice, they could still be best friends. But as happens in all friendships, Hawk and Chicken grew older. Soon it was time for them to make nests and lay their eggs. Chicken made her nest on the ground at the foot of a tree at the edge of a meadow. Hawk made her nest high in the branches of a tree deep in the woods.

It was then that Chicken realized that she had a problem. You see, this was a long time ago, and back then, when bird chicks hatched out of their eggs, they didn't have any feathers. Back then, mother birds had to sew feather suits for their children to keep them warm. Like I said, this was a long time ago. The problem was that Chicken had lost her sewing needle. She had looked all over for it, in the meadow near her nest, in the woods nearby, but she couldn't find it. But then she thought of an idea.

"I'll ask Hawk to lend me her needle. She won't be needing it for a few days anyway."

Chicken flew up to Hawk's nest.

"Hey Hawk, how's it going?" said Chicken.

"Fine, Chicken, fine," said Hawk, narrowing here large eyes. "How are things going with you?"

"Well to tell you the truth Hawk, I need a favor," said Chicken. "You see, I lost my sewing needle. Could I borrow yours?"

Now Hawk had a problem. She wanted to help her friend, but she also didn't want to lose her sewing needle. Everyone in the forest knew how scatterbrained Chicken was. After thinking about it for a while, she came up with an idea.

"OK, Chicken, I will lend you my needle, but you must promise to return it in two days. Remember Chicken, two days."

"No problem, no problem, I'll have the needle back to you in two days, Hawk, thanks a lot," said Chicken as she took Hawk's silvery needle in her beak and flew off to her nest.

Chicken sat down on her nest of eggs and immediately started sewing feather suits for her 10 children. She sewed all through the day and part of the night. The next day, just as Chicken was finishing the last of her 10 feather suits, she heard a "crack" from her eggs. She jumped up to see one of her chicks hatching from its egg. As soon as it was out, Chicken pulled a feather suit over its head. Then she heard more cracking sounds, and more chicks hatched from the eggs. Once Chicken had gotten feather suits on each of her chicks, the chicks were hungry, so she took them out to the meadow to look for seeds and bugs. Then they were thirsty, so she took them to the stream to drink some water. Then they were cranky. Can you imagine that, children getting cranky? So Chicken took them back to the nest for a nap. The next day they did the same thing all over again: the field for bugs, the stream for water, and back to the nest for a nap. Those of you who are parents know how difficult it can be caring for one child; imagine what it would be like if you had 10.

At the end of that busy day, Chicken had the feeling in the back of her head that she had forgotten something. You know the feeling, like you haven't done something important. Just as she was going to sleep, she remembered: Hawk's sewing needle! Chicken got up and looked around the nest for the needle, but it was a dark night and she couldn't see a thing. Finally she settled down and went to sleep.

The next morning, Chicken gathered her chicks.

"Now children, you need to help me look for a sewing needle that I borrowed from Hawk so I could sew your feather suits. It is small and silvery, so look closely at the ground," she said.

Chicken and her chicks scratched at the ground and looked closely all around the nest. But they didn't find the needle.

"You know, we have spent a lot of time in the meadow, too. Let's look there."

They searched all through the meadow, but looking for a sewing needle in a meadow is a lot like . . . looking for a needle in a haystack. They didn't find it.

"Let's go look by the stream," said Chicken.

They searched the stream banks and even looked into the crystal clear water of the stream, but they didn't find the needle. That night, Chicken told her chicks something she had never told them before.

"Tonight children, we aren't sleeping in the nest. I want you to go in the tall grass in the meadow and find a place to hide."

"But why, ma?" whined the chicks.

And Chicken told her children something that parents have told children from the beginning of time: "Because I said so."

These chicks were good chicks and they did as their mother told them, and it was a good thing, too. Just as Chicken was settling into her hiding place in the grass, she saw Hawk fly over and land near the nest. Hawk looked around for her needle.

"Chicken, Chicken, where's my needle," shouted Hawk. "I said you could borrow it for two days. Two. Now it has been four days and I still don't have it back."

Now some animals would just go up to Hawk and explain what happened. But Chicken wasn't that kind of friend. And maybe that was a good thing in this case.

"Chicken, we were friends once, so I will give you one more day to bring back my needle," said Hawk as she opened her great wings and flew off into the night.

The next day, mother Chicken and her children searched for Hawk's sewing needle around the nest, in the meadow, and at the stream, but the more they looked, the less they found, and when evening came, they went to hide in the tall grass.

As the sun was setting blood-red in the west, Hawk returned, circling three times over the meadow and landing near Chicken's nest. When Hawk didn't see her sewing needle, she called out to Chicken.

"Chicken, since you took my sewing needle and I cannot make feather suits for my children, then I will take the suits from yours. From now on, whenever I see one of your children, I will grab it and take it home and feed it to mine."

With that, Hawk opened her great wings and flew off. And that is why to this day, whenever a hawk sees a chicken, it swoops down and eats it for dinner. And since that day, whenever you see a chicken, it is scratching at the ground and pecking at the ground. Now some would have you believe that it is scratching the ground for bugs and pecking at seeds, but now you know the real reason. That chicken is scratching at the ground and pecking in search of Hawk's sewing needle. All of the chickens in the world are looking for that needle in the hopes that if they find it and return it to the hawks, the hawks will stop eating them and taking their feather suits. Who knows? Maybe someday they will find it.

**Teller notes:** I learned this story as part of an international classroom story exchange with a friend, Chrissy Watson, who was a teacher in the Peace Corps in Kenya in 1991. She had her students collect traditional Kenyan stories at home and translate them into English as part of their lessons. You can adapt this story to include chicken-like wild birds from your region such as quail, turkeys, or grouse.

*Themes:* competition, adaptation—songbirds mobbing owls

# The Birds Choose a King (India)

Long ago, in a deep, dark forest, Owl was sitting on the limb of a tree.

"You know," he thought to himself. "I am not getting any younger, and it would be a lot easier for me to fill my belly if the birds elected me as their king."

Owl gathered together the birds of the forest.

"My friends, our king, the Eagle, soars far in the sky," said Owl. "He is not here to protect you. I believe that we need a king who lives in our forest. We need a king who is strong enough to save us from our enemies."

The birds tweeted and chirped in the trees. They looked at each of the birds and finally decided that with his sharp beak and strong talons, Owl would be a strong king.

Owl smiled because his plan was working perfectly.

Just before Owl spoke up to ask his new subjects to get him some mice for dinner, Crow flew by. When he asked the birds what was going on and heard about Owl's upcoming coronation, he burst out laughing.

"Why would you want another king? Eagle keeps us safe enough even if he doesn't live in this forest. Just saying Eagle's name frightens our enemies," said Crow. "And if we were to choose a king, why choose a flat-faced, hooked-nose grouch like Owl. Besides, how can Owl protect you when he sleeps all day and only flies at night?"

The birds thought about that for a little while, chirping and tweeting in the trees. Then Sparrow flew up to Owl.

"Crow is right. We need no other king but Eagle."

Owl clenched his branch hard with his sharp talons and stared at Crow.

"Oops," thought Crow, "perhaps I spoke too soon."

Crow flew off into the darkness of the woods. After that, when Owl flew at night, he went looking for Crow and his children in their nests. Owl wanted revenge.

Soon, the crows gathered to talk about this new threat.

"We can't defeat Owl alone," said a wise, old crow. "But we can do it together."

All of the crows made an agreement. Since that time, whenever a crow sees an Owl sleeping in the forest, he gathers his brothers and sisters and friends and they chase that Owl into the light and out of their woods again.

**Teller notes:** Crows, blue jays, and other songbirds will mob and chase off any owl that they find in their part of the forest. Scientists think they do this because owls sometimes prey on young songbirds during the night.

*Theme:* adaptation

# Why Owls Hunt at Night (Puerto Rico)

Long ago, when the animals could talk like people do today, the animals liked to give parties and dances. One day, the birds decided that they wanted to have a dance. The birds wanted to make sure that all the birds would come and wear their best suits of feathers. So they sent Hawk to tell all of the other birds about the party.

When Hawk got to Owl's house, Owl burst out crying and told him that she couldn't possibly attend.

"Why not?" said Hawk.

"Because I don't have any feathers to wear," said Owl.

You see, back in those days, Owl was naked.

"All the other birds will be at the dance in their fine feather suits and I have nothing to wear so I can't possibly come."

Hawk went back to the other birds and told them about Owl's problem.

"No problem," said a small yellow songbird. "I'll lend some of my feathers to Owl. If each of you do the same, Owl will have a wonderful suit to wear."

The birds agreed that that's what they would do. Hawk took a basket of feathers to Owl's house.

"Now after the party, you have to give these back," said Hawk.

Owl agreed and then set about arranging the feathers in her new feather suit. When she came to the dance, all of the other birds agreed that Owl looked beautiful in her new feather suit. Owl enjoyed all the dancing. But soon she began thinking about how she would have to give back all of those borrowed feathers at the end of the dance. She began thinking of a plan to keep those feathers. When the band was starting the last song of the evening, Owl slipped out of the crowd and disappeared into the darkness of the forest. When the last song ended and the birds began looking for Owl so they could retrieve their feathers, but she was nowhere to be found. The birds became angry. They squawked and shouted, but Owl stayed hidden. Owl got frightened when she heard the other birds yell, but she didn't want to give up her fine feather suit. Owl worried that the other birds might see her bright-colored feathers in the dark. So she flew down and grabbed some dirt and ashes with her feet and rubbed it all over her feathers. The dirt and ashes hid the bright colors on her new suit. It made her coat look dull, but it helped her to hide in the branches of trees.

And that is why people say that Owl only comes out at night, when the other birds are sleeping. She is still afraid that if she flies during the day, the birds will come and pull out the feathers that they leant her such a long time ago. And that's the end of the story.

**Teller notes:** By flying at night, owls can more easily find and catch their mouse prey. Mice are more active at night as well. The owls' large eyes and excellent night vision make them excellent nocturnal (night-active) hunters. Some studies have shown that owls have the ability to detect and catch prey by sound alone, using their sensitive ears and listening their way to catching prey.

# Birds of Prey Facts

**Group facts:** Birds of prey include hawks, eagles, owls, and other meat-eating bird species. They generally have sharp beaks and sharp talons (claws) for catching and killing their prey. Most birds of prey will cough up pellets of undigested fur, feathers, and bones after eating a meal.

## Hawk

**Name:** red-tailed hawk (*Buteo jamaicensis*)

**Size and coloration:** 25 inches tall, 4½-foot wingspan; dark brown back, white belly, rust-red tail

**Senses:** Hawks have keen eyesight (at least five times sharper than human vision) and can see a mouse or rat on the ground from hundreds of feet in the air. They have good color vision, a poor sense of smell, and give a high-pitched "skreee" call that movie producers often dub in for eagle calls in movies.

**Food:** rabbits, rodents (mice, rats), reptiles, birds, insects; often catch their prey on the ground

**Predators:** none, except humans hunting illegally; harassed and chased by crows and other songbirds

**Travel:** flying; while migrating in the spring and fall they can soar on winds for thousands of miles

**Ecological niche:** predator, carnivore consumer

**Habitat:** swamps, woodlands, and meadows

### Other fun facts:

- Hawks are often portrayed as villains in stories because they are predators.

## Owl

**Name:** great horned owl (*Bubo virginianus*)

**Size and coloration:** 25 inches tall; black and brown with wing and tail stripes; two ear-like tufts of feathers on top of head

**Senses:**
- Owls have excellent eyesight and can probably see 10 times better in the dark than humans can.

- Owls have excellent hearing in laboratory experiments, sightless owls could catch mouse prey by hearing alone. Owls can hear a mouse squeak a half mile away and can hear a mouse scurrying under a foot of snow.

- Owls probably have little or no sense of smell or taste.

**Food:** mice, voles, small birds, skunks (remember, no sense of smell, so don't notice the skunk's smelly spray), rabbits, grouse, domestic cats

**Predators:** none, but crows will harass and chase this top predator

**Travel:** flies to hunt or travel; can also walk, but usually uses feet only to grasp branches or prey

**Ecological niche:** predator, carnivore consumer

**Habitat:** forests, forest edges, meadows, and farmsteads

**Folklore:** In some folklore, owls are birds of "bad omen." In Greek folklore, owls were portrayed as wise, and while American folklore portrays owls as "wise birds," they are actually not all that bright. Their eyes are so large that they take up most of the space in their skulls and leave little room for brains.

**Other fun facts:**

- Owls can't move their eyes; they have to turn their heads to look at something new. They can turn their heads 270 degrees.
- They give a "hoo-hoohoo-hoo-hoo" call.
- Their wings have a special frill on the front edge allowing them to fly silently through the night.

**Other owl stories in this book include:**

"How Rabbit Got Its Long Ears" (African American) (p. 87)

"How Birds Got Their Colors" (original) (p. 111)

# Small Birds

*Themes:* adaptation—bird colors

## How Birds Got Their Colors (Original)

Long, long ago, when the only place was here and the only time was now, every bird in the world, from the tiny finch to the huge heron, every bird in the world was gray. They were gray like the rocks or gray like the clouds, just before it rains. Every bird was gray. Now at first, the birds didn't mind being all the same color.

But one day, Hummingbird was flying over a grassy field and she looked down and saw Flowers! Red ones and blue ones and yellow ones and orange ones covered the meadow. She landed in a tree and looked at her feathers.

"I fly all over the place, and I am stuck with boring gray feathers. Those flowers just sit there and they have bright colors," said Hummingbird.

She decided to fly over to her friend Jay's tree.

"Hey Jay, how's it going?"

"Just fine, Hummingbird, how's it going with you?" said Jay.

"Not so good, Jay. You see I just saw a whole field of bright-colored flowers and I decided that I want a color for my feathers," said Hummingbird.

"You already have a color for your feathers, its called 'gray'," said Jay.

"No, I meant a bright color like red or yellow or green. Yeah, green would be the perfect color for a bird, green like the leaves and the grass," said Hummingbird.

Jay looked around at the leaves and grass.

"No, green's not a very good color for a bird," said Jay.

He looked at the tree bark and soil, and then he looked up at the sky.

"Blue, that's the color that I want, blue like the sky. That's the perfect color for a bird," said Jay.

But neither bird knew how to get a new color for its feathers, so they each flew off in a different direction, looking for a bird who knew how to change its color. Though they found many birds who wanted to have a different color, none of them knew how to get colors. Now sometimes, when people can't figure out the solution to a problem, people hold a meeting, and that's just what the birds did. They met in a big clearing in the forest. All the birds sat in the trees, and the wisest of the birds, Owl, led the meeting. Some people say that Owl is the wisest because he is the oldest bird, others say it is because he can fly at night, but I like to think Owl is the wisest bird because he is always asking questions, like "Who, who?".

Owl started the meeting. "Whoo has an idea? Whoo has a suggestion for how we can get some colors?"

Little Finch raised her wing. "I've got an idea, we should get some bright colors like red and yellow and green and orange and color ourselves with stripes and circles and dots and what do you think about that," said Finch.

Many of the birds weren't sure what Finch had said because she had spoken so quickly. But they had heard the word "colors" and they liked the sound of that.

"Yes colors, we like colors. Colors are a good idea," said all of the birds, nodding their beaks. But still, no one suggested how to get some colors.

"There are lots of colors in the flowers. Maybe they would share their colors with us," said Hummingbird.

The birds liked that idea and sent Hummingbird to ask the flowers for help. Hummingbird flew down to the field where the flowers lived and walked up to a particularly tall, red flower.

"Umm, Ms. Flower, we birds were wondering if you would be so kind as to let us use some of your bright colors for our feathers. You see, ours are just this plain gray color and you flowers seem to have lots of colors. What do you think?" said Hummingbird.

Now who knows why flowers act the way that they do, but this one folded her leaves across her chest, frowned with her flowery head, and said "No, you cannot have our colors. We got them fair and square, and we're not going to share them."

Hummingbird wasn't sure what else to do, so she flew back to the rest of the birds. They were still arguing about what would be the best color for birds. Some thought it was brown, others red, some even insisted that it was gray. When Hummingbird told the rest of the birds what happened, they fell silent for a while.

Then Crow spoke up.

"I know!" said Crow. "There is lots of color in the sky just before the sun goes down. Then the sky is pink and gold. There is so much color there, that I'm sure that the sky would share."

The birds knew that they could never fly high enough to reach the blue of the sky, but if these evening colors were just above the trees, they could fly that high. So they opened their wings. The little birds flapped their wings really, really fast, because they were excited to get some colors. The big birds, they took their time. "What's the rush, there's plenty of colors there. We'll get there eventually," they said.

But as the birds flew to the west, they saw the bands of pink and gold getting smaller and smaller and smaller until all that was left was a dark night sky.

"What do we do now?" asked the birds. Then Jay spoke up.

"I've heard that 'good things come to birds who wait'. Maybe we should sit in a tree and wait until morning," said Jay.

So the birds landed in trees and put their beaks under their wings and went to sleep. And the next morning Robin opened her eyes and do you know what she saw? Bands of pink and gold stretching across the eastern sky.

"Birds, birds, wake up! Wake up! We were flying the wrong way. The colors are in the east," said Robin.

When the birds heard this, they woke up and leapt into the sky, flying back the way they had come. The little birds flapped their wings very quickly, but the bigger birds flapped slowly and trailed behind. "No big rush. There's lots of color," said the bigger birds.

But as the birds flew back to the east, the bands of pink and gold colors got thinner and thinner, until those colors disappeared into the light of the rising sun. As the birds watched, the sun gathered up all those pinks and golds and climbed higher and higher into the sky, farther than any bird could fly.

"What are we going to doo now," said Owl, "whoo has another idea?"

The birds were silent for a while. Then they heard a quiet voice.

"Peent, I've got an idea." It was Duck. Now Duck didn't usually speak up at gatherings. She usually stayed at the back of the flock and just listened. But now she was talking.

"You see, I'm a duck, and you other birds don't know this because when it rains, you fly up to the trees to stay dry, but we ducks, we don't mind the rain. When rain falls on us, it just rolls right off like water off a duck's back. So it doesn't bother us at all. And when the rain stops, a huge band of colors stretches from one end of the sky to the other. That band isn't as high up as the sky, so I bet we could fly up there and get some colors."

Now the birds didn't have a name for those bands of color, but we call them the rainbow. But you need rain to get a rainbow. So the birds waited and waited. Some forgot about getting bright colors and went off to build nests and look for food.

One morning, Robin awoke early to see gray clouds filling the eastern sky. She heard a rumbling like the sound of running buffalo.

"Birds, wake up! Birds, wake up! It's going to rain! It's going to rain!" she sang. The birds all opened their beady little eyes. The little birds started stretching their wings and getting ready to fly. The big birds just put their bills under their wings and went back to sleep. "Call us when the colors appear," said Hawk.

Soon the rain was pouring down on the forest where the birds lived. The little birds were very excited. When the rain stopped and the clouds broke apart, just like Duck had told them, a huge band of color stretched from one end of the sky to the other: red, orange, yellow, green, blue, indigo, and violet. The little birds leapt into the sky and began flapping their wings as fast as they could, because they were so excited to get some bright colors. The bigger birds finally opened their eyes and opened their wings.

"What's the rush? There are lots of colors up there," they said.

The little birds reached the rainbow first. Finch flew right through a band of yellow and painted her feathers from bill to tail. Jay found some blue and flew right on through. Hummingbird found some green to paint her head and back. Gray bird couldn't decide.

"Should I be blue or red, blue or red, which should I be," he mused. "Wait, I could be both!"

Saying that, he flew right between a band of blue and a band of red, painting his back blue and his belly red.

Each of the small birds painted their feathers with the rainbow. But rainbows are like paint you might use on earth. As the small birds flew through the rainbow, they started to mix the colors, and when you mix all of the colors in the rainbow, you get a dull brown. So when the big birds got to the rainbow, the only color that Hawk and Grouse and Turkey and Duck could find was brown. Mallard Duck did find one small piece of green that he used to paint his head, but that was all.

From that day to this, the small birds are very proud of their colors, and every morning, they sit in the trees, singing loudly, because they want to show off their colors. But the bigger birds, they don't sing. They sit quietly in the trees or hide in the bushes because they are embarrassed that they were lazy on the day that the birds got colors from the rainbow.

**Teller notes:** In the bird world, males are more often brightly colored and females are more often dull colored. This is in part because male birds use visual displays to attract a mate and females need to be able to hide from predators while sitting on their nests. In North America, many of our smaller birds are more brightly colored than the larger birds. This may be because many of those larger birds, like hawks and owls, are hunters and take advantage of their dull coloration to hide in the forest while hunting or resting. Other large birds like grouse or turkeys use their dull colors to help them hide from predators.

*Themes:* adaptation—robin coloration, everyone can make a difference

# Robin's Red Breast (Ireland)

Long ago, at the beginning, there was only one fire in the whole wild world. That was all that people had to keep them warm and frighten off the creatures of the night. But people didn't know how to make fire, so they had to keep their one fire burning day and night. An old man and a boy tended the fire each night.

On a cold night, the boy, warm in his blanket, fell asleep on his watch. In the darkness, a wolf saw that both the boy and the man were asleep. Now was its chance to get rid of fire forever! It ran up and kicked dirt on the flames and stomped on the fire with its wide feet. The ash turned its fur gray. The wolf left to tell its brothers that the fire was gone. But a small brown bird saw what had happened. She flew down and brushed off the dirt with her wings. She found one glowing coal and she fanned it with her wings. Then she hopped off and gathered some twigs and placed them on the coal and fanned the coals until they burst into flame. She kept adding sticks until the fire was once again going strong. The boy woke up from the light and once again took care of the fire.

People say that the flames of that first fire were magic, for they burned that brown bird's chest and turned it red-orange like the flames. All of the robin's offspring still carry that color, and that is why robins have red on their chests today.

*Themes:* adaptation—woodpecker beak, food chain

# The First Woodpecker (Romania)

Long ago in a small village there lived a very nosy old woman named Katrina. Katrina wasn't happy just knowing her own business. She wanted to know everybody's business. She wanted to know who had quarreled, who was courting, who was keeping a secret from everyone else. She was one of those people who gathers gossip the way that a crow hoards shiny objects. And then she spends her secrets like gold.

One day she was walking down the road when she met a strange-looking old man walking the other direction. He wore a gray coat, had a white beard down to his waist, and was carrying a large green bag.

"Old woman, do you know the way to the sea?" asked the traveler.

"Of course," said Katrina. "It's not far from here."

"Could you do me a favor? I'd pay you well."

"What kind of favor?" asked Katrina, her interest piqued.

Taking a big bag off his shoulder, he told her: "All you have to do is throw this bag into the sea. Do that, and I'll give you a bag of gold. But you have to promise not to look in the bag."

"Sure, sure, no problem. I could do that and more for a bag of gold," said Katrina.

"I'll wait here under this tree for you to return," said the strange man.

Katrina set off down the road to the sea. But as she was carrying the bag, her curiosity began to gnaw at her like a mouse gnawing on a grain bin.

"I wonder what's inside the bag," she thought. "Maybe it's papers he wants to get rid of. Maybe it's evidence of a crime. Maybe it is old love letters."

Once she was deep in the woods, where no one could see her, Katrina stopped and shook the bag. It made a sound like dry grass inside. Then she began untying the knot on the bag.

"I'll just peek inside. The old man will never know that I looked. What harm could that do," said Katrina to herself. "It is really for the good of the community. Perhaps this man is a criminal and we'd better find that out right away."

Katrina untied the bag and opened it just a bit to look inside.

"Woosh" like a mighty wind a cloud of tiny creatures flew up into Katrina's face and covered her with a strange gold dust. There were buzzing things and flapping things and things with six legs and things with tiny wings. Katrina tried to grab them and stuff them back into the bag, but they were too fast. For every one she caught, two more escaped from the bag. Katrina knew that now the old man would know that she had opened the bag. She tried to chase the tiny creatures through the forest, but as she ran, she felt herself starting to change. Her nose grew longer and turned hard and sharp. Her legs shrank until they looked like the legs of a bird and her arms shrank and sprouted feathers. Her whole body shrank and her black dress became black feathers and her red kerchief became red feathers on her head. That magic gold dust had turned Katrina into the world's first woodpecker, and those creatures in the bag were the world's first insects.

From that day to this, Woodpecker and her children are searching cracks and crevices for bugs. They are hoping to gather all the bugs in the world and stuff them back into that big green bag.

# Small Bird Facts

**Group facts:** The songbirds or passerine (perching) birds are smallish birds that feed mostly on seeds, fruits, and insects. Woodpeckers feed primarily on insects that they find on or in dead and dying trees.

## Robin

| | |
|---|---|
| **Name:** | American robin (*Turdus migratorius*) |
| **Size and coloration:** | 7 inches tall; dark brown back and wings; orange-red breast |
| **Senses:** | good wide-angle vision, color vision, good hearing; probably doesn't have a good sense of smell |
| **Food:** | worms, insects, fruit |
| **Predators:** | owls (robins will mob and chase owls out of their territory) |
| **Travel:** | will fly to food sources; is also a strong hopper/walker when searching for food |
| **Ecological niche:** | predator and prey species; also spreads seeds when it consumes fruit and passes the seeds in its scat (droppings) |
| **Habitat:** | forests, fields, backyards |

### Other fun facts:

- When hunting, robins will cock their heads to look for worm movements in grass or soil.
- Robins are often seen as the first sign of spring in many areas.
- The robin is often seen as a "helpful" bird.
- There are several stories about how robins got their red breasts.

## Crow

| | |
|---|---|
| **Name:** | common crow (Corvus brachyrhynchos) |
| **Size and coloration:** | 19 inches tall; black feathers, beak, and legs |
| **Senses:** | good wide-angle vision, color vision |
| **Food:** | Crows eat everything from corn to garbage and carrion; they also eat grasshoppers, cutworms, mice, and voles. |
| **Predators:** | owls |
| **Travel:** | flies from place to place |
| **Ecological niche:** | mid-level predator, decomposer (carrion eater), and omnivore consumer |
| **Habitat:** | forests, meadows, farms, backyards, suburban areas, mountains |
| **Folklore:** | The crow has been seen as a bird of ill omen because of its black feathers, and has been seen as a clever bird in stories. |

### Other fun facts:

- The crow gives the common "caw, caw" call.
- It sometimes collects shiny things, possibly to "decorate" its nest.

- It is seen as a very "intelligent" bird that seems to display problem-solving ability. Crows have been observed to make a "hook" out of a twig and use this tool to get ants out of crevices.
- There is anecdotal evidence that crows can mimic sounds that they hear, like cell phone rings. Crows have been observed saying "giddy up" to get horses to run in a pasture.
- They are social birds that can gather in large groups of as many as 1 million members.

## Chickadee

| | |
|---|---|
| **Name:** | black-capped chickadee (*Parus atricapillus*) |
| **Size and coloration:** | 4½ inches long; 7-inch wingspan; gray-brown back and wings, black cap on head, white belly |
| **Senses:** | good wide-angle vision, color vision; poor sense of smell and taste |
| **Food:** | mostly caterpillars, spiders, beetles, carrion (dead animals) in the fall and winter; conifer seeds, sunflower seeds, berries, cherries, acorns, and maple sap |
| **Predators:** | sharp-shinned hawks, saw-whet owls, northern shrikes, nests raided by red squirrels, raccoons, weasels, and snakes |
| **Travel:** | Chickadees can fly up to 12 mph; stays in the northern United States all winter despite the cold weather. |
| **Ecological niche:** | mid-level predator, prey species, and omnivore consumer |
| **Habitat:** | forests and fields |

### Other fun facts:

- Chickadees will form winter multi-species "forage flocks" for security and to help search for food. Nuthatches, titmice (birds), and down and hairy woodpeckers will join this flock. The birds travel through the forest looking for food.
- It gives its "chicka-dee-dee" call in winter and a two-note "spring's-here" call in the spring.

## Blue Jay

| | |
|---|---|
| **Name:** | blue jay (*Cyanocitta cristata*) |
| **Size and coloration:** | 11 inches long; 16½-inch wingspan; blue back and wings, wings also have black stripes; white belly, crest on its head |
| **Senses:** | good wide-angle, color vision; poor sense of smell and taste |
| **Food:** | Blue jays will eat just about anything, but in some cases 80 percent of their diet is oak acorns. Blue jays bury acorns in the ground for safekeeping, and if the bird doesn't dig up the acorns, they may sprout into new oak trees; they also eat pine seeds, berries, caterpillars, and other insects, frogs, and minnows. |
| **Predators:** | hawks and owls; crows, squirrels, and rat snakes also raid nests |
| **Travel:** | Blue jays can fly at 20 mph and reach speeds of 32 mph in migration. Some blue jays migrate to warmer climates when winter reaches the northern states. |
| **Ecological niche:** | mid-level predator, prey animal, and omnivore consumer; also spreads seeds in its droppings and plants acorns in the soil; some of those acorns sprout into new trees |
| **Habitat:** | forests, fields, farms, and backyards, |
| **Folklore:** | The blue jay is portrayed as a clever bird in stories. |

**Other fun facts:**

- A single jay can cache (bury) up to 5,000 acorns in a single autumn. Jays can carry five acorns in their crops (throats) at one time

- A blue jay's "blue" feathers are not really blue. The color is due to light reflecting off special surface on the feather. If you hold a "blue" feather up to a light, you will see its natural gray-brown color.

- The Western Steller's jay is a relative of the blue jay. It has a dark blue body and a black head.

- Blue jays give a raucous "jay! jay!" call to warn other blue jays (and the rest of the forest as well) that a predator has entered the forest. They can also give a "queedle" call.

- They are seen by many biologists as a very "intelligent" bird species.

- The blue jay is in the same *Corvus* group as crows, ravens, and gray jays.

# Woodpecker

| | |
|---|---|
| **Name:** | downy woodpecker (*Picoides pubescens*) |
| **Size and coloration:** | 6 inches long; white belly; mottled black and white back, wings, and tail; black and white striped head; males have a red spot on the backs of their heads |
| **Senses:** | good wide-angle, color vision; good sense of touch with their long tongues |
| **Food:** | insects and insect larvae, seeds |
| **Predators:** | shrikes, sharp-shinned hawks, and merlins |
| **Travel:** | These birds climb up and down tree trunks with specially adapted feet that have two toes pointing forward and two toes pointing backward. Unlike many small birds in the northern United States, downy woodpeckers do not migrate, finding plenty of insect food in dead and dying trees year-round. |
| **Ecological niche:** | mid-level predator, prey animal, omnivore consumer |
| **Habitat:** | Woodpeckers live primarily in forest habitats and are especially common in older forests with dying trees that provide insect food. |

**Other fun facts:**

- Woodpeckers use their sharp beaks to peck holes in dead or dying trees that have been infested by insects. They also excavate nests in old trees. Many species make a new nest each year, leaving old nests for other songbirds or mammals to use.

- Woodpeckers have extremely long tongues. The tongue structure actually starts at their nostrils, wraps over the heads, and comes out their mouths. Woodpeckers use their very sticky or sharp tongues to gather insects.

- Woodpeckers have specially padded skulls, much like a "crash helmet," to protect their brains from the incessant pounding they do in search of food.

- Their stiff tails help them balance when pecking. The tails also help the bird climb up a tree.

- The spots on a woodpecker's back "break up" its body outline and help camouflage it in the woods.

# Bird Sound Survey Activity

**Grade Level:** 4–8

**Environmental Themes:** adaptation, habitat, diversity

**Curriculum Areas:** science, social studies, music

**Student Skills:** comprehension, problem solving, inferring, comparison

**Materials:** birdsong tape or CD, clipboards, paper, and pencils

## Instructions:

1. Go outside and listen for the birdsongs you hear in the area. Then choose up to five songs and record them on a tape or CD for the class to hear (reproducing a tape or CD for educational purposes is usually legal under the federal government's "fair use" clause as long as you only make one copy for school or library use, but check with your administrator to be sure).

2. Have students listen to the five bird songs over and over again over a few days. Post pictures of the birds that sing those songs in the room. Then go outside with clipboards, paper, and pencils and make a "sound map" of the area. Have students put an "X" in the middle of their pages to represent them. Then have them close their eyes and listen to the world for a few minutes. It is usually easier to hear things with our eyes closed. Have them use words or pictures to describe the sounds around them. How many bird individuals did students hear? How many bird species did they hear? Did they hear any bird sounds that weren't songs (e.g., a woodpecker tapping or a sparrow shuffling through the leaves)?

3. If time allows, survey two different areas, like a schoolyard and a park or a site in the middle of town and one in the country. Which site had more birdsongs and more species of birds? Why?

## Evaluation:

How many students could identify a bird from the classroom recording? Were they surprised by how much they heard when they listened?

From Kevin Strauss, *Tales with Tails: Storytelling the Wonders of the Natural World.* Westport, CT: Libraries Unlimited, 2006.
Copyright © 2006 by Kevin Strauss.

# Caterpillar Scramble Activity

**Grade Level:** 1–6

**Environmental Themes:** adaptation—camouflage, habitat

**Curriculum Areas:** science

**Student Skills:** inferring, comparison, evaluating

**Materials:** multicolored 1-inch pipe cleaners or toothpicks; different colors of yarn will also work

## Instructions:

1.  Spread the small pipe cleaners around the "search room."

2.  Talk with students about camouflage and how many animals have coloration that helps them blend into their environment. Tell students that for this activity they will be birds, and their job is to collect as many pipe-cleaner "worms" as they can for their food. Give students 30 seconds to search for worms in the "search room." How many worms did they find? What colors were the worms that they found? Generally, bright-colored pipe cleaners are more visible and easier to find. Give the students another 30 seconds to search for worms. Did the results change?

3.  Discuss how the process of "natural selection" indicates that if a particular animal is easy to find and eat, it is far less likely to reproduce. Choose some "camouflaged" worms that blend in with the "search room" floor and put more of them in the room to simulate the reproduction of these well-hidden worms. Do another 30–second search. Are the students getting better at finding the worms? The more experience a bird has, the better it seems to get at finding prey.

4.  Assuming that birds will eventually find ways to identify even camouflaged worms, how might these worms survive? One option would be for them to only come out at night. Darken the "search room" by pulling the blinds and turning off the light. How did this affect the search process?

    Both humans and birds use color vision to find food. In low light, our color vision doesn't work as well, and it is harder to find food. This could be why humans and many bird species are most active during the day and many worms are more active at night.

## Evaluation:

Did students take part in the activity and discussions? Can students describe how camouflage affects animal survival?

From Kevin Strauss, *Tales with Tails: Storytelling the Wonders of the Natural World.* Westport, CT: Libraries Unlimited, 2006. Copyright © 2006 by Kevin Strauss.

# Avian Adaptations Activity

**Grade Level:** 4–8

**Environmental Themes:** adaptation, habitat, diversity

**Curriculum Areas:** science, visual arts, language arts

**Student Skills:** creativity, comprehension, problem solving, inferring, comparison

**Materials:** paper, markers or crayons, pencils, modeling clay, popsicle sticks, and other art tools

## Instructions:

1. Define the term "adaptation" for students. An adaptation is a physical (tooth, claw, feathers) or behavioral (migration, nest-building) "tool" that helps animals to survive. Describe some adaptations of common birds: A bald eagle has talons for catching fish and a sharp beak for tearing up food to eat; a woodpecker has a sharp beak for pecking holes in trees and a long tongue to help it fish out insect food; chickadees gather in winter "forage flocks" with other chickadees, and even other species like nuthatches and woodpeckers, to look for food, and by traveling in a group, there are more birds watching for predators, so each individual is more likely to survive.

2. Tell students that they will create their own birds with their imaginative and artistic skills. Give them a habitat card, a size card, and a food card (see below). Ask students to draw or create a model of their bird, either singly, or for younger children, in small groups. It needs to have an adaptation to help it find and gather food, an adaptation to help it find a mate, and an adaptation to help it avoid an enemy (they can decide what enemies their bird has).

3. After 30 to 45 minutes of bird creation, have students give a presentation on their new bird species. Discuss how some of the adaptations they came up with are real adaptations for actual birds. Truth really is stranger than fiction in the natural world.

## Adaptation Cards

Write these terms down on cards or photocopy and cut out this page. Hand one of each category to each student or group of students.

| Habitat | Size | Food |
|---|---|---|
| Antarctica | tiny (2 inches long) | worms |
| Huge city | small (5 inches long) | seeds |
| Ocean | medium (10 inches long) | garbage |
| Desert | large (24 inches long) | rocks |
| Mountaintop | very large (48 inches long) | insects |
| Cave | huge (72 inches long) | mammals |
| Forest | gigantic (144 inches long) | birds |

## Evaluation:

Did students find creative ways to describe their new birds? What adaptations of the imaginary birds are similar to real bird adaptations? (Have students research bird adaptations and make comparisons.)

From Kevin Strauss, *Tales with Tails: Storytelling the Wonders of the Natural World.* Westport, CT: Libraries Unlimited, 2006.
Copyright © 2006 by Kevin Strauss.

# Chapter 9

## Animal Stories: Reptiles and Amphibians

Reptiles are cold-blooded animals with dry, scaly skin that lay hard or leathery-shelled eggs on land. Snakes, turtles, and lizards belong to this group. Many reptiles live on land, although many can swim if they have to. Some reptiles, like the painted turtle and snapping turtle, spend most of their lives in the water. Reptiles are most common and numerous in warmer climates because they are slow and sluggish in colder regions.

Amphibians are cold-blooded animals with relatively smooth skin that live part of their lives in the water and part of their lives on land. The name "amphibian" literally means "double life." Frogs, toads, salamanders, and newts are examples of amphibians. Their young (e.g., tadpoles), live in water and breathe through gills, then later metamorphose into adults (e.g., frogs) who have legs, can live on land, and breathe air. Amphibians need to return to ponds or rivers each year to lay their jelly-like eggs. Of the 1.2 million known animal species in the world, 10,500 are reptiles or amphibians.

Amphibians were some of the first vertebrates (animals with backbones) to live on land. Fossil evidence shows that amphibians evolved about 370 million years ago, long before the first dinosaurs. The earliest reptiles appeared 330 million years ago.

## Turtle

*Themes:* adaptation—turtle hibernation, turtle shell shape

### The Talkative Turtle (Adapted from India)

Long ago, in a deep green forest, there was a Turtle who loved to talk. He talked all day long to whomever he could find. He would walk right up to Rabbit and say, "Hey Rabbit, how's it going? I see that I'm here and you're here so why don't we have a conversation? We could talk about the weather or the trees or what you ate yesterday and how it tasted. What do you think?"

Of course, conversations with Turtle only went one way. He did all of the talking and everyone else had to listen. Rabbit quickly turned and ran off into the woods. Other animals were not so lucky.

One day, Turtle saw a flock of geese getting ready to migrate. They had flown to the lake and were waiting for the rest of the flock to arrive. They were just what Turtle wanted: a captive audience. He swam right up to them.

"Hey, geese, how's it going? Are you guys flying somewhere, because I love to fly and I've always wanted to fly. Are you guys going to fly south? Is it warm down there? Do they have forests like this one down there? Hey, could you guys take me with you when you fly?" said Turtle.

The geese had heard about Turtle and they knew that there was no way they were going to get rid of him, unless they gave him a job to do.

"Honk, Turtle, honk," said the Goose Leader. "We'd love to take you with us, but the problem is that, honk, you don't have any wings. But, we like to be fair, honk, so if you can think of a way that you could fly without wings, we'll help you do it. And to help you even more, I've got a suggestion for you. See that rock sticking out of the water way over there on the far side of the lake?"

"Yeah," said Turtle, squinting his nearsighted turtle eyes.

"Well that's the 'Thinking Rock'; any animal that goes and sits on that rock, and closes his mouth, is bound to think of a good idea. But remember Turtle, it's really hard to think and talk at the same time."

Of course, the geese were just trying to get rid of Turtle, but Turtle didn't know that. He swam right over to that Thinking Rock, talking to himself all the time about what a good thinker he was. When he got there, he climbed on top of the rock, sat down, and for five whole minutes, he didn't say a thing. It was a miracle. That was probably the first time in Turtle's life that he had been that quiet. But when he did that, Turtle realized something amazing: it really is easier to think when you aren't talking. Suddenly he had a plan on how he could fly without wings. Of course once he had his plan, he wanted to tell someone about it.

Turtle splashed into the water and swam right out to the Geese. When the geese saw him coming back, they frowned. They had hoped to get at least an hour of peace and quiet, but all they got was five minutes!

"I've got a plan. I've got a plan," called Turtle. "You see, I could go find a stick and then bite on the middle of the stick with my jaws, because we turtles have very strong jaws. I could bite the stick and then a goose could grab each end of the stick and carry it into the air. What do you think? You said that you'd help me, right?"

At first the geese were disappointed that Turtle had come up with a plan. But when they heard the plan, they smiled.

"You realize, Turtle, that for this plan to work, you can't talk the whole time you are flying?" said the Goose Leader. "If you open your mouth to talk, you'll let go of the stick and then you'll fall down and down and down and SPLAT! And we wouldn't want that to happen."

But Turtle wasn't worried.

"No problem," he said. "Some animals say that I have to talk all of the time, but I don't have to talk all of the time. I can stop talking any time I want. Besides, if I did fall, I'm sure that my strong, strong shell would protect me. No problem. So are you ready to go?"

The geese were still hoping to get rid of Turtle before they had to fly south.

"Well you know, Turtle, we'd be happy to help you, but you don't have a stick and there aren't any sticks out here in the lake, and we've got to leave bright and early tomorrow morning," said the Goose Leader. "So if you can go find a stick and be back here before dawn, we'll help you fly."

Turtle set off right away, swimming across the lake and back to the forest, all the time, talking to himself about what would be the perfect stick for this trip.

"It can't be too long, or it might get tangled in the trees and it can't be too short, or the geese won't have a good place to grab on," said Turtle. "It can't be too thick, or I won't be able to get my jaws around it, and it can't be too thin, or it will break when the geese lift me into the air."

Turtle talked and he searched all through the night. The geese went to sleep hoping that was the last they had seen of that talkative Turtle. They hoped that Turtle wouldn't be able to find the right stick. They hoped he would get lost in the woods. They even hoped that he might just give up. But as the sun rose pink and gold in the eastern sky, they realized that they weren't that lucky. There was Turtle, swimming across the lake and dragging the perfect stick, not too long, not too short, not too thick and not too thin, behind him.

"Here it is," said Turtle, "the perfect stick. Are we ready to go?"

The geese realized that now they had to make good on their promise. So two Geese volunteered to help Turtle fly. As the rest of the flock flapped their wings and lifted off into the sky, Turtle bit the middle of his stick and a goose grabbed on to each end. The geese that carried Turtle into the sky couldn't fly as high as their brothers and sisters in the flock, but they could get just high enough to clear the trees.

It wasn't long before they flew low over a village. In that village, one of the men looked up and saw something amazing. You see, they had all seen a horse fly before, and a deer fly, they had even seen a house fly. But no one in that village had every seen a turtle fly before. And that's exactly what they saw, a turtle fly, a flying turtle.

"Those must be the smartest geese in the forest if they could teach a turtle how to fly," said the man.

That made Turtle angry. It wasn't the geese's idea, it was his idea, and the geese were getting all of the credit. As they flew over the village he couldn't contain himself. He yelled out, "It was my ideaaaaahhh . . . ." As soon as Turtle opened his mouth, he let go of the stick and fell down and down and down and "Thump." The fall knocked him out cold, and when he woke up the next day, he only had the strength to crawl to a hole and climb inside.

The next spring, when Turtle came out of that hole, he was a very different turtle. His cracked shell had healed, so he could walk again. But wherever he went, he didn't say a word, having learned his lesson from the last time he spoke. And to this day, if you meet a turtle on a lake or in the forest, you can say anything you want to it, but it won't matter. That turtle won't talk back. Because every turtle mother tells her children this story and always ends it the same way.

"Remember children, there are times to keep your big mouth shut!"
And that's the end of the story.

**Teller notes:** Depending on my audience, I adapt the ending. If I am telling it to family groups, I emphasize the fact that turtles don't talk. If I am telling it to a school group, I emphasize the "pourquoi" part about why a turtle's shell has cracks in it.

*Theme:* habitat of turtles

## Turtle Wins at Tug-of-War (Adapted African American Tale)

One day Turtle was walking through the forest when she met Bear.

"Hi, Bear, how are you doing?" said Turtle.

Bear just stuck his nose in the air and walked by, pretending not to notice Turtle. Turtle ran after Bear (as fast as a turtle can "run") . It took her most of the afternoon to catch up with Bear at the side of a lake. By the time she reached Bear, Turtle was feeling very angry. She caught her breath and then walked up to the napping Bear.

"Hey, Bear, who do you think you are? Walking by and not speaking to me, you should be ashamed of yourself!"

Bear opened one eye and looked at the angry Turtle.

"I'm way too big and strong and important to bother with a puny animal like you," said Bear.

"Puny? Did you say Puny?" said Turtle. "I'm the strongest animal in the forest! Who are you calling 'puny'?"

Bear open both eyes and laughed. "Haw, haw, haw! You, the strongest animal in the forest? I doubt it."

Turtle had to think fast. "Well then I'll prove it to you. We'll have a tug-of-war, unless, of course you're scared of me."

Bear noticed that Blue jay and Squirrel were listening to this conversation. He couldn't back down now.

"OK, Turtle, where should we meet?"

"I'll meet you tomorrow at dawn at the bend in the river," said Turtle. "Since I challenged you, you should bring the rope."

Bear agreed and then Turtle set off into the woods. She had some thinking to do before the contest. News of the competition spread like summer rain through the forest. Every animal, from the smallest Mouse to the biggest Moose, was at the bend in the river at dawn.

When Bear arrived, he joked with his friends about how this would only take a minute. As the sun shone pink and golden through the trees, Turtle popped her head out of the water.

"Hey Bear, I will pull from the water and you can pull from land," said Turtle. "If you can pull me out of the water, then you win. If I stay in the water, I win."

"Whatever you say, Turtle. I'll beat you anyway."

Bear threw the rope out to Turtle. Turtle dove underwater and tied the rope to a big rock. Then she swam to the surface and grabbed onto the middle of the rope, pretending that it was the end.

"On your mark, get set, GO!" croaked Frog.

Bear yawned and pulled with one paw, but the rope didn't move. He grabbed the rope with both paws and pulled even harder.

"I haven't moved yet, " said Turtle.

Bear grunted and pulled even harder. Some of the animals started to snicker. Then some of them started to laugh. Bear pulled and pulled, but no matter how hard he pulled, he couldn't pull Turtle out of the river. Finally exhausted, Bear fell to the ground.

"OK, Turtle, you win," said Bear.

All the small animals like Chipmunk and Gopher and Salamander and Mouse cheered, but the big animals were quiet.

Turtle dove down to untie the end of the rope and swam in to shore. But as Turtle stepped on land, a shadow fell across the sky, and a huge hoof landed right in front of his head. It was Moose.

"OK, Turtle, you might be stronger than Bear, but you're not stronger than ME!"

Turtle looked up. She couldn't give up now. So she puffed out her cheeks, took a deep breath, and said, "I accept your challenge. Meet me here tomorrow morning."

"Fine!" said Moose. "But this time, I get to be in the water and you get to be on land."

"That's fine with me," said Turtle. "I'll even bring the rope."

That night Turtle swam across the river to a hill on the other side. She climbed the hill and tied the rope to a tree on the far side. Then she lay down on the top of the hill to sleep. The next morning, when Moose and all the other animals arrived, Turtle threw the rope out to Moose. Moose grabbed it in his teeth.

Once again, Frog croaked, "On your mark, get set, GO!" Moose pulled as hard as he could. Nothing moved. He pulled even harder and the rope stretched, but Turtle was still standing on the top of the hill, smiling.

"Are you ready to start yet?" said Turtle.

That made Moose even angrier. He wrinkled his nose, closed his eyes, and pulled like he had never pulled before. He pulled so hard that "snap!" the rope broke and he landed upside down with his antlers stuck in the mud. When he finally stood back up, a very muddy Moose looked up at Turtle and said, "You've won."

The little animals cheered and the big animals even clapped a little. But then Moose yelled above the noise.

"Turtle, you have proven you are a strong creature, so I invite you and your children to live in the water with us."

"Hey, wait just a minute," bellowed Bear. "I was the first one to lose to Turtle, I want to invite you and your children to live on land with the bears."

Turtle thought about the proposals for a moment, and then came up with a brilliant idea.

"You know, I have many children," said Turtle. "From now on, some of my children will live in the water and some of them will live on land."

And that is the way that it is to this day. Some turtles live in the water and some on land, and no one ever challenges them to tug-of-war.

# Turtle Facts

**Name:** painted turtle (*Chrysemys picta*)

**Other names:** Other North American species include the terrestrial (land-living) box turtle (*Terrapene carolina*) and aquatic snapping turtle (*Chelydra serpentina*).

**Size and coloration:** 4–9 inches long; dark olive green shell and legs; yellow and orange sides and yellow-striped head, legs, and tail

**Senses:** Painted turtles have wide-angle vision. They can sense movement, and when basking on a log can quickly slip into the water when a predator or a child sneaks up on them.

**Food:** Painted turtles eat a variety of plants and small animals, including algae, small fish, snails, lily pads, duckweed, mayfly and caddis fly nymphs, beetles, crayfish, fish eggs, and carrion.

**Predators:** Most (70 percent) of painted turtle nests fall prey to nest-raiders like raccoons, foxes, and mink; turtle hatchlings are also food for those animals, as well as for crows, gulls, herons, bullfrogs, snakes, and large fish. Adult turtles are relatively safe from predation.

**Travel:** Painted turtles are relatively slow walkers on land, but they are graceful swimmers.

**Ecological niche:** mid-range predator and plant eater, omnivore consumer

**Habitat:** ponds, lakes, and wetlands; likes to sun itself on rocks and half-submerged logs

## Other fun facts:

- Painted turtles can breathe in water by drawing water in through their nostrils and into their mouths to extract the oxygen in the water.

- Painted turtles are the most wide-ranging turtle in North America.

- Turtle shells are actually modified ribs.

- In autumn, painted turtles bury themselves in up to 3 feet of mud under lakes and hibernate throughout the winter. The turtle's metabolism slows down considerably during hibernation.

- This turtle can freeze solid and then thaw out again without harm.

- Painted turtles are long-lived organisms, living an average of 10 to 15 years, but they have been known to live up to 40 years.

- Incubation temperature determines gender in painted turtle young. If the temperature of the eggs is 77 degrees F or cooler, the young are male. If it is 87 degrees F or warmer, the young are female, and if it is around 84 degrees F, the young are a mix of males and females.

- Painted turtles spend much of their summer basking in the sun on logs or rocks. Scientists think this helps warm their bodies, get rid of leeches and other aquatic parasites, and make vitamin D, an essential nutrient for absorbing calcium from their aquatic plant food.

## Other turtle stories in this book:

"Why Deer Has Split Hooves" (adapted from the Philippines) (p. 78)

"How Rabbit Lost Her Tail" (China) (p. 88)

# Snake

*Themes:* adaptation of snake and frog bodies, metamorphosis, food chain

## How Snake Lost Her Legs (Original)

Long ago, Snake had four legs and could walk around the way that lizards and foxes do today. One day while Snake was walking through the forest, rain clouds stretched across the sky and rain poured on the land. This wasn't unusual, but what was strange was that when the rain stopped, the Sun didn't come out again. The land was starting to get cold. Snake began walking through the forest asking the other animals what was going on. She heard from Eagle that the Cloud People had kidnapped the Sun and locked him in a cave. When news spread that the Sun was trapped behind a huge iron gate, the animals gathered to discuss the problem.

The snakes and turtles were most concerned about the loss, since without the sun's warmth, they are slow and sluggish. But the insects were worried as well. With no sunlight, the plants won't grow. Eagle took charge of the meeting and sent the mosquitoes and flies to survey the situation. Soon they returned to report that they had found the key to the cave door, but it was hidden in a small hole and they weren't strong enough to carry it out.

The animals traveled to the hole. Most of the animals couldn't even fit their heads into the hole. But Snake could. Unfortunately, her legs made her too wide to slip into the hole and grab the key. Snake tried and tried, but she just couldn't fit through the hole. Rat had the same problem, as did Weasel. That night, as the animals sat at the edge of a pond, they discussed their problem.

"Wait a minute," said Tadpole, sitting in the water. "If your legs make you too wide, why don't you just take off your legs?"

No one had ever thought of that before. All of the animals looked at Snake, Rat, and Weasel.

"No way," said Rat. "My legs are staying right where they are."

Weasel mysteriously disappeared into the shadows. That left Snake. She knew what was at stake. If they couldn't free the sun, soon she and all of her children would freeze.

"OK, I'll do it," said Snake.

Tadpole smiled to himself.

The next day, Snake walked to the hole. When she saw that all of the animals had gathered around the hole, she sneaked off behind some bushes to take off her legs. You see, back then, animals could take off and put on their legs just like we take off or put on a pair of pants today. Snake hid her legs under a bush when she thought no one was looking. Then she wiggled out into the crowd.

"Snake's here! Snake's here!" all of the animals cheered.

Snake looked at the crowd, looked at the gray sky, and then wiggled into the hole. It was tough going, wiggling on her belly, but Snake was strong and she didn't give up. Finally, she found the key and put it in her mouth.

"This way, this way," said the Mosquito guide.

Snake wiggled and Mosquito flew through the cracks and caves in the mountain until they reached the great iron gate that trapped the Sun.

"Who are you?" said Sun.

"Just a friend who wants to see you fly in the sky once again," said Snake.

When Snake turned the key in the lock, Sun burst out into the sky, blowing the Cloud People far and wide.

All of the animals cheered when they saw that Snake had freed the Sun. They ran or hopped or flew into the hilltops or meadows to enjoy the Sun's warmth. But when Snake slithered back out of that tiny mountain hole, no one was around to greet her. What was more, Snake's legs weren't there either!

"Hey! Who stole my legs!" yelled Snake.

She searched far and wide. Finally she slithered up to the top of a tall hill and asked the Sun for help. Sun searched all across the land and he finally spotted Snake's legs on Tadpole's body! Tadpole had stolen Snake's legs when no one was looking, and now he was hopping around in the forest for the first time.

Of course now that he had legs, Tadpole got to thinking.

"I'm not just a 'tadpole' anymore. I'm a new animal, an animal with legs, so I need a new name. Something snappy, something clever, something with one syllable."

You probably know what name he chose, right? He chose "Frog," and that's what we call him today.

When Snake heard what Tadpole had done, she tried to catch up with Frog and take back her legs, but Frog was just too fast. Sun looked down from the sky and wanted to help his friend.

"Snake, from now on, when you are feeling slow and sluggish, call up to me and I will warm the land and give you the energy to chase that Frog," said Sun.

Snake never forgave Tadpole or Frog for stealing her legs. From that day to this, whenever a snake sees a tadpole or frog, she bites it and eats it for dinner, legs and all. And since that day, when clouds gather and storms rage, if there is a snake in the land, the Sun will always return to bring warmth to the forests and fields and hills. You see, the Sun never forgets his friends.

**Teller notes:** Snakes use their very muscular bodies to slither through their forested or grassland homes. Since a snake's skeletal system contains what appear to be hips, some scientists believe that the snake's ancient ancestors had legs like a lizard.

*Themes:* adaptation of snake poison, food chain

# How Snake Got Her Poison and Rattles (African American)

Long ago, when the animals were first made, the Maker made every creature and gave it a job to do. Deer was supposed to eat the bushes and trees, so they don't get too tall. Wolf was supposed to chase and eat the Deer, so they don't deforest the world. Mouse was supposed to eat seeds and chew on the bones left over from the dead Deer, and Snake was supposed to eat the Mice, so they didn't eat too many seeds.

But Snake had a problem. Since she didn't have any legs, she couldn't move all that fast. And since she was so low to the ground, sometimes animals trampled right over her without a second thought. She didn't think most of them were doing it on purpose, but she couldn't be sure sometimes. She did know that her brown and green scales made her hard to see on the ground. That was handy when Broadwing Hawk was in the neighborhood, looking for a meal, but annoying when a herd of deer came tramping by.

One day, after being trampled half to death by a Black Bear, Snake decided that she needed to do something about it.

"I'll go find the Maker," she said. "He made us, he should be able to help solve our problems, and if he doesn't, we snakes might just go on strike and stop doing our job in the world."

Snake had heard that the Maker lived on a high mountain in the west. So she crawled on her belly, day after day, until she got to the top of that mountain. There she found the Maker sitting on a chair and admiring his work.

"Well Snake, what brings you to these parts?" said Maker.

"Well, to tell you the truth, I come here with a problem," said Snake. "You see, I can't move all that fast and from time to time, I get trampled by the other animals. I have tried talking with them, and some of them, especially the smaller ones like Rabbit and Raccoon, have promised to be more careful, but the bigger ones like Bear and Deer don't really seem ready to be neighborly. They act like they are way to busy to bother with the likes of a lowly snake."

"That might have been a design flaw," said Maker.

"A what?"

"A design flaw," said Maker. "You see I made all animals, including people, a bit selfish. I figured that was a good way to make sure they survived. But I might have overdone it in a few cases. You know, too much of a good thing, is not a good thing . . . ."

Maker thought for a few moments.

"Well, no use crying over spilled milk. Let's give them a reason to be a little more careful around snakes."

With that, Maker reached up into the sky and came down with two sharp fangs and a jar of clear liquid.

"Open wide," said Maker.

And he put the fangs into Snake's mouth and gave her a drink of that liquid.

"Now, if anyone bothers you, you can bite them and the poison in your fangs will give them a good reason to avoid you. You shouldn't have any problems with those bigger animals after this."

Snake thanked the Maker and set off back to her forest.

Now after all of those years of getting stepped on by the other animals, Snake was looking for a little payback, and she had a way to collect. She would lie down in the middle of the path, and when an animal came by, even if it didn't step on her, she would bite it on the ankle, and more often than not, gave it a dose of poison. Pretty soon, forest animals were dropping like leaves in October and everyone was afraid of Snake because she had power.

Pretty soon, all the animals had a meeting, but they didn't invite Snake. Rabbit led the meeting.

"We've got to do something about that Snake," said Rabbit. "I've been to 15 funerals this week and it's only Tuesday. What's more, Snake isn't killing for food, like most animals do, she's just killing and leaving them there, lying on the ground."

"Yeah," said Frog. "Snake already killed four uncles, two brothers, and a second cousin. We can't leave the pond to catch bugs with that Snake around."

So the animals talked and talked about what they should do. Some wanted to talk to Snake, others wanted to just get together and finish her off. But a few of the more sensible ones had a different idea.

"How about we talk to Maker?" said Owl. "He's the one who gave Snake those fangs and poison in the first place."

You know how it is when you're on a committee. If you make a suggestion, then you become the one to carry it out. So Owl had to fly up and talk with Maker on the mountaintop. It didn't take long for Owl to get there.

Maker saw him coming.

"How's it going there, Owl?" said Maker. "How are those 'night vision' eyes working for you?"

"Oh, the eyes, they're doing great, Maker, I can find a mouse in the starlight. Couldn't ask for anything better," said Owl.

"So what brings you up here?" said Maker.

"Well, Maker, it's Snake," said Owl. "With those fangs and poison you gave her, we animals are dropping like ripe fruit. If this keeps up, soon there won't be many of us left, and I know that wasn't your plan. Do you think you could take away the poison?"

"Now I can do a lot of things," said Maker. "But I'm not sure I just want to take away Snake's poison until I look into this matter a little further. Tell Snake to come back up here right away."

Owl flew off and told the birds about the Maker's message, since birds are one of the few animals that can get close to Snake without getting bit. A few weeks later, the slow-moving snake reached the mountaintop.

"Snake, it appears that you and I need to talk about that poison I gave you," said Maker.

"What about it? It works great. I haven't been stepped on in weeks," said Snake.

"That's just it, Snake, from what I hear, you're using it for insurance instead of protection," said Maker. "I didn't mean for you to kill every animal in the forest just to keep them from stepping on you. They got jobs to do, too, and with you killing them left and right, they can't get much done."

"I'm sorry, Maker, but I guess I'm a little gun-shy after getting stepped on all those years," said Snake. "Me being so low to the ground means that it's hard to tell who is my friend and who might be an enemy, so I just bite whomever comes by."

"Well, maybe this was a little bit my fault, as well. Making you all camouflaged like you are certainly doesn't help things," said Maker.

He thought for a minute and then reached into his pocket.

"Here, Snake, take these rattles and put them on the end of your tail," said Maker. "If you hear someone coming, just shake your rattles. That will be a warning. If the animal is smart, it will go the other way. But if it isn't, then it probably deserves to get bitten."

That's why, to this day, we call those snakes "rattlesnakes." They still have their poison and they still shake their tails to warn us when they are near.

# Snake Facts

**Group facts:** Snakes are legless reptiles. About 30 percent of snake species are venomous, meaning they can inject poison into prey. Snakes are predators who smell the world with their tongues and have poor eyesight. Some snakes, known as "pit vipers," also have an organ that lets them "see heat" the same way that infrared goggles and cameras can see heat. Rattlesnakes are one example of a pit viper. Snakes shed their skin several times a year.

Like all reptiles and amphibians, snakes are "cold-blooded," meaning they can't generate their own body heat. They need to warm up in the sun before they can be active. By comparison, "warm-blooded" animals like mammals can generate their own body heat.

In most cases, venomous snakes have heads that are wider than their bodies, and nonvenomous snakes have heads that are the same width as their bodies. The brightly colored coral snake is one of the few venomous snakes with a narrow head.

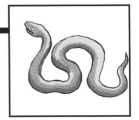

## Garter Snake

**Name:** garter snake (*Thamnophis sirtalis*)

**Other names:** common garter snake, grass snake, gardner snake

**Size and coloration:** 1–4 feet long; black, brown, or dark green coloration;, often three yellow stripes on the back, which helps it hide on the forest floor

**Senses:** good sense of smell (snakes "smell" with their tongues); has a "vibration sense" that lets it feel approaching creatures; is probably nearsighted and almost deaf; like many predators, it probably has little or no sense of taste

**Food:** toads, salamanders, frogs, tadpoles, earthworms, insects, mice, voles, and fish

**Predators:** broad-winged hawks, herons, ravens, crows, owls, mink, weasels, foxes, and larger snakes

**Travel:** The garter snake shelters under rocks and logs and hunts during the day except in the hottest part of summer, when it hunts at night. Garter snakes can swim as well as slither on land.

**Ecological niche:** mid-level predator, prey species, and carnivore consumer

**Habitat:** The garter snake prefers to live in areas with moist ground near ponds and rivers, but it is very adaptable and can live in forests or grasslands as well.

## Other fun facts:

- Garter snakes got their name because of their resemblance to the "garters" that men used to wear to hold up their socks.

- Their jaws can open up to 180 degrees to help them swallow large prey.

- These snakes can release a bad-tasting and bad-smelling liquid from their tails to discourage predators. It doesn't work well against bird predators like hawks and owls, who have poor senses of smell and taste.

- Unlike most snakes, which lay eggs, garter snakes give birth to live young.

- Garter snakes can live up to 20 years, but the average lifespan is much shorter. Up to 80 percent of garter snakes die in their first year.

- Large meals may take several days to digest. During that time the snakes hide in logs or underground shelters. Their slow metabolism lets them go for weeks without eating.

- Unlike most snake populations, the highly adaptable garter snake populations are stable. They live farther north than any other snake species and eat any food they can get their jaws around.

## Rattlesnake

|  |  |
|---|---|
| **Name:** | timber rattlesnake (*Crotalus horridus*) |
| **Other names:** | rattlesnake, pit viper, rattler |
| **Size and coloration:** | 3–4½ feet long (a record rattlesnake was 6 feet long). This species has two color patterns: a "yellow phase," with black or dark brown crossbands on a lighter background color of yellow, brown, or gray; and a "black phase," with dark crossbands on a black background. The timber rattler has a wide, triangular head. |
| **Senses:** | "Pit" heat sensors let rattlesnakes "see" heat so they can catch prey in complete darkness. They smell with their tongues and have a great "vibration sense" when they lower their jaws on the ground; they can determine the size of an approaching animal by how the ground vibrates. Rattlesnakes have poor eyesight that only lets them detect motion at short distances, and they are probably deaf to airborne sounds. |
| **Food:** | Timber rattlesnakes are carnivores that eat mice, voles, shrews, chipmunks, tree squirrels, ground squirrels, rats, rabbits, and sometimes birds. |
| **Predators:** | Juvenile rattlesnakes are the prey of hawks, owls, fox, coyote, and raccoons. Adult rattlesnakes' few natural predators include humans and eagles. |
| **Travel:** | Rattlesnakes can swim as well as slither. |
| **Ecological niche:** | top predator, carnivore consumer |
| **Habitat:** | Timber rattlesnakes prefer deciduous forests in rugged terrain. |

### Other fun facts:

- Of the 8,000 people bitten annually by venomous snakes in North America, only 15 die each year. That is similar to the number of people killed by dog attacks in North America annually.

- Biting is how rattlesnakes defend themselves. If frightened, snakes will try to escape or hide. If that doesn't work, a rattlesnake will hiss and rattle its tail. But when startled, a snake might bite without warning.

- Timber rattlesnakes are disappearing from most of their range in eastern North America and are the subject of much debate over how best to protect declining snake populations. Other species of rattlesnakes are also in decline.

- Young rattlesnakes follow their mother's scent trail to hibernate in their mother's hibernation burrow. Snakes migrate 1⅓–4½ miles to hibernate.

- Rattlesnakes have two hollow fangs, which are connected to a venom gland in the mouth. Snakes periodically shed and replace these fangs. Rattlesnakes use their venom to immobilize prey and to aid in digestion. Since this venom is relatively slow acting and a snake can only produce a certain amount each day, rattlesnakes don't seem to use their venom as a defense. A defensive rattlesnake bite only carries a fraction of the venom that the same snake would inject into prey.

# Frog

*Themes:* food chain

## The Wide Mouth Frog (United States)

Once there was a little sister Frog, and this little Frog had questions. She always wondered why frogs ate flies. So she went up to her older brother and said, "Brother, why do we eat flies?"

"Because we do," said her older brother, before hopping into the pond.

That wasn't a very good answer, so the little Frog went to her older sister, thinking that maybe sisters are smarter than brothers.

"Sister, why do we eat flies?"

Her older sister looked at her sideways and said, "Because we do," before hopping out into the tall grass.

The second answer wasn't any better than the first.

"Well, if my older brother and sister don't know the answer to this question, maybe I have to find it for myself," thought the little Frog. "I'll go ask other animals what they eat, and then I will be able to figure out why I eat what I eat."

So she hopped out of the marsh to go in search of some answers.

She hopped through the woods until she came to the edge of a river.

And then she saw it. It had dark brown fur all over its body.

It was big like a log! (Remember, frogs are pretty small.)

It had a flat, scaly, pancake-like tail.

It had long orange teeth.

And it was eating a birch tree.

The little Frog hopped over and asked her favorite question.

"Hi, I'm a Wide Mouth Frog. Who are you and what do you feed your babies?"

The Beaver looked over at the little Frog and smiled.

"Well . . . I'm a Beaver and I feed my babies birch bark and aspen bark and ferns and pond lilies."

"OH!" said the little Frog. "Thank you very much."

You see she was a very polite little Frog.

And the little Frog hopped off.

She hopped through the forest until she came to a clearing. And then she saw it.

It was huge like a mountain! (Remember, frogs are really small.)

It had black fur all over its body.

It had claws at the ends of its paws.

It had sharp teeth and it was eating . . . berries. The little Frog hopped up and asked her favorite question.

"Hi, I'm a Wide Mouth Frog. Who are you and what do you feed your babies?"

The big Black Bear looked down at the little Frog and told her, "Well, I'm a Black Bear and I feed my babies berries; that's how we got our names, you know . . .

berries—bears. I also feed them acorns and ants, and your garbage, if you don't lock it up at night, ho, ho, ho."

"OH!" said the little Frog. "Thank you very much." Then she hopped off toward a lake.

And then she saw it.

It was tall like a tree. (Remember, frogs are really short.)

It stood on two scaly legs, ankle-deep in the water.

It had blue-gray feathers all over its body.

It had two wings.

It had a long, snake-like neck and a long, spear-like bill.

The little Frog hopped up and asked her favorite question.

"Hi, I'm a Wide Mouth Frog. Who are you and what do you feed your babies?"

The creature looked down its long bill and said in a high voice:

"I am a Great Blue Heron, and I feed my children Wide Mouth Frogs!"

Right then, the little Frog knew that she was in trouble. So she created a disguise! She took two fingers and made her mouth very, very small and said in a high, squeaky voice, "Really, Wide Mouth Frogs, well I haven't seen any of those around here. The only kinds of frogs I have seen in this lake are frogs with itty-bitty mouths like this one. Hey, wait a minute. I think I hear my mom calling, I'll see you later, bye!" And she hopped off, "Hop, hop, hippity hop-hop. Splash." And she was back in her own home pond.

After that, little Frog didn't worry so much about what other animals ate. She knew that she liked flies just fine, and knew to stay away from that Great Blue Heron.

**Teller notes:** You can adapt this story to animals that live in your region. I have heard Southern storytellers tell this story with an alligator instead of a heron.

*Themes:* adaptation—frog tails, metamorphosis

## How Frog Lost Its Tail (Ashanti)

Long ago, Frog was hopping though the forest when he met the Sky God. Sky God was handing out gifts to the animals. The first gift that Sky God gave Frog was a long tongue, so Frog could catch bugs for dinner. But then Frog got into line behind the other animals to ask for another gift. When Sky God saw Frog again, he asked Frog what he wanted.

"Sky God, I would really, really, really, really, really like a tail," said Frog. "All of the other animals have tails and I would like one too."

"All right, Frog, I will give you a tail, if you promise to guard my well. It's a pool of water that never runs dry," said Sky God. "Your job is to make sure that everyone can drink there, but don't let anyone muddy the water."

Frog agreed. But as time went by, Frog forgot his job. He forgot that his job was to make sure that animals didn't waste or muddy the water. But after a while, he began to think that the well was really his well. Soon he would meet animals on the path and tell them lies like "the well is dry, no water here," or "watch out, there is a lion at the well. You'd better run!"

When Sky God heard what Frog was doing, he was angry. A cloud covered the sun and the god's voice boomed like thunder.

"I gave you a gift and you have shown your true nature: rude and mean," said Sky God. "Since you have not done your job, you will lose your tail!"

A bolt of lightning struck Frog's tail and the tail disappeared. From that day to this, all Tadpoles have tails for swimming in the water, but once they become frogs, their tails disappear.

But the frogs do still remember part of their job in ponds and lakes. If you listen carefully, you will hear the frogs calling: "keep it clean, keep it clean, keep it clean." That's the way it was and that's the way it is and that's the end of the story.

**Teller notes:** Frogs and toads go through a process of "metamorphosis" in which they grow from an egg to a tadpole (with a tail) to an adult (with legs and no tail). Because the process of metamorphosis in insects and amphibians is so amazing, many cultures have developed stories to explain it through folklore or science.

# Frog and Toad Facts

**Group facts:** Frogs and toads have a lot of similarities and a few differences. Most toads have dry, rough skin, plump bodies, and shorter back legs suited for hopping. Most frogs have smooth, moist skin, and more slender bodies. They have long legs well suited for leaping. There is currently a worldwide decline in many frog and toad species, possibly due to pollution, loss of habitat, or destruction of the ozone layer.

## Frog

**Name:** leopard frog (*Rana pipens*)

**Other names:** grass frog

**Size and coloration:** 2–5 inches long; green body with black irregular spots that give it a "leopard-like" appearance; tadpoles are 5½ inches long and olive black

**Senses:** Leopard frogs have wide-angle vision and good vision for finding prey; frogs have eyes on top of their heads so they can hide in the water while looking for prey. They have a poor sense of smell.

**Food:** Adults eat grasshoppers, crickets, beetles, flies, spiders, snails, and smaller frogs; tadpoles eat algae and decaying plant material.

**Predators:** Predators of adults include raccoons, weasels, garter snakes, bullfrogs, great blue herons, kingfishers, bass, and trout; predators of tadpoles include dragonfly nymphs (young), fish, and leeches.

**Travel:** Leopard frogs will travel from 200 yards to 2 miles to go from shallow breeding ponds and feeding ponds to deep winter hibernation ponds and lakes.

**Ecological niche:** mid-level predator, prey species, carnivore consumer (adults)

**Habitat:** shallow ponds, grassy fields, and deep ponds for hibernation

**Folklore:** • Frogs are often seen as "helpful" creatures.

• In many stories, talking frog characters are humans under a spell.

## Other fun facts:

- This frog's call is a deep, staccato snore

- Tadpole mortality is 95 percent in the first six weeks. About 60 percent of adult frogs die each year.

- Chemical pesticides seem to have been responsible for a leopard frog population crash in the 1970s. In the 1990s, students in a southern Minnesota school found deformed frogs in a pond. Scientists believe that the deformations may be due to a new parasite or the effect of new pesticides or new combinations of chemicals in the environment.

## Other frog stories in this book:

"How Snake Lost Her Legs" (original) (p. 129)

# Toad

| | |
|---|---|
| **Name:** | American toad (*Bufo americanus*) |
| **Size and coloration:** | 3–4 inches long; mottled brown, tan, rust, and green with bumpy warts on dry skin; tadpoles are fat, black, and fishlike |
| **Senses:** | wide-angle vision and good eyesight for finding prey; poor sense of smell |
| **Food:** | beetles, ants, grasshoppers, spiders, flies, worms, insect larvae (caterpillars), slugs, millipedes, and moths; by some estimates, one toad eats up to 3,300 insects each month |
| **Predators:** | skunks, raccoons, garter snakes, broad wing hawks, crows, owls. Some of the "warts" on toads are actually poison sacks that contain a poison that leaves a bad taste in the mouth of a predator. |
| **Travel:** | Toads hop to get around, but usually hunt by ambushing insect prey and catching it with their long tongues. They hibernate in chambers up to 4 feet underground. Toads spend more time on dry land than frogs do, often traveling to ponds and marshes only for breeding. |
| **Ecological niche:** | mid-level predator, prey species, and carnivore consumer |
| **Habitat:** | moist upland forests, meadows, shallow ponds, and marshes |

## Other fun facts:

- The mottled skin helps camouflage the toad in its forest floor habitat.

- This toad has a high "trilling" mating call in the spring.

- Toads are often connected to witches and other evil forces in stories.

- Toads are reputed to spread warts, but you can't get warts from toads. A virus causes warts, not contact with toads; toad warts are actually protective poison sacks on the toad's skin.

- All toads are poisonous, but some predators have developed resistance to toad poisons.

# Who Am I? Activity

**Grade Level:** 3–6

**Environmental Themes:** adaptation, habitat, animal groups

**Curriculum Areas:** science

**Student Skills:** problem solving, inferring, comparison

**Materials:** pictures of reptiles, amphibians, and other animals, tape or safety pins

## Instructions:

1.  Discuss the differences between reptiles and amphibians. Also discuss examples of reptiles and amphibians. Then tape pictures of various reptiles and amphibians on the backs of students. Tell them that they can only ask "yes or no" questions about the animals on their backs. Their job is to determine what kind of reptile or amphibian is on their backs.

2.  For older students, repeat the process, but use any kind of animal, including insects, mammals, birds, and fish. If students are very familiar with the animals you are using, challenge them to determine the species of the animal on their backs (e.g., "garter snake" rather than just "snake").

3.  Discuss how this process of asking "yes or no" questions is what scientists do to help them divide animals up into groups. In effect, with this activity students are using the same process as scientists do with a tool called a "dichotomous key." Look for some easy ways to divide different kinds of animals into groups by their appearance. Body covering, leg design, and way of giving birth are three categories that scientists use. What are some other aspects of animals that you could use?

## Evaluation:

What sorts of questions were most effective in determining the kind of animal on a student's back? Was everyone able to determine the name of his or her animal?

From Kevin Strauss, *Tales with Tails: Storytelling the Wonders of the Natural World.* Westport, CT: Libraries Unlimited, 2006.
Copyright © 2006 by Kevin Strauss.

# Snake Myths and Frog Facts

**Grade Level:** 4–8

**Environmental Themes:** adaptation, habitat, diversity

**Curriculum Areas:** science, social studies

**Student Skills:** evaluating, comprehension, problem solving, inferring, comparison

**Materials:** list of "reptile and amphibian facts," note cards (see below), "true" and "false" signs

## Instructions:

1. Divide students into groups.

2. Discuss how the realities of the natural world are often more amazing than fictional things that authors dream up. Hand out four "reptile and amphibian facts" cards to each group and have students work in small groups to determine if the statements on their cards are true or false and come up with reasons for their answers.

3. Have students tape their fact cards under either a "true" or "false" sign on the chalkboard or wall. Then go through the list and briefly discuss each statement and whether it is indeed true or false. If a group has put a card in the wrong spot, move the card and discuss the reason for moving it.

4. For older students: backing up the facts. Now that you have discussed which statements are true and which are false, challenge the students to find two independent sources of evidence to prove that statements on four cards are either true or false.

## Evaluation:

Did students take part in small group or class discussions? Were students able to find evidence to back up the truth or falsity of their fact cards?

### True

- Frogs swallow with their eyes.
- Toads have poison sacks in their skin that make them taste bad.
- Amphibian (frog, toad, salamander) populations are decreasing worldwide.
- Some people eat frog legs and say they taste similar to chicken.
- Wood frogs can freeze solid during the winter and then thaw out in the spring.
- Turtle "shells" are actually just external ribs.
- Some frogs breathe through their skin.
- All amphibians need to lay their eggs in water.
- Reptiles can shed their skin all at the same time.
- Snakes have "hip bones" similar to those on animals who have working legs.
- Snakes have no outer ears and probably can't hear airborne sounds.
- Snakes can feel the vibrations of an animal's footsteps on the ground.
- Snakes smell with their tongues.
- Crocodiles and large tortoises can live to be over 150 years old.
- Dinosaurs are related to lizards.
- Birds are related to lizards.

### False

- Toads can stun their insect prey with their high-pitched calls.
- Toads can give you warts.
- Every rattlesnake bite is fatal.
- Turtles are immune to fire.
- Turtles can crawl out of their shells.
- Frogs aren't an important part of the natural world.
- Snakes are slimy.
- Frogs hatch out of their eggs with arms and legs.
- Frogs can live to be 100 years old.

From Kevin Strauss, *Tales with Tails: Storytelling the Wonders of the Natural World.* Westport, CT: Libraries Unlimited, 2006. Copyright © 2006 by Kevin Strauss.

# Chapter 10

## Animal Stories: Insects

Insects are by far the largest group of creatures in the world. They are generally small (less than 3 inches long) creatures with six legs and exoskeletons (a hard "skeleton" on the outside of their bodies). Insects have three body parts: a head, a thorax (middle, with the legs and sometimes two to four wings), and an abdomen (tail, with stinger or egg-laying "ovipositor") . Insects hatch from eggs and may go through a "metamorphosis" to change from a wormlike larvae (like a caterpillar) into an adult (like a butterfly). Insects can molt or shed their hard skin as they grow.

Of the 1.2 million known animal species in the world, 75 percent (963,000) are insects. There are more beetle species in the world (300,000) than any other group of organisms. There are more kinds of beetles in the world than all other noninsect species combined. Although spiders are a closely related group of animals, they have eight legs and two body parts and never have wings. They are not insects; they are arachnids.

## Butterfly

*Themes:* adaptation—butterfly wings, food chain

### Where Butterflies Come From
### (African American)

Back in the beginning of time, Creator made the world with his own two hands, shaping the mountains and the valleys and the rivers and the lakes. He placed the oak trees and pine trees and aspens and maples. But when he was done, he breathed on the world to form the clouds and the sky. Rain came to fill the rivers and the lakes and the sea.

Creator rose up to the sky to look over creation. But it looked a little bare to him. There was just land, a few trees, and a lot of ocean. What's more, when the rains fell, they washed soil into the rivers and turned the lakes a dingy brown.

"That's not the way things should be," said Creator.

So he snapped his fingers and created a pair of pruning shears. He snipped bits off of each of the trees and they fell to the ground. These magical bits of the first trees turned into the bushes and the grass and the flowers that we have today. As the sun set in the western sky, Creator rose into heaven.

The next day, Creator looked over the world and heard the flowers talking.

"It is so lonely down here. The grasses are jealous of our beautiful colors, so they won't talk to us, and the trees feel that they are far too uppity and important to speak to lowly 'flowers.' And besides, how in the world will we get our pollen to the other flowers in the field. It is too heavy for the wind."

Creator heard all of these complaints and got to feeling a little frustrated. He wasn't even done creating the world yet and already there were complaints!

"Well, I'll fix them!" thought Creator.

Creator snipped off bits from every part of creation—bits of sky, bits of clouds, bits of flowers and trees and sunsets and rocks. He gathered the bits and breathed life into them, commanding: "You will fly from flower to flower, keeping them company and carrying pollen wherever you go."

Those magical pieces of the sky, clouds, flowers, trees, and sunsets sprouted wings and began flying all across the world. Blue ones came from pieces of the sky, white ones from clouds, green ones from the trees, and red ones from the sunset.

After that, Creator made all of the other animals and finally the people in the world. When the first people saw the small, flying creatures flitting and fluttering from flower to flower, being logical people, they called them "flutterbys" because they were "fluttering by."

But that name, even though it was descriptive, was hard to say, and if something is too hard to say, eventually, people will change it to make it easier. That's what happened with "flutterbys." Over the years, people changed it bit by bit, to call them "butterflies" and that's the name that we use today.

Now the flowers were so happy to have the butterflies for company, and so pleased that butterflies would carry pollen from flower to flower, that the flowers used their magic to turn sun, soil, water, and air into sugar water (nectar) as a gift to the butterflies, and that's what the butterflies drink to this day.

**Teller notes:** This story tries to answer questions about why butterflies look the way they do and why we call them "butterflies." Other stories describe butterflies as witches who take the shape of butterflies to steal butter (a valuable commodity when you had to make it by hand) and fly off with it. While it is likely that a butterfly might land on a block of butter and taste it with its feet, rest assured that no butterfly could carry off a stick of butter.

*Themes:* metamorphosis, self-confidence

# The Ugly Worm (Original)

Long ago in a deep, dark wood, on the bottom of a great green leaf, a tiny insect egg hatched and Little Green Worm (larva) came out. The Little Green Worm crawled and crawled all over the leaf, until she got hungry. The leaf smelled good, so she ate and ate and ate until she was full. Then she climbed down to the ground. As she walked on the forest floor, she saw lots of animals that looked a lot like her, well, sort of like her. Some had six legs, some had eight, and a few even had a hundred. Some of them crawled on their bellies, some hopped, others flew. She had never seen so many creatures before. One of the animals she saw looked a lot like her, except that it was covered in brown fur. The Little Green Worm walked up to the Fuzzy Caterpillar.

"Are you part of my family?" asked the Little Green Worm.

"Hah! Me, related to an ugly little worm like you, ha? Never. My parents were beautiful brown moths and I will be a moth some day as well, not an ugly green worm," said the brown caterpillar.

Black Beetle laughed as well.

"Look at those bulging eyes and short, stubby little legs," laughed the Beetle, holding his belly. "You look like a bird snack just waiting to be eaten. Hah, hah."

That made the Little Green Worm feel sad. She crawled off into the tall grass, so no one would see her cry. But then she saw something glowing in the grass. As she got closer, she saw that it was another beetle, but not like the last one. This one had a tail that glowed! The Glowbug walked up to the Little Green Worm.

"Don't listen to them," said Glowbug. "Those bugs always act that way. It's because they are insecure. They think they will never amount to anything and will just end up food for some bird."

"But they're right," said Little Green Worm. "I am an ugly little worm."

"Well you are little, and you are green, but I think you are a cute little larva."

"Larva, what's that?" said the Little Green Worm.

"Well that's a baby bug. That's what you are right now. But when you grow up, you'll probably change into something else."

"Really, what kind of thing?" said the Little Green Worm.

"I don't know," said Glowbug. "That's something you'll have to find out for yourself."

After that, the Little Green Worm felt better about herself. She spend her whole day chewing on leaves and exercising her muscles until one day, when she had grown much bigger, she climbed to the top of a branch and fell into a deep sleep. Her skin turned hard and became a chrysalis (KRIS-a-liss), sort of a hard cocoon. Green Worm (she wasn't little any more) slept and slept. When she awoke, she stretched her muscles and that hard skin split. She climbed out of her chrysalis and felt something strange on her back. She flexed her back muscles and felt herself rise into the air. She did it again and again and she was flying over the forest. All of the other insects looked up in amazement. Green Worm landed on the edge of a puddle to look at her reflection.

It was then that she realized that she wasn't a green worm at all any more; she was a Monarch Butterfly, the queen of the forest bugs. She joined her brothers and sisters in the sky as they sang and danced and flew through the trees.

**Teller notes:** "The Ugly Duckling" by Hans Christian Anderson inspired me to write this story. While swan cygnets are homely, their transformation into adults is nothing compared to what caterpillars go through.

# Butterfly and Moth Facts

**Group facts:** There are about 200,000 species in the butterfly and moth order; 10 percent are butterflies and 90 percent are moths. While in general butterflies are more colorful, are active in the day, and have skinny bodies and skinny antennae, and moths are dull-colored, night-active, and have thicker, furry bodies and feathery antennae, there are exceptions. Some moths, like the luna moth, are very colorful.

Butterflies pupate (change from caterpillar to adult) in a hard chrysalis (KRIS'-a-liss) that forms from their outer layer of skin. Many moth larvae are furry caterpillars that spin a silken cocoon to pupate in. While it is not technically correct to talk about butterfly "cocoons," among non-naturalists and some children's authors, this is a common practice.

Although this group of insects might seem small and unimportant, pound for pound, the caterpillars in the average northern forest outweigh all the forest birds, moose, bears, chipmunks, and other animals put together. Most of the agricultural forest pest species in the world are moth larvae.

## Butterfly

**Name:** monarch butterfly (*Danaus plexippus*)

**Size and coloration:** adult—4-inch wingspan; bright orange wings with black veins; black bodies. larva (juvenile)—2-inches long; often has bands of yellow, black, and white

**Senses:** good color vision; wide-angle vision; "tastes" with its feet

**Food:** Adults drink nectar from flowers with their long, straw-like tongues. The larvae eat milkweed leaves.

**Predators:** birds, mice, shrews, wasps, and spiders

**Travel:** diurnal (day-active); can fly up to 11 mph and can travel 44 miles per day when migrating

**Ecological niche:** pollinator, prey species, and herbivore consumer

**Habitat:** meadows, forest edges, marshes, and shorelines

## Other fun facts:

- Monarch caterpillars have a high tolerance for the poisons in milkweed plants; the poisons stay in the insect's body and make them unpalatable (taste bad) to most vertebrate predators. Blue jays quickly learn that orange and black butterflies taste bad and leave them alone.

- A monarch butterfly's bright colors probably warn predators that the monarch tastes bad. Monarchs also look for mates based on coloration, so they can find the right species of butterfly.

- Each fall, monarch butterflies start their migration south, some traveling up to 2,000 miles. By November, hundreds of millions of monarch butterflies converge on mountaintops in Mexico and on trees in southern California. The really amazing thing is that none of those butterflies made that trip before. Researchers think that instinct and magnetite (a magnetic mineral) in their cells help them to navigate. Once they reach their winter area, monarch butterflies go semi-dormant. In the spring they start the return journey. But it takes several generations before the monarchs return north.

- Monarch numbers seem to be dropping in the wintering grounds in Mexico. Recent news reports estimate a 75 percent drop in the number of wintering butterflies. Habitat destruction in Mexico (illegal logging) and the United States (due to intensive agriculture) seem to be the primary reasons for the decline. Chemical and biological (genetically modified) pesticides may also be part of the threat to monarch survival.

# Moth

|  |  |
|---:|:---|
| **Name:** | luna moth (*Actias luna*) |
| **Other names:** | moon moth |
| **Size and coloration:** | adults—5-inch wingspan; pale mint-green wings |
| **Senses:** | excellent sense of smell with their antennae; males use smell to find females in the night |
| **Food:** | Adults don't eat at all (they don't even have mouths), and their sole job is to mate and lay eggs (all of the eating happens when they are caterpillars). Larvae eat birch, aspen, and willow leaves. |
| **Predators:** | bats, birds, mice, beetles, wasps, ants, and spiders |
| **Travel:** | night-active flyers |
| **Ecological niche:** | herbivore consumer (plant eater) and major prey species |

## Other fun facts:

- Their green wings act as camouflage when luna moths land in the green foliage of deciduous trees.

- Researchers think that streetlights attract moths because moths use distant light sources like the moon to help them fly in a straight line. Unfortunately, nearby light sources disorient their navigation instincts; moths keep adjusting their flight pattern and end up circling and sometimes running into streetlamps.

- In fall, luna moth larvae spin silken cocoons for the winter; adults emerge in May (or earlier in Southern states) to lay eggs for the next generation.

- Some moths pollinate flowers and drink nectar with long, straw-like "tongues."

- A male luna moth can smell a female moth up to 5 miles away.

- Many moth species are dull in color; because they don't find their mates by sight (it is dark at night, after all), bright colors are not necessary. Instead they use scent to find their mates. Dull colors provide moths with camouflage as they sleep on bark or on branches during the day.

# Ant

*Themes:* habitat, adaptation, diversity

## Why Ants Are Everywhere (Burma)

Long ago, King Lion called all of the animals to a banquet. Ant, with her short legs, was the last one to arrive. When she got there the larger animals just laughed at her.

"What took you so long," laughed Woodpecker.

"We thought that Snail was slow, but you took even longer to get here," joked Rabbit.

"Of course, you are so small, it's not like we missed you," howled Prince Lion.

Ant was so embarrassed, she turned and ran off into the woods. She ran all the way to her underground nest.

The next day King Lion awoke with a terrible pain deep in his ear. It felt like some small creature was biting him. Lion tried to use his claws to remove the creature, but only succeeded in scratching himself. Then he called all the animals together to help him with his pain. Doctor Owl did his best, but couldn't do anything. Even Woodpecker and Heron, with their long beaks, couldn't help. Lion was at his wit's end.

"Can no one cure this pain?" he roared.

Just then, Rabbit spoke up.

"You know, King Lion, not everyone is here yet. Perhaps one of the missing animals could help you."

"Go get them, NOW!" howled Lion.

Rabbit ran off as fast as she could go. When she reached Ant's nest, she called out very politely.

"Ms. Ant, our King has a terrible pain in his head. It appears to be a worm or something. Could you come and help him?"

Ant thought about how the animals had treated her. But rather than holding a grudge, she agreed to help. Ant jumped onto Rabbit's back and Rabbit ran like the summer wind to Lion's house. Some of the animals snickered, "What can a tiny ant do?" But King Lion silenced them with a look.

Ant hopped down, bowed to the king, and then climbed up his mane and into his ear. Ant crawled way to the back of the ear and grabbed the biting worm with her jaws. Ant pulled the worm out of Lion's ear and the pain disappeared as well.

Lion was so grateful for the help that he offered Ant any gift that she wanted.

"Well, your majesty, all that I really want is the freedom to live wherever I want to live."

"So be it!" roared Lion. "From now on, ants can live wherever they want to live in the world."

And this is why to this day, no matter where you go, if you look carefully, you will find ants living there.

# Ant Facts

**Group facts:** There are almost 2,500 species of ants in the world. They are found everywhere in the world, with the exception of the north and south poles. Ants are social insects (colonial); a queen lays eggs and worker ants collect food, care for the young, and protect the nest. The queen, all workers, and all soldier ants are female. The workers and soldiers are sterile females. In some species, soldier ants also defend the nest. Ants winter in their underground nests. Some worker ants live to be six years old. Some queens live to be 15 years old. Ants will bite with their mandibles, and some species will sting with abdominal stingers to defend their nests form bears, humans, or other animals that threaten their home. In many cases, ants will store plant or animal food in their nests for the winter. Some ants protect and "milk" aphids in much the same way that humans care for and milk cows. Some ant species can lift 50 times their body weight. That would be like a 200-pound human lifting a pickup truck!

## Field Ant

**Name:** field ant (*Formica* species)

**Size and coloration:** ¼ long; dark reddish-brown to black

**Senses:** excellent sense of smell and taste; relatively poor eyesight

**Food:** leaves, insects, human foods, fruit

**Predators:** woodpeckers, black bears, predatory insects, and spiders

**Travel:** Field ants use their six legs to walk. Most ants are wingless sterile females, but young queens and drones (males) hatch with wings on their bodies and fly off on mating flights. After mating, the male dies and the queen finds a nest site, pulls off her wings, and digs the start of her colony's nest. Ants can climb up trees and buildings with ease. They can also fall a great distance and walk away unharmed. Those exoskeletons really are something.

**Ecological niche:** predator, prey species, and omnivore consumer; important food source for some bird and insect species

**Habitat:** forest and field areas; builds nest mounds in loose or sandy soil

### Other fun facts:

• Some species of field ants tend aphids and caterpillars and "milk" them for the honeydew they excrete.

• In groups these ants can attack creatures much larger than themselves. They can deliver a painful, pinching bite to humans.

## Carpenter Ant

**Name:** carpenter ant (*Camponotus pennsylvanicus*)

**Size and Coloration:** ½ inch long; black

**Senses:** excellent sense of smell and taste; relatively poor eyesight

**Food:** insect prey

**Predators:** woodpeckers, black bears, predatory spiders, and insects

**Travel:** Carpenter ants use their six legs to walk. Most ants are wingless females, but young queens and drones (males) hatch with wings on their bodies and fly off on mating flights. After mating, the male dies and the queen finds a nest site, pulls off her wings, and digs the start of her colony's nest. Ants can climb up trees and buildings with ease. They can also fall a great distance and walk away unharmed. Those exoskeletons really are something.

**Ecological niche:** predator, prey animal, decomposer, and carnivore consumer; they build nests in wood, hollowing out standing trees and fallen logs and speeding up the decomposition process

**Habitat:** logs or wooden structures; can damage buildings with their nest-building activities

# Mosquito

*Theme:* food chain

## Who Has the Sweetest Blood? (Jewish)

Long ago, Snake wanted to find the tastiest food to eat. He caught Gnat (mosquito) one day and ordered it to taste every creature in the world and report back to Snake. If he failed, Snake said he would eat gnats for the rest of his days. Swallow heard Snake's order and decided she should follow Gnat to make sure it didn't cause any trouble. Gnat traveled all over the world, tasting each creature. In the end, Gnat decided that humans taste the best. Swallow was a friend of the humans. She built her nest on their houses and she certainly didn't want to see snakes eating them. So she quickly made a plan.

Before Gnat could report back to Snake, Swallow ambushed Gnat and pulled out its tongue, so it couldn't talk. When Gnat tried to tell Snake that humans tasted best, all it could do was "buzzzzz." Snake was outraged.

Swallow swooped down to Snake. "You know, Snake, I heard Gnat saying just yesterday that frogs are the best-tasting animal in the world."

Snake's eyes narrowed. "Perhaps you're right," said Snake. "But before I decide on that, perhaps I should taste a BIRD!"

Snake lunged for Swallow, but she was too quick and leapt into the air. Snake bit down on Swallow's tail, but she just flew off, leaving feathers behind in Snake's mouth.

From that day to this, snakes have eaten frogs for dinner, swallows have had a V-shaped cut in their tails, and gnats have fed on humans, the tastiest food in the world. So if you hear a buzz in the air, get ready to slap that gnat.

**Teller notes:** A gnat is a biting fly, much like a mosquito. The "hum" that mosquitoes and gnats make comes from the sound of their wings. Male mosquitoes can find female mosquitoes just by following the sound of their wings.

*Themes:* food chain, habitat

# Mosquitoes and the Night Monster (Original)

Long ago the world was very different than it is today. Back then, people say, the animals could talk. Back then, monsters roamed the world. One day, long ago, a darkness came over the land. Now at first the animals thought that it was just regular night. But then it stayed. The sun never rose, or if it did, the animals couldn't see it. The stars never shone and the moon never crossed the sky. Without the sun, the wind didn't blow. Without the sun, the plants couldn't grow. Without the wind, the water turned stagnant and smells hung in the air. Without the sun, animals had trouble finding their food. This darkness was a problem. But none of the animals had ever seen anything like it before. Who had ever heard of a night that doesn't end?

But then, one night, Barred Owl was sitting in a tree when he saw a pair of glowing orange eyes in the sky and he could just make out the shape of a midnight arm reaching down to grab a clump of trees for dinner. With her sharp ears, Barred Owl could hear the chomping of teeth. Then Owl knew that the thing in the sky wasn't night; it was a Night Monster. Owl leaped from the tree and flew on silent wings through the forest calling all of the animals.

"Whooo can gather? Whooo can come quickly? There is a danger in the woods!" called Barred Owl.

The animals gathered in the deepest, darkest grove in the forest. Some of the daytime animals had trouble finding the place, as dark as it was, but the night animals helped them along. Once they had all gathered, Barred Owl told them what she had seen.

"There is a monster blocking the sun!" cried Barred Owl. We've got to do something about this, but whooo's going to do it."

"Maybe if we just leave it alone, it will move on and leave us alone, too," said Woodchuck hopefully.

"Not likely," said Bull Moose. "It seems to be in no hurry to go. And it has already eaten four of my family. I am the biggest and strongest of the animals. I will get rid of the Night Monster."

Moose climbed to the top of the highest hill.

"Night Monster, your time here is done, leave our land and bring back the sun," yelled Bull Moose. Then he took his sharp pointed antlers and thrust them up into the sky. He struck something that felt like an animal.

"Ho, ho, ho. Do you think that your tiny antlers can hurt the great Night Monster? I could just eat you now, but I am feeling full after eating your brother. So I will just teach you a lesson."

Saying that, the Night Monster used one of his huge midnight hands to push down on Moose's antlers. Bull Moose tried to resist, but Night Monster was so strong that he pushed Moose right down to the ground and flattened out his antlers. After that, Moose slunk off into the woods.

Barred Owl saw the whole thing. When she reported back to the other animals, they all looked at their paws.

"If the biggest and strongest of us can't get rid of the Night Monster, then who can?" they all thought.

"Perhaps what we need here is cleverness," said Raven. "I am the smartest of the birds. I will try to trick the Night Monster into leaving."

The black-feathered Raven was difficult to see as she flew up into the sky.

"Night Monster, I know that you are up here, even if I can't see you, but I have something important to tell you," said Raven.

"What could a puny creature like you ever have to tell me?" said Night Monster. "I travel all over the world. I see everything and I take what I want. What could you tell me that I don't already know?"

"I could tell you that there is a land not far from here where honey drips out of the trees and the land is covered in apple trees and strawberry bushes. Surely that land is much richer than our poor forest with its pine trees and aspen," said Raven.

"You ravens are a clever lot," said Night Monster. "You are trying to lure me away from your land. But I know that if there were such a wonderful place, you would all live there instead of here."

Then the Night Monster swung one of his arms and knocked Raven out of the sky.

When the animals heard what had happened, they were worried.

"If the strongest animal and the smartest animal can't get rid of the Night Monster, who can?" squeaked Chipmunk.

"Perhaps we should just leave the forest," said Woodchuck.

"And go where?" said Fox. "We don't even know how big the Night Monster is. He might cover the whole sky."

At that thought, the animals went silent.

But then, amid the crowd of animals, a tiny voice spoke up.

"Zzzzzz. I'll chase off the monster. Zzzzzz. I'll chase off the monster," said a tiny, high-pitched voice.

The animals looked around to see who was speaking, and then they saw that it was tiny Mosquito. The birds just shook their heads.

"Mosquito, you can't even hurt a bird," said Chickadee. "How could you get rid of the Night Monster?"

"Zzzzzz. I'll try. Zzzzzz. I'll do it. If he has skin and eyes, there's nothing to it," Mosquito replied.

The animals thought that Mosquito didn't have a chance against the monster, but they didn't have a plan, so they agreed to send her. Mosquito flew up into the sky until she bumped into the soft skin of the Night Monster. Mosquito took her time. She smelled the air and found the creature's mouth. Then she smelled some more and found that the creature had a nose and ears as well.

Mosquito flew into the Night Monster's ear and buzzed as loudly as she could.

"Hey!" yelled the monster. "Stop that racket or I'll eat you for lunch."

"You've got to catch me first," buzzed Mosquito. She buzzed even louder.

"Get out of my ear!" yelled Night Monster and his voice sounded like thunder.

On the ground, the animals were trying to watch the battle, but only Owl's eyes were good enough to see it.

"At least Mosquito got the monster's attention," thought Owl.

Night Monster scratched at his ear with one clawed hand. But Mosquito was hidden deep inside. Then Mosquito started to bite the monster's ear.

"Ow!" yelled the monster. He dove out of the sky and stuck his huge head in a lake, hoping to wash Mosquito out of his ear. For a few minutes, the animals could see the stars and the quarter moon in the sky. Mosquito swam out of the monster's ear and climbed onto his back. Mosquito was so light that the monster couldn't feel her. Soon the monster flew up into the sky, sure that Mosquito had drowned. Then Mosquito flew up into the monster's nose and began to bite it.

"Ow! I thought I killed you already," howled Night Monster.

"It will take more than water to get rid of me," buzzed Mosquito.

The monster blew air though his nose and sent Mosquito flying into the night. But before she hit the ground, Mosquito turned and landed on a tree leaf. She was so small that when Night Monster came looking for her with his huge orange eyes, he couldn't find her. When Night Monster looked away, Mosquito flew up and bit him on the shoulder. But this time, the monster was ready. He swung out with one of those midnight arms and "slap" hit Mosquito like a charging bear.

"Ha, ha, ha. That's the end of that puny bug," thought Night Monster. But he didn't know Mosquito.

When he lifted up his paw, his orange eyes didn't see a squashed mosquito, they saw two very alive Mosquitoes. You see, back then Mosquito had magical powers, and if you slapped it, it would break into two new mosquitoes. Now two mosquitoes buzzed in Night Monster's ears and eyes, biting and buzzing like a tiny whirlwind. Night Monster slapped and slapped, but the more he slapped, the more mosquitoes appeared, until he was sharing the sky with a storm cloud of angry mosquitoes.

"Ahh, leave me alone, leave me alone," pleaded Night Monster as he felt their bites all over his body. Then the monster started to think. "If water and wind can't hurt these creatures and slaps just make more of them, then what can I do?"

"Maybe I should just burn you little bugs in a fire," threatened Night Monster.

"Try it. Fire only makes us stronger," lied Mosquito.

Night Monster tried to suck in his breath and swallow the mosquitoes, but there were just too many of them and they bit his mouth and throat as he swallowed. Finally the monster turned and began flying to the east, toward the sea. The mosquitoes stayed with him until he reached the salty sea air. There on the shore, they watched the Night Monster disappear over the ocean, never to be seen again.

As for Mosquito, when she had finished chasing the monster, she returned to the forest to a hero's welcome. All of the birds and squirrels and deer and foxes cheered for the brave little Mosquito. But then Deer noticed that Mosquito had been injured in the fight. She had lost some of her blood.

"Mosquito," said Deer. "Since you lost some of your blood protecting us, now whenever you need some blood, you can take some of mine."

The other animals agreed as well. And that is why it is to this day that female mosquitoes drink blood from the animals that live in the forest. That is also why mosquitoes come out at night. They are always on watch in case the Night Monster returns, ready to chase him from the woods. They buzz as a warning to frighten off any monsters who want to visit this land.

Some people might think that it is annoying to have to deal with mosquitoes in the forest, but imagine what the world would be like with the Night Monster here.

**Teller notes:**  Only the female mosquitoes bite people and other animals and suck blood. They use the protein in our blood to give them enough nutrition to produce eggs. Human blood is rather nutrient-poor, so some scientists theorize that until humans wiped out many other mammal species, mosquitoes may have preferred feeding on other species that have more nutrient-rich blood. Since we are now the most common large mammal in some areas, mosquitoes feed on us instead.

*Themes:* everything goes somewhere, food chain

# The Hobgoblin's Revenge (Japan)

Long ago, in a faraway land, a hunter was walking through the woods. Game was scarce that month and he had to go deeper and deeper into the forest than he ever had before. He soon came upon a cave that had bones at its entrance. The hunter knew what kinds of bones they were; some of them were human bones. He realized at once that he had found the lair of the Hobgoblin, a one-eyed ogre with shaggy hair and yellow teeth who carried off people for food. His legs started to shake from fear. He was about to turn and run into the woods when he heard the most terrific crash behind him. He heard the deep laugh that could only be from the Hobgoblin. The monster had pushed a tree down over the hunter's trail. He was trapped! The hunter ran into the cave and crawled to the very back. The Hobgoblin just laughed.

"Ha, ha, ha. You can't escape that way. You're just making it easier to catch you."

The hunter racked his brain for any advice he had heard about dealing with hobgoblins. That's when he remembered that hobgoblins only had one eye. The hunter chose his straightest arrow. He spit on it, for luck, and then notched it and drew his bow.

The ogre came closer with its arms outstretched, its yellow claws reaching for the hunter.

The hunter let the arrow fly, right into the Hobgoblin's eye.

"Rrrrrroar" yelled the Hobgoblin. "I'm going to catch you and drink your blood, human!"

"You'll have to find me first, blind one," said the hunter and he ran off into the woods.

The Hobgoblin used its giant-sized ears to listen for where the hunter was going. It followed the hunter though the woods with big strides. The hunter ran to a steep cliff, and as he walked down a narrow trail he taunted the Hobgoblin.

"You'll never hurt me, or my family," yelled the hunter.

The Hobgoblin lunged for the hunter. He tripped and fell down, down, down the cliff yelling, "I'll get you yyyet!"

When the hunter reached the bottom of the cliff, he saw that he Hobgoblin was dead. But he didn't want to take any chances, so he piled wood on top of the body and set the monster ablaze. He figured that would keep the Hobgoblin from coming after him.

The next day, the hunter left that part of the forest, never to return. But that Hobgoblin made good on its promise. It was a magical creature and couldn't just stay dead from a fall or a fire. Those ashes blew up into the wind and sprouted wings. They turned into the mosquitoes, blackflies, and deerflies that torment us to this day. The Hobgoblin was right; he will drink our blood, that is, if he can catch us.

**Teller notes:**   Biting flies, like mosquitoes, blackflies, horseflies, and deerflies, bite humans and other mammals for a blood meal. Blood is much easier to digest than plants or even meat. Only the females bite. They use the blood meal to produce their eggs. While many biting flies are an annoyance to people and livestock, they are an important food source for birds, bats, and fish (many biting flies live as larvae in water). This is another example of the importance of understanding the interconnections or the "web of life" in nature.

# Mosquito Facts

**Name:** mosquito (*Ades* species)

**Other names:** little fly, gnat

**Size and coloration:** ¼ inch long; gray

**Senses:** wide-angle insect vision; very acute senses of smell and hearing.

- Female mosquitoes can smell the carbon dioxide from human breath up to 100 feet away; they follow that smell until they get close, then use a form of infrared (heat) vision to find their food source.

- Male mosquitoes use their antennae to listen for the wing beat buzzing sound of a female mosquito, so they can approach and mate.

**Food:** Males and females drink flower nectar and plant juices; females also need a blood meal for extra protein when laying eggs.

**Predators:** bats, dragonflies, spiders, warblers, swallows, flycatchers, and wasps

**Travel:** They can fly up to 3 mph (slower than a person can walk), but usually seek shelter in windy weather; they are most active at dawn and dusk.

**Ecological niche:** prey, parasite, and omnivore consumer; are a critical food source for many bird, bat, and fish species. Many of the birds that migrate to the northern United States each spring are going to feed on the prolific mosquitoes and mosquito larvae.

**Habitat:** forested and wetland areas close to water where females can lay their eggs

## Other fun facts:

- Mosquitoes seem to be attracted to dark colors like brown, gray, and navy blue.

- A female mosquito can feed up to eight times in her lifetime and produce 60 to 300 eggs per meal.

- Many people are allergic to mosquito saliva, and that is what causes mosquito bites to itch.

- Mosquitoes inject the saliva into us to act as an anticoagulant (to keep the blood flowing) and an anesthetic (to reduce the pain).

- The AIDS virus is too fragile to survive and be transmitted by mosquitoes, but in the southern United States, mosquitoes can carry and spread diseases like malaria and yellow fever.

- DEET insect repellants seem to "jam" mosquito's antennae sensors. This means that when a mosquito gets close to someone wearing DEET, it goes "blind" and can't find its prey. Medical authorities report that repellants with 25 percent concentrations of DEET are just as effective and much healthier for humans than repellants that are 100 percent DEET. Just like when using other chemicals, read and follow the instructions on the label.

## Other mosquito stories in this book:

"Why Wasp Has a Small Waist" (African American) (p. 159)

"The Frog Hunt" (Zaire) (p. 194)

# Bee and Wasp

*Themes:* adaptation—bee's sting, there is no such thing as a free lunch

## Bees Get Their Sting (Aesop)

Long ago, the bee people had a problem. No matter how hard they worked to gather nectar and make their honey, thieves like humans and bears would break open their hives and steal their honey. After one attack, the hive members gathered for a meeting.

"Bzzzzzz. We have to do something or people will always destroy our homes," said Worker Bee.

Queen Bee spoke up, "I have an idea. Help me gather up a cup of honey to take up to Zeus. Surely the king of the gods can help us."

Queen Bee flew up to Mount Olympus with the honey. When Zeus tasted the sweet honey, it was like nothing he had ever tasted before.

"Ah, Queen, if you will bring me a cup of honey every day, I will give you whatever you want," said Zeus.

Queen Bee knew that she had him now.

"Well King Zeus, all I really want is a sting, a weapon that we can use to kill our enemies."

"Done, " said Zeus. And like magic, a stinger appeared on Queen Bee's rear end.

"Ha, now we will teach those humans a lesson," she said as she turned to leave.

Suddenly, Zeus realized what he had done. It was too late to take back the stingers, but he could dull their points a bit, because Zeus loved the humans and didn't want to see them die at the hands of bees.

"Perhaps I was a bit hasty, Queen Bee. You do have the stinger you asked for, but I have to tell you that you will only be able to sting once and then you will die. And while your poison will hurt people, it will not kill them. You see, revenge may feel good at the moment, but at best it is a two-edged sword."

And that's how it is today. Although bees can sting, they save their stings for protecting the hive.

**Teller notes:** Bee venom is painful, but not normally fatal to humans (unless you are allergic to bee stings). Although bees can sting only once, a hive consists of several thousand bees, and several thousand stings can make even large animals uncomfortable. Bears, who love honey, have thick fur and skin that protects them somewhat from bee stings. Besides, honey is so good, it is probably worth a little pain for the bears.

*Theme:* adaptation—wasp bodies

# Why Wasp Has a Small Waist (African American)

People say that Wasp was once quite a joker. He was always telling jokes and playing the fool. But one day he was walking down the road when he ran into Mosquito. Now Mosquito was one of those insects who took himself very seriously and back then, mosquitoes were farmers. It just so happened that a frost had hit the crops that year and all the farmers had to dig up their half-grown sweet potatoes while they were still good. Wasp decided he would rib Mosquito about his misfortune a little.

"Say Mosquito, how did your potato crop do?" said Wasp.

"Oh, the crop was just fine. It was our biggest crop ever," said Mosquito.

"Really? How big were your potatoes?"

"Well, they were huge," said Mosquito. "They were each as big as my thigh."

Wasp stopped. He looked at Mosquito's skinny, mini leg. The smile crept across his face. His eyes started to water, his belly tightened up, and he burst out laughing. Wasp laughed and laughed until his sides got sore. His sides started to hurt so much that he had to hold them with four legs. He started rocking his body back and forth.

"What's so funny?" asked Mosquito, feeling a little hurt.

Wasp got hold of himself for a moment and was able to blurt out, "Mosquito, when you talk about the thickest part of your thigh, it is like talking about the heaviest part of a hair! Those potatoes must be huge if they are as big as that. Ha, ha, ha!"

Wasp's sides hurt even more, and he wrapped his arms even tighter around his middle. Now Mosquito knew when he'd been insulted. He clenched his fist and thought about taking a swing at Wasp, but when Mosquito looked at how big Wasp was and remembered how ornery Wasp could get when he got into a fight, Mosquito got himself under control.

Mosquito's face was hot when he yelled at Wasp, "Just go ahead and laugh you no-mannered fool. But I just hope that no one ever laughs at you the same no-mannered way. Because mark my words, it will happen some day."

Mosquito turned on his heels and stomped off, leaving the laughing Wasp behind. Wasp kept laughing as he walked all the way home. He had to stop a couple times to catch his breath. But when he walked in the front door, his wife just looked at him.

"What happened to your stomach?" she said.

Wasp looked down at his waist and realized that all of that laughing and all that pressing on his stomach had made his belly as skinny as Mosquito's thigh. When he saw that, Wasp got serious right away. He remembered what Mosquito had told him. He started worrying that when animals saw his new skinny waist, they would laugh at him as well. That made Wasp angry. He started getting short on patience and after that, he didn't go around telling jokes and laughing any more. From that day to this, he is always on the lookout to see if animals were laughing at him. And if another animal so much as looked at Wasp, he was ready for a fight. So be careful when you see Wasp coming by and make sure never to laugh in his vicinity.

**Teller notes:** Many members of the Hymenoptera (bee, ant, and wasp) insect order have skinny waists. Scientists theorize that a skinny waist may be an adaptation that helps ants and wasps twist and turn, the better to sting their enemies.

Despite what this story says, male wasps are quite rare. Most of the wasps that we see are female wasps. Males are only born in the fall; they mate with new queens and then die.

# Bee and Wasp Facts

**Group facts:** Bees and wasps both come from the insect order Hymenoptera, the same group as ants. Most bee and wasp species are solitary, but we notice the large colonial species like the honeybee and the bald-faced hornet. Bees and wasps cause about 50 sting fatalities each year in the United States. This is about half of all deaths caused by venomous animals. Many of the fatalities are people who are allergic to bee or wasp stings.

## Honeybee

| | |
|---|---|
| **Name:** | honeybee (*Apis* species) |
| **Size and Coloration:** | ½ inch long; black and yellow stripes |
| **Senses:** | good sense of smell; wide-angle, compound color vision |
| **Food:** | Honeybees eat flower nectar, pollen, and honey. A honeybee colony needs 55 pounds of honey in its hive to survive the winter. |
| **Predators:** | crab spiders, bee flies, robber flies, flycatchers, skunks, mice, raccoons, and bears |
| **Travel:** | A honeybee travels 500 miles in its lifetime. |
| **Ecological niche:** | pollinator, prey species, and herbivore consumer |
| **Habitat:** | Wild honeybees build their hives in tree cavities and crevices in woods and forest edges near meadows. |

## Other fun facts:

- Honeybees are a colonial species with a strict division of labor. The queen bee sits in the hive and lays the eggs, while the worker bees care for the young and gather nectar and pollen for food. Honeybees dehydrate nectar to make honey.

- Settlers from Europe brought honeybees to North America in the 1600s to pollinate their field crops and orchards. The bees spread quickly into the wild.

- A honeybee colony has 40,000 to 80,000 members in the summer and 5,000 to 20,000 members during the winter.

- Since 1984, a parasitic mite from Europe has decimated much of the North American wild honeybee population. The mite is also affecting domestic honeybee hives.

# Wasp (Hornet)

|  |  |
|---|---|
| **Name:** | bald-faced hornet (*Vespula manculata*) |
| **Other names:** | wasp, yellow jacket |
| **Size and coloration:** | 1 inch long; black and yellow or black and white body |
| **Senses:** | good sense of smell: wide-angle, compound color vision |
| **Food:** | Adult hornets eat flower nectar and tree sap. They hunt flies, mosquitoes, spiders, insect eggs, or carrion to chew up and feed to their larvae (young) back at their rounded paper nest. |
| **Predators:** | crab spiders, predatory flies, and bears |
| **Travel:** | flies to get from place to place; can also walk on six legs |
| **Ecological niche:** | mid-level predator, prey species, pollinator (when consuming nectar), and omnivore consumer |
| **Habitat:** | forests and forest edges; colony builds a 2-foot diameter round paper nest in tree branches |

**Other fun facts:**

- Especially in the fall and when defending their nest, bald-faced hornets can be very aggressive, stinging a person several times. Away from their nests and when not threatened, hornets are not aggressive.

- Hornets were some of the first creatures to make paper from wood fiber. They chew up the fiber, mix it with their saliva, and then use the mixture to make the grayish paper for their nest. Some historians contend that paper wasps showed humans how to make paper out of wood fiber when we were still using cotton rags to make paper in the 1700s. Now wood pulp paper manufacturing is a billion dollar industry in the United States and Canada.

- This is a "social wasp," with a colonial structure in which the queen lays the eggs and worker wasps find food, care for the young, build the paper nest, and defend the nest.

- Unlike honeybees, hornets can sting multiple times, injecting painful venom into humans and fatal venom into insect prey.

# Wildlife Here, Wildlife There, Wildlife Everywhere Activity

**Grade Level:** 1–4

**Environmental Themes:** adaptation, habitat, diversity

**Curriculum Areas:** science, social studies, language arts

**Student Skills:** comprehension, inferring, comparison, observation

**Materials:** hand lenses (optional), clear plastic containers

## Instructions:

1. Discuss how animals, especially insects, have adapted to live in a wide variety of places. Ask students if insects live indoors. Make a list of the ways you would know if an insect (or spider) were living indoors. The list could include seeing the insect, seeing a dead insect, seeing a spider web, hearing an insect (like a cricket), or seeing holes in an indoor plant where an insect was feeding.

2. Search the room for these signs for two minutes. Make a list of what you find. Then search again (using hand lenses if you have them) for five minutes. Which search yielded more findings? Why? (Generally speaking, the more you look for something like animal signs, the more you are likely to find something. This activity is a good way to demonstrate that persistence pays off.)

3. Repeat the activity at an outdoor location near your school or library or at a nearby park. Where did you find more insect signs, indoors or outdoors? Why do you think this was so?

4. For older students, have the group describe and sketch the insect signs that they have found. Have them take on the role of a naturalist to describe and make up original insect names for their creatures. Have them compile a one-page report about the creature and what they could learn just from its animal signs. After students have described and named their find, have them use guidebooks to learn more about their creatures.

## Evaluation:

What sensory information did students use to find signs of insects? Could students "make connections" between an insect sign and the kind of insect that might leave it behind? Were older students able to describe their insects for their report just from their observations?

From Kevin Strauss, *Tales with Tails: Storytelling the Wonders of the Natural World.* Westport, CT: Libraries Unlimited, 2006.
Copyright © 2006 by Kevin Strauss.

# Wildlife Want Ads Activity

**Grade Level:** 4–8

**Environmental Themes:** adaptation, habitat, interdependence, food chain

**Curriculum Areas:** science, social studies

**Student Skills:** analyzing, inferring, comparison

**Materials:** "Wildlife Want Ads" handout, wildlife guidebooks and ecology books

## Instructions:

1. Working in small groups, have students read the "Wildlife Want Ads" card (below) and brainstorm animals that could do the jobs requested.

2. Have them do book or Internet research to find evidence that animals on their brainstorm lists could really do the job needed.

3. Have groups make presentations about their findings. How many different kinds of animals do the same sorts of jobs in nature? Although there are many "pollinators" in the world, some plant species only have one or two pollinators who can successfully pollinate their flowers. When just one kind of animal can do an important job in nature, we call that a "keystone" species. A beaver is an example of a keystone species. In ecosystems where beavers have disappeared, there are far fewer ponds and wetland areas than in areas where beavers are common.

---

### Wildlife Want Ads

1. Wanted: Delivery animal. Seek well-traveled individuals to spread seeds around the forest. Willing to offer juicy fruits as payment. Seasonal position. Apply in person at 3401 Orchard Avenue.

2. Wanted: Pollen packer. Seek small creature to carry pollen to other flowers. Willing to pay with sweet, sugary nectar in exchange for services. Seasonal position. Apply in person at 101 Blooming Lane.

3. Wanted: Predator with a view to a kill. Hope to develop long-term relationship with carnivore who could supply me with a ready supply of deer or moose meat. Needs to be willing to make a kill and clean off thick skin. May be willing to help predator locate prey or may just follow along and make noise. Year-round position. Apply in person at 345 Avian Way.

4. Wanted: Aquatic engineer. Looking for animal to block streams and make ponds for upright marsh plant. Would be willing to provide starchy plant stems and roots as payment for engineering services. Year-round position. Apply in person at 2117 Cattail Drive.

---

From Kevin Strauss, *Tales with Tails: Storytelling the Wonders of the Natural World.* Westport, CT: Libraries Unlimited, 2006.
Copyright © 2006 by Kevin Strauss.

# Wildlife Want Ads Activity, *continued*

*Answers:* There are several acceptable answers for each of these want ads; following are some examples:

1. Any fruit-eating bird (like robins, blue jays, and crows) and many fruit-eating mammals (like bears and squirrels) could answer this want ad. Many animals eat the entire fruit and the seeds pass unharmed through their bodies. They deposit the seeds in their scat (droppings) in a new location, complete with a ready source of fertilizer. Some ant species also carry fruit to their nests, spreading the seeds in the process.

2. Most pollinators could apply for this job. Butterflies and bees are the most well-known pollinators, but some beetles and flies pollinate flowers as well. Flowers have sticky, pollen-filled "anthers" on their flowers, and when an insect comes to the flower to collect sugary nectar, it brushes up against the anthers and the pollen sticks to its back. When the insect flies to another flower of the same species, it carries the pollen with it. Some of that pollen sticks to the new flower and pollinates it so it can grow fruit and seeds.

3. Many predators could fill this bill. Wolves, bobcats, cougars, and coyotes (not to mention cars on the highway) are all capable of killing adult deer or fawns. Often these predators can't eat the whole kill, so scavengers like ravens, crows, blue jays, gray jays, bald eagles, and turkey vultures get to eat as well. While the larger creatures are eating their fill, scavenger insects feed on carcasses and lay their eggs on dead animals as well. Many fly species lay eggs that grow into maggot larvae on dead animals. Dermestid beetles eat the meat off bones. Some museums and nature centers use colonies of dermestid beetles to clean bones for museum displays and research.

4. A beaver is the only animal that could do this job. Beavers cut down trees with their sharp rodent teeth and use sticks, mud, and rocks to build a dam across a stream or river and create a pond. Beavers probably build dams instinctively to provide a "moat" around their aquatic homes and to create a pond deep enough so it doesn't freeze solid during the winter. These ponds also provide ideal growing areas for cattails, pond lilies, and other aquatic plants that beavers will feed on during the summer.

## Evaluation:

Were students able to use clues to determine which animals could answer the want ads? Could students come up with more than one animal for most of the want ads?

From Kevin Strauss, *Tales with Tails: Storytelling the Wonders of the Natural World.* Westport, CT: Libraries Unlimited, 2006. Copyright © 2006 by Kevin Strauss.

# Mosquito Hunter Activity

**Grade Level:** 4–8

**Environmental Themes:** adaptation, habitat, food chain

**Curriculum Areas:** science, physical education

**Student Skills:** comprehension, problem solving

**Materials:** shaker (made from a plastic jar and some rice) (optional)

**Instructions:**

1. In this adaptation of the call and response game "Marco Polo," a blindfolded bat will try to catch one or more mosquitoes in an enclosed play area. Have students join hands and make a circle. Choose one student to play the bat and one to play a mosquito. Blindfold the bat with a bandanna. Point out to children that bats aren't really blind. They can see as well as we do, but at night, when there is very little light, they rely on their sonar-like "echolocation" ability to "see" insect prey in the dark.

2. Tell the bat that she needs to find the mosquito by saying "bat" to "send out a sound wave." The mosquito has to either shake her shaker or say "mosquito" whenever the bat says "bat." The rest of the people in the circle are the boundary. Their job is to keep the blindfolded bat safe. When the bat tags the mosquito, she wins the round. If the mosquito can avoid being caught for three minutes, she escapes and the round ends.

3. Try several rounds of the game. Also try adding a second mosquito. Does that make it easier or harder for the bat to find food? What do you see the mosquito doing to avoid capture? What do you see the bat doing to detect her food?

As bats are homing in on an insect, they often send out more sound waves so they can zero in on a prey animal. Some insects will land on trees or on the ground so the sonar echoes from trees or the ground will help the insect hide from the hungry bat.

**Evaluation:**

Discuss whether it was easy or hard to be the bat. One defense that many insects have against predators is a high reproduction rate. How did the game change when a second mosquito entered the game? Do you think this happens in the real world?.

From Kevin Strauss, *Tales with Tails: Storytelling the Wonders of the Natural World.* Westport, CT: Libraries Unlimited, 2006. Copyright © 2006 by Kevin Strauss.

# Chapter 11

## Plant Stories: Trees, Lichens, Fungus, and Algae

## Trees

*Themes:* adaptation—pine needles, nature knows best

### The Little Pine Tree (Denmark)

Once there was a small Pine Tree growing in the forest. The little tree looked at all of the other trees and bushes and felt even smaller than she was.

"If only there was something special about me, something that would make the trees and animals take notice," said the Little Pine Tree.

Right then, a carriage came down the road. It had beautiful gold trim on the doors and glass windows that sparkled in the sun.

"That's what I need! If I had gold needles, then the plants and animals would have to notice me," she said.

So that night, she thought and she thought and she hoped and she wished. And who knows how it happened. Maybe there was a magic fairy nearby, but when the Little Pine Tree woke up, she was covered in solid gold needles! The needles sparkled in the sunlight and they got the little tree a lot of attention. Squirrels and deer came up for a closer look. Even the big maples and spruces bent over for a better look at the beautiful gold-needled tree. The Little Pine Tree liked all of the attention. But just after noon, a poor merchant walked by, and when he saw the gold-needled tree, a smile crept across his face.

"Gold needles, well my luck has changed! I can sell these in town and with the money left over, I can start my business again."

He tore every needle off the Little Pine Tree. That night, the Little Pine Tree stood bare in the moonlight.

"Obviously gold was the wrong thing to wish for," she thought. "It is far too valuable, and some people will steal valuable things. I need to think of something that would make my needles beautiful, but not be worth a lot of money . . . ."

Then she remembered the carriage once again.

"Glass, that's what I need!" said the Little Pine Tree. "I need needles made out of glass. Glass is beautiful and sparkly and it isn't very valuable."

So that night, the Little Pine Tree thought and she thought and she hoped and she wished. And that fairy must have still been nearby, because when the Little Pine Tree awoke the next day, she was covered in needles made from crystal clear glass. The light danced on her needles and a rainbow of colors shown on her branches. Once again the squirrels and deer came up for a closer look. Even the big maples and spruces bent over for a better look at the beautiful glass-needled tree. The Little Pine Tree liked all of the attention. But just after noon, the wind picked up and shook the tree's branches back and forth. Soon there was a crash and all of the Little Pine Tree's needles broke and showered the ground with their glassy shards.

That night, the Little Pine Tree once again stood bare in the moonlight.

"Obviously glass was the wrong thing to wish for," she thought. "It is far too fragile for my needles. I need to think of something that would make my needles beautiful and flexible . . . "

The Little Pine Tree looked around her and saw the leaves of a huge maple tree.

"That's what I need to look important—maple leaves!"

So the Little Pine Tree thought and she thought and she hoped and she wished. And when she awoke the next morning, her branches were covered in lush green maple leaves. As the day wore on, animals didn't take a second look at the Little Pine Tree, they just thought she was another small maple, just like the hundreds of other small maples in the forest. The trees didn't pay any attention either. But when the Sun sent his rays through the forest, they warmed up the Little Pine Tree. Suddenly she felt water evaporating out of her broad leaves. She was drying out.

"If this keeps up, I will die of thirst," she said.

The Little Pine Tree used her branches and twigs to pull off each and every maple leaf. It wasn't easy, but when she was done, once again her branches stood bare in the moonlight.

"Gold needles are too valuable, glass needles are too brittle, maple leaves make me dry out," thought the Little Pine Tree. "What kind of needles do I need?"

She thought back over the past few days, and then it hit her. It was so simple that she was surprised that she hadn't thought of it before. But then again, the best solutions often are the simplest ones.

"I wish that I had ordinary green pine needles," said the Little Pine Tree. "Pine needles aren't valuable, except to me, they are flexible in the wind, and their waxy coating keeps me from losing too much water in the hot sunshine."

So the Little Pine Tree thought and she thought and she hoped and she wished and when she woke up the next morning, she was covered in beautiful, flexible, green pine needles. And after that, the Little Pine Tree didn't worry so much about getting noticed by the animals and the other trees. She decided it was best to just be a pine tree.

Now if you go looking for this Little Pine Tree in the forest today, you'll see that she's not little any more. Now she is a great big enormous pine tree. And if you sit down at her roots, and listen to the wind in the branches, you will hear this story.

**Teller notes:** This is one of my favorite "self-acceptance" stories. It is also a good example of an "adaptation" story that demonstrates why evergreens are the way they are. The waxy coating on pine needles helps them conserve water so they don't dry out.

*Themes:* adaptation—evergreen needles, cooperation

## Why Trees Are Evergreen (Denmark)

Long ago, when animals and trees would speak to people, a flock of redwings gathered for their flight to the warm land in the south. But one bird, excited about her first migration, tripped on a branch and tumbled to the ground, breaking her wing. The other birds left her some seeds, but could do nothing else. The cold North Wind was already blowing and they had to fly.

Redwing hopped over to a birch.

"Could you shelter me in your branches," said Redwing.

"I am far too busy being beautiful to bother with the likes of you," said Birch.

Birch swayed in a dance with the breeze.

Willow made no reply to Redwing's request. Willow just leaned over the stream seeming to nurse some deep and secret sorrow. When Redwing asked Oak for help, he just scoffed.

"A strong tree like me help a puny little featherball like you? I don't think so. Be off with you!" said Oak.

Redwing was just about to give up when she heard a soft voice say, "Don't listen to him. He's just showing off for the other trees. I'll help you."

Redwing looked up to see Spruce opening up her branches. Pine tree offered up her seeds and spread her branches to block more of the wind and dark Juniper stretched her branches and offered Redwing some of her blue berries. The seeds and berries kept Redwing's strength up during the cold winter days and the shelter from the trees kept the bird warm throughout the cold winter nights.

When the South Wind blew back into the forest in the spring, she noticed Redwing shivering under the Spruce Tree. When South Wind heard what Spruce, Pine, and Juniper had done for the little bird, and how Birch, Willow, and Oak had treated Redwing, South Wind conjured up a storm and cast a spell on those selfish trees.

"Rude is as rudeness does. So from now on, when I leave the land, I will take your beautiful green leaves with me and you will stand as shivering skeletons in the snow."

Then South Wind turned to Spruce, Pine, and Juniper.

"Because of your kindness, my friends, you shall always keep your leaves, so you can shelter the birds and beasts that live here."

That is why the spruces, pines, and junipers are evergreen to this day.

**Teller notes:** "Evergreen" trees do lose their needles; they just don't lose them all at once. Throughout the year a pine tree will drop some of its rust-colored, dead needles. A waxy coating helps evergreens keep their needles so they don't dry out during the cold, dry winters. Evergreens do go dormant in the winter like broadleaf trees, but by hanging onto their needles, they can start growing much more quickly in the spring.

# Tree Facts

**Group facts:** Trees are large, woody plants. They grow in the soil, and like all green plants they use the special green chlorophyll (KLOR-o-fill) cells in their leaves to turn sunlight, soil minerals, water, and carbon dioxide ($CO_2$) into sugar. Most of the paper that we use and many of the construction materials that we use come from trees. Trees also provide important food and shelter for many animals. Dead trees act as "wildlife hotels," with large and small animals living inside them at several levels.

## Maple Trees

**Name:** maple trees (*Acer* species)

**Other names:** sugar maple, silver maple, red maple

**Size and coloration:** Maples are medium to tall trees reaching a height of 98 feet; they are deciduous (DEE-sid-you-us) or broadleaf trees with leaves that are hand-shaped with three or five lobes.

**Predators:** Many herbivores, including deer, squirrels, and insects feed on maple leaves, seeds, twigs, bark, or sugary sap.

**Travel:** Maple trees spread their seeds by dropping propeller-shaped seeds that coast on the wind to a new growing location.

**Ecological niche:** Maple trees are producers, turning sunlight into sugar through a process called "photosynthesis" (FOTO-sin-thee-sus) or literally "making something out of light." Many animals use maple trees for food or shelter.

### Other fun facts:

- The sugar maple produces very sugary sap in the spring that is the source for our natural maple syrup.

- The red and sugar maples turn brilliant red in the fall. They are the most showy fall color trees.

- Maples can grow so thickly that they shade out competitor trees.

- The Canadian flag sports a red sugar maple leaf.

## Pine Trees

**Name:** pine trees (*Pinus* species)

**Other names:** white pine, red pine, lodgepole pine, longleaf pine

**Size and coloration:** Pine trees can grow up to 230 feet tall, although trees average about 110 feet; pines are needle-leaf conifers (cone-bearing) and are also "evergreen," meaning that they don't lose all their needles in the fall. They do shed old needles, but only a few at a time all year long. They have their needles in bundles of two, three, or five needles.

**Predators:** Many herbivores including porcupines, deer, squirrels, and insects, feed on pine leaves, seeds, twigs, or bark.

**Travel:** Pine trees grow their seeds in pine cones, which squirrels often bury as a food source for later. If the squirrel doesn't return, the seeds could grow into a new pine tree. Cones also open on the tree, and when this happens, the winged pine seeds carpet the forest floor. If a seed lands in a spot with the right amount of soil, sun, and moisture, it may grow into a tall pine tree some day.

**Ecological niche:** Pine trees are producers, turning sunlight into sugar through a process called "photosynthesis" (FO-TO-sin-thee-sus) or literally "making something out of light." Many animals use pine trees for food or shelter.

## Other fun facts:

- We often use pine trees for Christmas trees. Another common Christmas tree is the balsam fir, an evergreen tree with short, single needles.

- When England administered the 13 colonies in North America, the English Navy confiscated many tall white pine trees to build the masts of their huge warships. The royal confiscation of these trees was one of the grievances that the colonists took to King George and one of the reasons for the American Revolution.

- Conifers are a very old group of trees, having been around for about 280 million years. By comparison, flowering plants like daisies and most "broadleaf" trees like maples first appeared 140 million years ago.

- Conifers include coast redwood trees, which can live up to 3,000 years, and the bristlecone pine, with a lifespan of 4,600 years.

# Lichen and Funguses

*Themes:* adaptation—lichens, funguses, habitat, natural succession

## The Rise of the Plants (Original Natural History)

Long ago in the northland, after the mountains of ice had scraped the land down to rock, the Rock people looked around at the world. Nothing moved, and they liked it that way. But as time went by, tiny creatures came blowing on the wind. They landed like dust on the rocks and grew very slowly. They were flat and gray and they spread over the face of the rocks. They whispered "grow, grow" day and night. They weren't much faster than the rocks, but slowly the Lichen people grew across the rocky land. They didn't need soil to grow, all they needed was sun and rain, and the land had plenty of that. As the Lichen people grew, they broke up bits of rock with their fingers. When they died, they made a bit of dirt. Some of that soil fell into cracks in the rock.

After a while, more creatures arrived. The next ones were taller than the Lichen people. They were tall and green. They were faster than the Lichens and they grew across the new soil like a slow green wave. They were the Moss people. The Moss people chanted "grow faster, grow faster" as they stretched an inch into the air. As the Moss people grew, they shaded out the Lichens so the Lichens moved on to other sunny rocks. When the Moss people died, they turned into even more soil.

Soon seeds blew in on the wind and landed on that soil. The first seeds came from the Grass people. The Grass people chanted "grow fast day and night, grow fast to reach the light," and that is just what they did. They grew tall, for this world, and shaded out the Mosses. The Mosses moved on to shadier rocks. When the Grasses died, the soil from their bodies covered the rocks. Next came the trees, at first scrubby pines and oaks, but later the big maples.

Now people come to the North Country to visit the lakes and fish for walleyes and camp under the white pines. But most people don't realize that long ago, there was nothing here but rock, and it was the tiny plants—the lichen, the moss, and the grass—that made the land green and made it grow such a long, long time ago.

**Teller notes:** This story describes the plant colonization of glaciated parts of North America. But similar plant succession happens on mountaintops and rocky regions cleared by intense fires. Adapt the story to your own region.

*Themes:* adaptation, symbiosis

# Alice Algae and Freddy Fungus (United States)

Long ago there was a fungus named Freddy. Now Freddy Fungus was very good at building houses, but he wasn't a very good cook. In fact, he couldn't even make his own food; like all funguses, he had to find dead plants or animals to eat, and sometimes he couldn't find much food. One day, while Freddy Fungus was sitting on a tree stump, he looked over at a rain puddle and saw something green growing there. The green thing looked up at him and smiled.

"What's your name?" the green thing asked.

"I'm Freddy Fungus. What's your name?"

"I'm Alice Algae, and I was just making some food out of sunshine. Are you hungry?"

Freddy Fungus blew right over there, and people say that Freddy Fungus and Alice Algae took a lichen (liking) to each other. They decided to get married. And from then on, Freddy Fungus would make a house and Alice Algae would make food and they could live wherever they wanted, as long as there was sunlight.

That's why to this day, when we see a lichen plant, we tell the symbiotic story of a fungus and algae that fell in love. Keep that in mind the next time you see lichen on a rock.

**Teller notes:** I have heard this story told as "Fran Fungus" and "Andy Algae." That way the story isn't reinforcing human gender stereotypes. It really doesn't matter to the funguses and algae. They don't have gender.

# Lichen and Fungus Facts

## Lichen

**Name:** lichen family

**Lichen basics:** Lichens are symbiotic (co-living) organisms consisting of an alga (similar to green pond scum) and a fungus. The alga uses photosynthesis to make sugars out of water and sunshine, and the fungus provides the "home" for the alga and keeps it from drying out.

**Size and coloration:** Lichens vary widely in color and size; some are like a flat coat of crusty paint on a rock, while others are like miniature green trees up to an inch tall. They range in color from green to yellow to orange to gray and black.

**Food:** Lichens are producers, making their own food from the sunlight and water they absorb. Some lichens use acid compounds to break up a host rock and extract minerals.

**Predators:** Many insect species, caribou, deer, and flying squirrels feed on lichens.

**Travel:** Lichen reproduce by sending spores into the wind. When the spores land in a sunny place, they often begin to grow. Some lichens only grow one millimeter in diameter per year.

**Ecological niche:** producer, soil builder

**Habitat:** sunny, soil-free surfaces like rock faces, tree trunks, or dead lower tree branches

### Other fun facts:

- Lichens have been used by humans as dyes, antiseptics, antibiotics, and an emergency food source.

- Lichens are some of the first organisms to colonize a bare rock surface and begin the process of making soil.

- Lichens can grow almost anywhere that has sunlight and clean air. Lichens can't survive in the relatively polluted air of many cities.

## Mushroom

**Name:** funguses (mushrooms)

**Other names:** toadstools, foxfire

**Mushroom basics:** Funguses are made up of two components—hair-like "hyphae" that are the body of this "plant," and a fruiting body (often a mushroom) that is the reproductive part of the fungus. We often only notice mushrooms because they stick above the ground or out of a log. The real mushroom "plant" is hidden underground or in a decaying log.

**Size and coloration:** Mushrooms come in a wide range of colors from white to tan to yellow, but because they don't make their own food, they are seldom green.

**Food:** Most funguses are saprophytes (SAP-row-fights), meaning that they eat dead things. Funguses use their hair-like hyphae to digest dead wood and animal matter and turn it into dirt.

     **Predators:** Mice, squirrels, and insects eat funguses; some funguses are poisonous to humans.

         **Travel:** Funguses release spores into the air from their mushrooms, and these spores float in the air until they land on something dead. If they land on something dead, they begin to grow and digest the dead material.

**Ecological niche:** decomposer (recycler)

## Other fun facts:

- Some funguses, often termed "foxfire," glow in the dark.

- If it weren't for funguses, we would be buried in dead trees and dead animals, and would have little or no soil for growing our food. As recyclers, funguses are critical to the earth's food systems.

# Looking for Lichens Activity

**Grade Level:** 4–8

**Environmental Themes:** adaptation, habitat, diversity

**Curriculum Areas:** science, social studies

**Student Skills:** comprehension, inferring, comparison, identification

**Materials:** pictures of mushrooms and lichens (from the Internet or books)

**Instructions:**

1. Describe how to identify lichens. They are usually a crust-like plant growing on the bark of trees and on rocks, tombstones, or buildings. They grow very slowly and can range in color from red and yellow to green or gray. Lichens can grow almost anywhere they can find sunlight and clean air. Some lichens have a "leafy" appearance, others grow in small stem-like clumps, but the most common ones look like a crust of paint.

2. Have students do a lichen survey of the school yard or other outdoor area. Look for lichens, especially on tree trunks. How many different colors of lichen can you find? Do you find more lichen on one part of a tree than on the other?

3. Describe mushrooms (think back to the last time you had a pizza). Do a mushroom survey of the same area. Do you find mushrooms growing in the same places as lichens? Not necessarily; since mushrooms digest dead plant material, they don't need sunlight to grow, so they can grow in the shade while lichens can't.

**Evaluation:**

Did the students all take part in the search? Did you have a lot of different kinds of lichens in the area, or few? What could that tell you about how clean the air is in your area? (All else being equal, the cleaner the air, the higher the diversity and density of lichen in an area.)

From Kevin Strauss, *Tales with Tails: Storytelling the Wonders of the Natural World.* Westport, CT: Libraries Unlimited, 2006.
Copyright © 2006 by Kevin Strauss.

# Color Search Activity

**Grade Level:** 3–8

**Environmental Themes:** diversity

**Curriculum Areas:** science, visual arts

**Student Skills:** inferring, comparison

**Materials:** paint "color cards" from hardware store

## Instructions:

1. Discuss how there are many colors in plants and funguses. We often think of these organisms as being only green or brown, but they have lots of other colors as well. If we observe plants carefully, we can often find amazing things.

2. Hand each child a paint card and ask the students to find all of the colors on that card indoors. Was it hard? Could you find every color?

3. Than take the children outdoors, preferably to a park area with trees, bushes, grasses, and flowers. Ask them to find all of their colors there. Which place was more "diverse" as far as colors go? (Generally a natural habitat is more diverse, with varying shades of color.) While you were looking for your color, what other things did you notice? Had you noticed all of these colors before?

## Evaluation:

Did everyone take part in the activity? What unusual things did people discover? Which colors were easiest to find in the building? Which colors were easiest to find outdoors? Why?

## Extension for older children:

Thomas Carlyle said "The great tragedy in life is not what [we] suffer, but what [we] miss." How does that apply to this activity?

From Kevin Strauss, *Tales with Tails: Storytelling the Wonders of the Natural World.* Westport, CT: Libraries Unlimited, 2006.
Copyright © 2006 by Kevin Strauss.

# Tree Leaf Key Activity

**Grade Level:** 4–8

**Environmental Themes:** adaptation, habitat

**Curriculum Areas:** science

**Student Skills:** problem solving, inferring, comparison

**Materials:** green tree leaves (and needles) collected by students

**Instructions:**

1. Combine all of the tree leaves (and needles) that students gathered from their yards or the school yard. Look for similarities among the leaves. Put all the needle-like leaves together. Put all of the round leaves together. Put all of the oval leaves together. Put all of the lobed leaves (with large bumps on them) together. Now give one group of leaves to each small group of students. Have students use guidebooks to figure out what kind of leaves are in that group. Give each group a name. If the group has several kinds of trees in it, divide the tree group into subgroups. If you have older students, work your way down to the genus or species level of identification (with specific kinds of maples or specific kinds of pine trees) in more advanced guidebooks. These are the steps that scientists use to classify tree families. Now that students know how to identify trees, give them sample leaves and ask them to identify them.

2. A quicker way to identify leaves is to use an already developed dichotomous key. Look at the example below. Describe dichotomous keys to students. A dichotomous key is a tool that biologists use to identify animal or plant species. As students read through the key, the key asks "yes or no" questions and gives students instructions on what to do next. See the demonstration generic key below. Have students use this key to identify the leaves that they have collected.

3. With older students, develop your own tree key specific to your region. After the class has developed the key, test it out on trees in the schoolyard.

From Kevin Strauss, *Tales with Tails: Storytelling the Wonders of the Natural World.* Westport, CT: Libraries Unlimited, 2006.
Copyright © 2006 by Kevin Strauss.

# Tree Leaf Key Activity, *continued*

**Generic Demonstration Tree ID Key (Designed for Northern Forests)**

1. Is the leaf needle-shaped (thin)?

    If yes, go to 2.

    If no, go to 3.

2. Does the needle-shaped leaf have long needles?

    If yes, it is part of the pine tree family.

    If no, it is part of the spruce, fir, cedar group.

3. Is the leaf made up of little "leaflets"?

    If yes, it is part of the ash and locust group.

    If no, go to 4.

4. Does the leaf have lobes ("thumbs") that stick out from the leaf)?

    If yes, go to 5.

    If no, got to 6.

5. Is the leaf "hand shaped," with three to five lobes?

    If yes, it is part of the maple group.

    If no, it is part of the oak group.

6. Does the leaf have a flat petiole (leaf stem)?

    If yes, it is part of the aspen group.

    If no, go it is part of the birch and elm group.

Dichotomous keys are tools designed for a particular habitat. A key made for one area may not work in another area. But the principles on which the keys operate always apply. By building a key with "yes or no" questions, scientists, naturalists, and the general public can develop ways to categorize and understand the diverse animal and plant life on the planet.

## Evaluation:

Could students identify trees with either the tree groups or the dichotomous key? Do students seem to understand the process of making a key? Have students describe why it might be important to develop categories for animals and plants.

From Kevin Strauss, *Tales with Tails: Storytelling the Wonders of the Natural World.* Westport, CT: Libraries Unlimited, 2006. Copyright © 2006 by Kevin Strauss.

# Chapter 12

## Sky Stories

*Themes:* nature knows best, be careful what you ask for

## Why Sun and Moon Live in the Sky (Efik-Ibibio, Nigeria)

Long ago, in a land far from here, Sun and Moon were married and lived in a house just like people do today. And back in those days, Sun was friends with Water. On many days, Sun would visit Water at the shore and they would talk for hours. One day Sun asked Water a question.

"My friend, why is it that I visit you several times, but you never come to visit me?"

"I would love to visit you, Sun, but your house is so small that if I came and brought all of my children, we would push you out of your house," said Water.

"Nonsense," said Sun. "I will go home today and add on to my house. A week from now we will have plenty of room for you. Come to my house then and my wife and I will welcome you."

"If you are sure you have room, I will come in one week," said Water.

Sun went home and told his wife, Moon, about his plans.

"Water is very large and he has a large family, are you sure you can build a big enough house for him?" said Moon.

"Don't worry, I know what I am doing. Have I ever failed before?" said Sun.

Moon just shook her head and went on about her work. All that week Sun worked to add on to his house. When he finished his house was huge. Surely this would be big enough for Water and his children.

When the sun rose the next day, Water began flowing across the land. When Water arrived at Sun and Moon's door, Water asked, "are you sure you have room for us?"

"Sure, we have room for many visitors, come in, come in," said Sun.

Soon Water rose to Sun and Moon's knees. The couple moved to their second floor. But Water kept coming with all of his fish, whale, and water snake children.

"Are you sure you have enough room?" said Water.

Sun was getting nervous about how big Water really was, but he couldn't go back on his invitation, so he crossed his fingers and stammered, "yes, please come in."

Moon glared at Sun.

The Water rose to the second floor of the house. Sun and Moon climbed onto their roof.

"You said you knew what you were doing," said Moon. "This is the last time I will listen to you."

The Water kept rising.

"Water, Water, you are too big, you can't visit our house," shouted Sun.

But it was already too late. Water couldn't stop. As the water rose over the roof, Sun and Moon looked for someplace they could go, but everything was underwater.

"We have to jump into the sky," said Sun. "Jump this way."

But Moon was still angry with Sun, so when Sun jumped into one part of the sky, Moon jumped into the other. That is why to this day, Sun and Moon are on opposite sides of the sky. It is also why most of the world is covered with water to this day. Moon is so angry at Sun that she still won't talk to him.

That's the way it was and that's the way it is and that's the end of the story.

**Teller notes:** The sun and moon are often in opposite sides of the sky, from Earth's perspective. When the sun and moon are in the same part of the sky, we sometimes get a lunar eclipse, in which the moon blocks light from the sun. But this is a very rare occurrence.

*Themes:* nature knows best, interdependence

*Pronunciation guide:*

Skoll (SKOAL)

Hati (HAT-ee)

# The Sky Wolves (Norse Inspired)

We often think that things have always been the way they are now. We often assume that the Sun always rose in the morning and the Moon always rose at night. But in Norway, they tell a very different story.

At the beginning of time, the god Odin, the All-Father, put Sun and Moon into magical chariots to fly across the sky. The god told Sun to cross the sky once each day and he told Moon to cross the sky once each night, but that wasn't how it worked out.

Sun liked watching waves crash on the shore, so he would hold his chariot for hours on the seashore. The Sun's heat turned the land into a desert and left the rest of the world dark and cold.

Moon liked the sight of the deep forests with their leaves and branches waving in the wind. She tied her horses for hours on end in the center of the deep, green woods. Her glow lit up the forests, but brought no warmth to the creatures there.

Because of Sun and Moon's disobedience, the animals, the people, and even the gods didn't know when to wake and when to sleep. Some places had daylight all of the time and some places were always dark. The gods in Asgard sent messengers to Sun and Moon, and they offered them gifts of gold and jewels, but those sky children just laughed at the gods.

"We shine more brightly than gold or jewels," jeered the Sun.

Loki, the red-haired god of mischief, smiled as he watched Odin and the other gods rage over the childish antics of Sun and Moon. But his smile turned to a frown when he realized that Sun had stopped his chariot right above the volcano home of Surt, the fire giant king. Loki had long been plotting to sneak into Surt's mountain and steal the fire diamond, a huge and beautiful gem made of living fire. Now, with the sun always shining, the giants that guarded the mountain were always awake, and even Loki couldn't sneak past them.

Loki was thinking about this problem as he walked through the forest when he heard a howl. He saw a pair of wolves chasing an exhausted deer through the woods. That gave Loki an idea.

Loki knew that no ordinary wolves would do for his plan, so he traveled to the Ironwood, a land of giants and trees as strong as steel. There he found two giant wolves, Skoll and Hati.

"Are you wolves hungry?" asked Loki.

"We're always hungry," growled Skoll. "The animals here are too small for our large bellies."

"In that case, I have a gift for you," said Loki. "Do you see those lights in the sky? They are two of the largest deer in the world. Catch them and you will eat for weeks."

"Grrr, what good does that do us? We can't fly," growled Skoll.

"Now I can help you there," said Loki. He took out the pouch of magical flying powder that he had stolen from Odin and sprinkled it on each of the wolves.

The giant wolves leapt into the sky.

"Grrr, I want the Sun," growled Skoll, heading for the ocean.

"Fine, but I get the Moon," shouted Hati, turning to the deep woods.

And the wolves were off.

When Sun and Moon saw the huge wolves coming, they drove their chariots up into the sky as fast as they could go. But the wolves kept up the chase, thinking all the time that they were chasing delicious food. Since the wolves never caught the Sun or Moon, they never learned the truth.

From that day to this, the Sun crosses the sky to make day, and the Moon crosses the sky to make night, and all parts of the world get at least some light and some darkness, so animals, people, and even the gods all know when to wake and when to sleep.

But you may have noticed that at some times of the year, the Sun moves more quickly over the sky, and at other times it moves more slowly. That is because during the summer, when the south wind blows, Skoll gets tired, and his fur feels warm, so he slows down and rests. But in winter, when the north wind blows, and cold winds waft over the world, Skoll feels stronger and chases the sun even faster than before, making our winter days shorter. But now, at least, everyone knows when to wake and when to sleep.

**Teller notes:** There are many references in Norse literature to how the wolves Skoll and Hati chase the Sun and Moon through the sky. But the surviving stories seem incomplete. Some versions talk about how Gulveig, "the hag of death," threw the giant wolves into the sky. But even that version doesn't fully explain why she did that or why the wolves chase the Sun and the Moon in the first place. My story attempts to use what we know about Norse mythology to answer that question.

*Themes:* cooperation, interdependence, adaptation

# The First Fire (Zaire)

Long ago, at the beginning of times, the people had no fire. When the sun went down at night and the winds blew, people had to wrap themselves in animal skins and shiver through the dark. Without fire, people couldn't cook their food. They couldn't harden their tools. Every once in a while, lightning would send a bolt of fire into the forests, but it never lasted very long. The people began to talk about this fire; they began to dream about this fire.

"We have to find a way to get fire from the sky," said Grandfather.

"We will need help for that," said Grandmother. "We must ask the animals for their help. They can do things that we cannot."

The people called together all of the animals for a meeting and described their problem.

"Hah," said Elephant. "You have no problem. If you grow thick gray skin like mine, you won't be cold, and if you grow big muscles and eat only plants, you won't need to make tools."

"Grow long teeth like mine and you won't need spears to catch your food," hissed Snake.

"Just grow more hair, like me," chattered Monkey. "Then you won't ever be cold."

Finally the people couldn't take the advice any more.

"We can't live like you," said Grandfather. "We are as we are and that won't change. But we know what we want, and we want fire."

At that, most of the big animals left the meeting, shaking their heads. "It would be so simple if people just listened to us," they thought.

But a few animals stayed behind. Jumping Spider scurried up to Grandfather and Grandmother.

"I will help you. If fire lives in the sky, I will help you get it."

Spider climbed to the top of a tree and began spinning a long silken thread.

"Wind, carry this thread into the sky," said Spider.

Wind came and carried Spider and her thread "kite" into the sky. She flew to the top of the sky. Then she tied the thread to the top of the sky. She tried to break through the sky, but it was too hard. Spider climbed down the thread. She spun more thread and tied it to the top of a tall tree.

"Woodpecker, I need your help."

Woodpecker followed Spider up the thread and used her beak to "tap-tap-tap" peck a hole through the sky. Light began to shine through. Woodpecker pecked several more holes in the sky. These were the first stars. Spider looked through the holes in the sky and talked to the Fire inside.

"Fire, will you come down to earth for the people?"

"I will," said Fire. "But I will only come down for someone brave enough to come up and get me."

When Spider came down and told the people this, some of them looked at the ground.

"We'll never be able to climb that high," they said.

But one young woman was willing to try. She tied a pottery jar to her waist and she climbed hand over hand up Spider's web. It was a long climb, but she was strong and light and Spider climbed along with her, encouraging her all the way. When the woman got tired, Spider spun a rope and tied her to the strand so she could rest. It felt like it took days for the woman to climb so high, but as the sun was starting to rise in the east, the woman reached the Fire in the sky. She broke off a small piece with a rock and placed the fire in her jar. Then she began the long climb down to the ground. It was dark before she reached the ground, but the starlight helped to light her way. The people cheered and rejoiced when they saw the fire that the woman carried in her jar.

Since that day, people have had fire to warm them, give them light, make their tools, and cook their food, all because of a helpful spider and strong woodpecker and the bravery of one young woman.

**Teller notes:** Young spiders can disperse by "ballooning" or standing on a fence post or treetop and spinning a thread into the air. When the thread is long enough, the wind pulls it like a kite and the light spiders float into the air. By traveling this way, young spiders can fly miles from where they were born. This dispersal method might help ensure that there aren't too many young spiders eating up food in any one area.

*Themes:* interdependence, why the wind blows

## Who Freed the Wind? (Original)

Long ago, the people say, Wind flew through the sky like a giant crimson bird. He would flap his arms and gusts of wind would shake the trees and blow dead leaves into the air. He would blow the clouds ahead of him and when he was especially excited, he would mix the clouds into thunderstorms and lightning. Because he loved to fly and blow and show his power, the young Wind was always blowing the trees and the grasses and the clouds. The animals just had to get out of his way if they didn't want to be blown this way and that.

There was one group of creatures that especially hated Wind and his wild antics. They were the bugs. The Bug people were so small that the slightest wind knocked them out of the sky or sent them sprawling across the ground. The bugs decided to make a plan. They decided that they would catch Wind and end all of his trouble-making. So they gathered together the best weavers in the land and they worked day and night to weave a huge net out of spider webbing, bee's wax, and caterpillar silk. It was the strongest net ever made. Then the dragonflies and the houseflies with their huge eyes flew off into the sky looking for Wind. They found him asleep deep in the forest. So the bugs gathered up the net and quietly sneaked up on him. As Wind lay there, the bugs anchored the net to trees and rocks and then covered Wind with the net. When Wind awoke and tried to get up, he couldn't move.

"Hey, what's going on here?"

Beetle hopped up onto Wind's chest and looked him in the eye.

"We've had enough of your blowing and huffing and puffing. From now on, we are going to keep you trapped in this net."

Wind tried to break free. But not only was the net strong, it was also flexible. Wind couldn't get through it. The bugs left Wasps to guard Wind so no one would set him free. Spider agreed to bring him food and water.

Wind pleaded with his captors.

"You have to set me free," pleaded Wind. "Without me, the clouds won't move and the land will shrivel and dry out. Without me the water will turn stagnant. Without me seeds won't soar through the air and birds can't soar on my gusts and the seasons will never change. You have to let me free."

But the Wasp guards just laughed.

"Without you, we can fly where we like. We can sting who we like and it will always be summer."

Spider felt a little guilty about what they had done. It just didn't seem natural. And the world was a very different place without the Wind. But she had made a promise to the bugs to help them catch Wind and "a promise is a promise" to a Spider at least.

The days went by and the weeks went by and still, the air was still. It was starting to get stagnant in the forest and the lake started to reek.

Spider began thinking, "Maybe Wind is right. Maybe we do need him out here in the world." But then Spider remembered his promise and "a promise is a promise," to a Spider at lest.

But finally one day, when Spider was giving Wind some berries and water, and the Wasp guards were standing at Wind's feet, Wind whispered to Spider.

"Please set me free. I'll give you whatever you want. Just cut these chords."

"I can't do that," said Spider. "I promised the bugs that I would help catch you, and a promise is a promise, to a Spider at least."

"Yes, but you have already fulfilled your promise. You caught me. But you never promised them that you would keep me prisoner, right?"

"Well, I guess that's true," said Spider.

After Spider left, she thought about what Wind had said all night long. It was true that the world was different without Wind and she wasn't sure that it was any better. The next night when Spider brought food to Wind, she whispered to him, "If I set you free, you have to promise me two things."

"Anything, anything, just set me free," pleaded Wind.

"You have to promise that you won't blow hard all the time," said Spider. "You have to be calm and quiet at least part of the time."

"Done. What is your second request?"

"Whenever my children need to travel, you have to carry them on your back."

"Done."

"You have to promise."

"Yes, I promise that I won't blow hard all the time and that I will carry your children on my back."

With that Spider turned to leave.

"Wait a minute, you said you would free me," said Wind.

"Shhh! Can't you see the Wasps at your feet? I have to wait for the right time. I promise I will help you, and a promise is a promise, for a Spider at least."

That night, Spider wove nets, and the next night when the Wasp guards were getting sleepy, Spider sneaked up behind them and threw a net over the guards. Then she jumped on their backs, tied them up, and gagged them so they couldn't call for help. Then Spider cut through the netting and freed the Wind. Wind flew out of the net with a rush.

After that day, Wind knew that he needed a change. He flew to the Northern Islands of Magic and traded his beautiful crimson coat for a magic coat that made him invisible, so the bugs could never find him and trap him in a net again. So today, you can't see the Wind, you can only see what he does as the trees sway or papers blow in the wind.

But Wind seemed to learn his lesson. Some days he blows hard, other days soft, and some days not at all. And to this day, when spiders need to travel, they throw web up into the sky, and Wind carries them miles and miles from home, because a promise is a promise for a Spider and the Wind, at least.

**Teller notes:**  Many spider species do "balloon" or fly when they are young. After hatching from its egg, a young spider will climb to the top of a fence post or tall piece of grass when the wind is blowing. It will put its abdomen (tail) into the air and begin spinning out silk. Young spiders are so light that when the spider sends out enough silk, it acts like a kite and the spider flies up into the air and carry it miles away. Scientists theorize that this technique allows spiders to disperse far and wide and avoid food competition with their siblings.

# Sky Facts

*Outer space*

- The sun is a medium star, 91 million miles from Earth (in July of each year).
- The moon and planets "glow" because they reflect light from the sun.
- Some people see a rabbit on the moon. Others see a coyote or two children carrying a bucket between them.
- The moon is about 240,000 miles from Earth. The moon always shows the same side to Earth as it rotates.
- Stars seem to "twinkle" because dust in our atmosphere occasionally blocks the light coming from these faraway stars. Astronauts tell us that in outer space stars don't twinkle.

*Sky*

- Sunlight is white and contains a rainbow of light waves. The sky appears blue because as sunlight enters the atmosphere, air particles scatter the blue wavelengths into the sky. At the same time, the sun looks yellow to us because white light minus the scattered blue wavelengths appears yellow. At sunrise and sunset, the sun's light travels through a thicker part of the atmosphere (from our perspective). At the horizon, the air is so thick that it scatters even the longer red wavelengths of light, creating a colorful sunset.

*Wind*

- Wind happens when air rushes from high-pressure areas to low-pressure areas. A vacuum cleaner operates under the same principle. A fan in the vacuum creates an artificial low-pressure zone. The air around the vacuum rushes in to fill the "vacuum" created by the vacuum cleaner, carrying the dust, dirt, and cereal into the vacuum cleaner bag. This rushing air is an artificial wind. In the atmosphere, the sun warms the earth, creating "thermals" of warm air that rise into the sky (like a hot air balloon). As warm air rises, air from surrounding areas rushes in to fill the "space" left from the rising air and creating wind on the surface of the earth.

# Finding the Wind Activity

**Grade Level:** 5–8

**Environmental Themes:** interdependence

**Curriculum Areas:** science, social studies

**Student Skills:** comprehension, inferring, comparison

**Materials:** thermometers, tissue paper

## Instructions:

1. Temperature in the classroom. Warm air rises and cold air sinks because warmer air is less dense and colder air is more dense. Check this out. Use thermometers to measure the temperature in your room. Also measure the temperature near windows and away from them. Which area is warmer? Why?

   Warmth comes to the earth from the sun. The sun's heat travels through space and then warms the earth's surface.

2. Indoor wind. In fall, winter, and spring, you can create wind indoors. Tape tissue paper to the bottom of a window. Then open the window and see what happens. Usually, if it is colder outside, denser, cold air will flow through the window and create a "wind" from outside to inside.

## Evaluation:

Think of examples from your life that demonstrate how heat and cold work in the atmosphere (steam rises, a cooler wind blows through the window on a hot summer day). Are there any times when these weather patterns don't seem to make sense?

From Kevin Strauss, *Tales with Tails: Storytelling the Wonders of the Natural World.* Westport, CT: Libraries Unlimited, 2006.
Copyright © 2006 by Kevin Strauss.

# Wind Direction Forecasting Activity

**Grade Level:** 4–8

**Environmental Themes:** adaptation, habitat

**Curriculum Areas:** science, social studies

**Student Skills:** prediction, comprehension, inferring

**Materials:** state and national maps

**Instructions:**

1. Wind brings weather with it, so you can use wind direction to help predict the weather. If the wind is blowing hard, the weather is likely to change. In the eastern United States, a wind out of the north brings colder weather. A wind out of the east often brings wetter weather. A wind out of the south brings warmer weather, and a wind out of the west brings drier weather. Mountains can affect how winds bring weather, and the rules are different in the Western United States.

2. Spend a week using wind direction to predict the next day's weather. How accurate was that? If it didn't work in your region, can you come up with some wind forecasting rules that do work for your area?

**Evaluation:**

Look at a map of your state and at the United States. Can you find geographic reasons why wind from a certain direction brings a certain kind of weather? (Weather is normally colder at the north pole and warmer at the equator. In the United States, there are usually large lakes or an ocean to the east and dry plains and mountains to the west.)

From Kevin Strauss, *Tales with Tails: Storytelling the Wonders of the Natural World.* Westport, CT: Libraries Unlimited, 2006.
Copyright © 2006 by Kevin Strauss.

# Moon Watching Activity

**Grade Level:** 4–8

**Environmental Themes:** cycles, interdependence

**Curriculum Areas:** science, social studies

**Student Skills:** observation, comprehension, inferring, comparison

**Materials:** clear evening with a visible moon, binoculars

**Instructions:**

1. Look at the "dark rabbit shape" on the face of the moon. Some cultures describe this as the "man on the moon" or a "coyote on the moon." Those dark areas are flat plains of basalt, a dark rock that also makes up much of our ocean floor. If you imagine the dark shape as a rabbit, the ears are on the right side of the moon. With binoculars or naked eyes, look for the "head" of the rabbit. That area is called the "Sea of Tranquility," and it is the place where Apollo 11 landed in 1969, where American astronaut Neil Armstrong was the first human to walk on the moon.

2. Sometimes the moon looks big when it is right above the horizon. This is an optical illusion. Use your hand to block your view of houses and trees and the moon will "shrink" back to its former size.

**Evaluation:**

Have students draw the shapes that they see on the moon.

From Kevin Strauss, *Tales with Tails: Storytelling the Wonders of the Natural World.* Westport, CT: Libraries Unlimited, 2006.
Copyright © 2006 by Kevin Strauss.

# Chapter 13

## Ecological Lesson Tales

# The Four Laws of Ecology

### Everything Is Connected (Interdependence)

*Themes:* interdependence, there is no such thing as a free lunch

### The Tinker's Clock (Original)

Long ago, but not so long that we can't remember, there was a man who was a tinker. He was a man who was always fixing things—broken pots, pulleys, and damaged knife blades. His house was always full of bits and pieces of gears and pulleys and boxes of parts. People always brought the tinker things to fix.

One day after working all day in his workshop, the tinker walked into his living room and noticed the loud "Tick-Toc, Tick-Toc, Tick-Toc" from the mantle clock on the shelf above the fireplace.

The tinker thought to himself, "I bet I could fix that." He took the clock into his workshop and unscrewed the back and began taking out gears and springs and moving things around until he thought that he had fixed the problem. As he was putting the clock back together, he had a couple gears left over.

"Oh well, I probably don't need these anyway," said the tinker and he threw away the gears.

When he finished putting the clock together, he wound it up and listened to it. It didn't make that "Tick-Toc, Tick-Toc, Tick-Toc" noise. The tinker smiled to himself and went on with his work until late in the night.

The next day, when the tinker looked at the clock, he noticed that the hands no longer moved.

"The first law of intelligent tinkering is to save all of the parts." —Aldo Leopold

**Teller notes:** This is one of those stories that I developed by starting with the proverb and working backward (see Chapter 4).

*Themes*: interdependence, nature knows best, there is no such thing as a free lunch

# The Frog Hunt (Zaire)

Long ago there was a village near a large marsh. For years, the people fell asleep to the spring calls of the frogs that lived nearby, "r-ribbit, r-ribbit, r-ribbit-ribbit." One night the chief of the village awoke from a bad dream. He got up and took a drink of water. But when he lay down again to go to sleep, he couldn't get back to sleep. All he could hear on that still night was the "r-ribbit, r-ribbit, r-ribbit-ribbit" of the frogs. He got up and yelled out his door "Be quiet!" But would you know, the frogs just kept on singing.

"I said BE QUIET," said the chief.

But the frogs didn't listen. The chief lay awake all through the night, thinking up ways to get rid of the frogs. As the sun crept over the tops of the trees, the chief called together all the people in the village.

"Am I the ruler of this village?" he bellowed.

All of the people shouted, "Yes."

"Am I the ruler of all this land?"

The people shouted, "Yes!"

"The frogs are not listening to me, so as ruler of this land, I command you to kill every frog in the land," called the chief. "And you know what will happen if you fail me."

All of the villagers grabbed their sticks and spears and ran out to the marsh to kill the frogs. They all went except for one old grandmother.

"Since you are so old, you can stay here in the village," said the chief.

"I am not standing here because I am too old. I am standing here because you are wrong," said the grandmother. "And since you are such a fool, I will tell you something that you need to learn."

"Me? Learn something? Ha!" laughed the chief. "What can an old woman like you teach me?"

"Being a chief doesn't mean that you know everything," said the grandmother. "Your actions show what you do not know."

Now the chief was getting angry with the grandmother.

"What do you have to teach me, old woman?" growled the chief.

"Everything is connected."

"What does that mean?" said the chief.

"You will see. You will see."

When the sun set on that spring day, an eerie silence settled on the land. There were no frog songs to lull the people to sleep. The people were restless. They didn't like the change in the night. But that chief slept soundly, sure that he had been right.

"Ha! What does that old woman know," he thought as he closed his eyes.

A few days later, the people heard another sound as darkness fell on the village. It was a high-pitched "zzz-zzz-zzz." It was the mosquitoes. The mosquitoes swarmed over the village, biting all of the villagers and keeping them awake.

The chief awoke, angry. "Get out of here or I'll kill you too."

The mosquitoes just buzzed in his ears and his nose and his hair. They didn't care.

The next morning, the chief called together the villagers.

"Am I the ruler of this land?" he bellowed.

The people looked at the ground and gave a half-hearted, "yeah."

"Then I want you to go into the marsh and kill all the mosquitoes."

A few people half-heartedly walked out to the marsh. Others went home to pack their belongings. They were going to leave. They knew it was impossible. There were too many mosquitoes. With no frogs to eat the mosquitoes, there would be more and more every day. The old woman waited as the crowd dispersed.

"Do you see what I mean?" she said.

"Everything is fine!" yelled the chief as he stomped off.

The next day there were more mosquitoes and the next day there were more. Soon not only the people were suffering , so were the animals. More families began to pack and leave the village during the night. Soon the village was empty. The chief had no one to rule and it was then that he realized the wisdom of the old woman's words.

"Everything is connected."

*Themes:* cooperation, interdependence

# The Parable of the Stomach (Aesop)

Long ago, all the parts of a body got to talking about how hard their lives were and each of them had a worse story than the last one.

The Eyes said, "All I do all day is look for things to eat, and what do I get for that? Nothing."

The Hands said, "You think you have it hard? I have to lift food to the mouth all day long, and do the hard work to make money for the food."

The Legs said, "You think that's hard? I have to walk mile after mile to work and to find and gather food. What's more, once I get to the food, I have to carry it back home. I'm always on the job."

The Mouth said, "I have to chew at the meals and that takes work, especially with muscles as small as mine. You may feed me, but I enjoy the food for only a moment and then it slides down my throat to the Stomach. That is who really profits from all of our labor."

Then Eyes said, "I've had enough of this. It is time that we teach that lazy Stomach what it means to pull his weight around here. I say we all go on strike and don't feed him any more food."

All the parts cheered, that is except for Stomach, who stayed quiet. For the first few days, everything went fine. But then as time went on, Stomach started to growl. The parts just ignored it. Then the Eyes started to get blurry. The Hands started to shake. The Legs felt weak and the Mouth was dry and sore.

It was then that the parts realized all of the things that Stomach did for them. Even though they couldn't see it happening, Stomach kept them strong.

"Maybe we should feed Stomach," suggested Hands.

Everyone else agreed, and after that, Eyes stayed clear, Hands and Legs stayed strong, Mouth could chew, and Stomach kept doing whatever it is that Stomach does to keep that whole body working right.

## Everything Goes Somewhere (There Is No Such Place as "Away")

*Themes:* recycling, reusing

# Just Enough . . . (Jewish)

Once long ago there was a tailor who sewed and cut and made coats and clothes for the people of his village. After many years of working, the tailor bought himself a bolt of warm wool cloth. So one evening, he took out his scissors and needle and thread. He took that cloth and made himself a beautiful long coat. Oh how the tailor loved his new coat! He wore it everywhere. He wore it downtown. He wore it on trips to the countryside. He wore it in fall and in winter and in spring. But after many years, the coat began to wear out. The sleeves and coat bottom frayed.

One day, the tailor looked at his coat. It was worn, but it still had just enough good cloth left to make something else. So one night, he took out his scissors and needle and thread. He took that cloth and made himself a short jacket. Oh the tailor loved his new jacket. He wore it everywhere. He wore it downtown. He wore it on trips to the countryside. He wore it in fall and in winter and in spring. But after many years, the jacket began to wear out. The sleeves and jacket bottom frayed. The shoulder tore. The tailor looked at the jacket and saw there was just enough good cloth left to make something else.

So one night, he took out his scissors and needle and thread. He took that cloth and made himself a vest. Oh the tailor loved his new vest. He wore it everywhere. He wore it downtown. He wore it on trips to the countryside. He wore it in fall and in winter and in spring. But after many years, the vest began to wear out. The vest bottom frayed. The tailor looked at the vest and saw there was just enough good cloth left to make something else.

So one night, he took out his scissors and needle and thread. He took that cloth and made himself a cap. Oh the tailor loved his new cap. He wore it everywhere. He wore it downtown. He wore it on trips to the countryside. He wore it in fall and in winter and in spring. But after many years, the cap began to wear out. The cap got holes in it. The tailor looked at the cap and saw there was just enough good cloth left to make something else.

So one night, he took out his scissors and needle and thread. He took that cloth and made himself a button. Oh the tailor loved his new button. He sewed it on his new coat. He wore that button everywhere. He wore it downtown. He wore it on trips to the countryside. He wore it in fall and in winter and in spring. But after many years, the tailor looked down and realized that he had lost his beautiful button.

At first, the tailor felt sad, until he realized that he had just enough cloth left over to make . . . this story. And he gave this story to someone he knew. And that person gave it to someone else, and now I have given it to you.

*Themes:* everything goes somewhere, stewardship

# Even Stones Go Somewhere (Jewish)

Long ago, in a hot, dry land, there was a rich merchant named Jacob who owned a fine mansion, surrounded by a fine brick wall on a hill. One day while Jacob was walking in his front yard, he thought to himself, " I like beautiful plants and birds. But it is such a bother to go for a walk in the woods. Besides, it might be dangerous. I should plant a garden here."

His yard was rocky ground, so he hired some laborers to remove the stones and plant the flowers and trees. Jacob ordered the workers to just throw the stones over the garden wall. The stones rolled down the hill and stopped on the public road. One day a rabbi walked by. He walked up to Jacob's house.

"Jacob, don't you know that you should never throw something from 'Not Yours' to 'Yours'?"

"What are you talking about?" yelled Jacob. He was not used to criticism and it made him angry. "I can do whatever I want. These stones are mine; this land is mine. I can do whatever I want with them. If a few of them roll onto the road, you can move them if it is so important to you. It's not my problem."

It was then that the rabbi realized that Jacob probably didn't walk on the road anyway. A rich man like him would ride a horse or at the very least, a donkey. The Rabbi shook his head and walked down the road.

Soon Jacob had a beautiful garden with trees and flowers and a fountain. But as the weeks went by, Jacob began hearing from his workers. His business was going badly. Bandits had raided one of his caravans. Some of his trading ships never returned. Soon Jacob had to sell his fine furniture and his horse and finally he had to sell his house and garden. He had to seek work as a common laborer.

One day he was walking down the road with a heavy bundle on his back when he stumbled over a rock, dropped his burden, and fell to his knees. Jacob cursed the stone, but then he noticed that sharp stones were scattered across the road. Then he looked up and saw a hill and a brick wall. It was his mansion.

Then he remembered the rabbi's words, "Don't throw stones from 'Not Yours' to 'Yours'." Jacob looked down at the ground. Then he reached down and began collecting the stones and throwing them off the road.

*Themes:* pollution, sustainability

# Putting Feathers Back in the Pillow (Jewish)

Long ago, in a village, there was a tailor named Hershel who loved to gossip. From morning to night, as Hershel sewed, he would leave his window open and listen to the conversations of the people outside. If he heard something particularly interesting, he would write it down and save that bit of gossip for later. Day after day Hershel would collect and share gossip with his friends.

Hershel liked gossip. It let him feel like he knew more than other people, and that made him feel important. He didn't have big muscles, he figured, so he could have a big brain. At least that is what he thought.

One day, the old rabbi in the village died, and a young rabbi came from a neighboring village to work with the community. The rabbi's name was Jacob. Now Jacob spent a lot of time listening to the people in town. He listened to their problems. He listened to their fears. And rather than telling people things like "do this . . ." or "the Talmud says . . ." he always asked them, "what do you think?"

Now Hershel never came to Rabbi Jacob. Hershel figured that he knew so much about the world that he didn't need to talk with a rabbi. So one day, Jacob made a visit to Hershel's tailor shop.

"Hershel, I hear that you are a person who knows what is happening in this village," said Jacob.

"Yes, I know a thing or two," said Hershel. "If you have questions about anyone, I could help you with them."

"No, I don't need that kind of help, but I do have one thing I would like you to do," said Jacob. Saying that, Jacob picked up one of the feather pillows waiting to be patched and tore it open.

"When the sun sets, take this pillow and run to my house just as fast as you can."

Hershel thought that the request was strange, but Jacob was a rabbi, so Hershel agreed to do it. As the sun set, Hershel quickly grabbed the pillow and ran to Jacob's house. When he got there, the pillow was almost empty. When he knocked on the door, Jacob smiled and told him, "Now I want you to put all of the feathers back in the pillow."

Hershel tried to find a few feathers on the way home in the dark. The next day he searched far and wide, but could only find a handful of feathers. They seem to have blown everywhere when he wasn't looking. Finally he went back to Jacob's house.

"It's impossible, I can't put feathers back into a feather pillow once they have blown into the world," said Hershel.

"It is the same way with gossip, Hershel," said Jacob. "Gossip is like poison. Once you release it into the world, it is almost impossible to clean it back up. The most important thing is to not to let those 'feathers' into the world in the first place. A little prevention is worth a mountain of cure."

**There Is No Such Thing as a "Free Lunch"
(Everything Costs Something)**

*Themes:* stewardship, there is no such thing as a free lunch

# Why the Sky Is Up So High (Nigeria)

It used to be that people didn't have to work. Whenever they were hungry, all they had to do was reach up into the Sky, break off a piece, and eat it. Some people said it tasted like melons, others said it tasted like yams. But as time went on, the people got lazy. Sometimes they would break off a piece of the Sky, eat half of it, and throw the rest on the ground to rot.

Now Sky is very forgiving, but as time went on, the people wasted more and more of what the Sky offered.

"Life must be too easy for these people, I will give them more of a challenge," said Sky. Sky moved up just out of reach of the people. Now they had to use boxes or rocks to reach the Sky. For a while, they were more careful and respectful about the Sky that they ate.

But one day, after traveling all day long, a man was so hungry that he climbed up onto a rock, broke off a piece of the Sky, and ate . . . half of it. He threw the rest on the ground.

Now the Sky had had enough. In a fit of anger it rose high into the air. The next day, when the people came out of their houses, they reached up into the air, but they couldn't reach the Sky. They climbed up on rocks and up into trees, but still they couldn't reach the Sky to break off a piece for their meals. From that day on, the people had to plant crops and weed fields and water fields to grow their food. And whenever a child would ask why they had to work so hard for their food, a mother or grandmother would tell him this story.

*Themes:* costs of human action, common sense

# Four Who Made a Lion (India)

Once there were four brothers who were all sons of a wealthy merchant. When it was time for them to make their way in the world, they all agreed that five years later, they would return to their town and discuss what they had learned. Each brother went off in a separate direction to seek his fortune and learn a trade in the world.

When they met five years later, they each spoke of the skills that they had learned, boasting of their skill. Finally, the oldest brother said, "Talk is cheap, let's demonstrate our skills. I remember seeing bones scattered in a clearing in the forest. Let's try our skills with them."

The brothers agreed and went into the forest. The first brother was an expert in anatomy and reassembled the bones into the skeleton of a Lion. The second brother used his skill to cover the skeleton with muscle and skin. The third brother piped up, "I can breathe life into this lion."

"Wait a minute, brothers, is this a good idea? Do we really want a living lion here?" said the fourth brother.

"We need to show our skill and knowledge," said the fourth brother. "What good is a skill if you never use it?"

"Then let me climb a tree first," said the only brother with common sense.

The fourth brother climbed a high tree. Then the third brother breathed life into the Lion. To everyone's amazement, the Lion opened its eyes and rose to its feet.

"Hmmmm," thought Lion. "I'm hungry."

And without a thought, Lion devoured the three brothers.

After the Lion had left, the fourth brother grieved for his brothers, but he never forgot their lesson.

## Nature Knows Best

*Themes:* sustainability, renewable resources

# The Goose That Laid the Golden Eggs (Aesop)

Long ago, a farmer went to the barn to collect eggs from the chickens and his goose. But this day was different; as he collected the eggs from the nest boxes, he saw something glint in the sunlight. He reached down and picked up something cold and heavy. It was a golden goose egg.

The farmer was so excited about the gold that he built the goose a special house, with a strong fence to keep out foxes.

"With this gold, I can build a grand mansion house," said the farmer. He went to town that morning and sold the egg and bought wood and nails and paint. But the money didn't buy as much as he thought it would.

"I'm going to need five more eggs before I can build my new house," thought the farmer.

Each day after that, the farmer searched through the straw for another golden egg. But days went by, weeks went by, and no more eggs appeared. Finally, a month later, he found another egg.

"At this rate, I'll never get my house built," thought the farmer.

But then he had an idea. He took his ax to the barn and killed his goose.

"If all that gold is in this goose, maybe I can get it all at one time," he thought.

But when he cut the goose open, it was just a regular goose on the inside, and he never saw another golden egg.

Teller notes: I sometimes end this story with "now some people talk about our forests or our lakes and our farmlands as being 'the goose that lays the golden eggs.' So the question for us is: How do we keep it alive?"

*Themes:* overproduction, there is no such thing as a free lunch

# Big Daddy Frog (Aesop)

Once there was a pasture right next to a pond. In the pond, among the cattails and reeds, there lived a frog family. One day, one of the young frogs went hopping into the pasture. A little while later, she came hopping back to the pond.

"Daddy, daddy, I just saw the biggest creature in the world! It is standing right there in the pasture. It has two curved knives on its head and it has a ring in its nose," said the little frog.

"Don't worry honey," said Daddy Frog. "That is just a bull, and to tell you the truth, that bull isn't much bigger than me."

"No daddy, it was much bigger than you."

So the frog puffed himself up and he seemed to grow.

"Was he bigger than me now?" asked Daddy Frog, trying to hold his breath.

"Yes daddy, much bigger."

The frog took another deep breath and puffed himself up even bigger.

"How about this big?" said Daddy Frog.

"No daddy, it was much bigger."

So Daddy Frog puffed himself up even bigger, when suddenly his daughter heard a loud "BANG!" and when the dust cleared, her father was nowhere to be seen.

That was the last frog that tried to be bigger than a bull; at least that's what the frogs say.

*Themes:* nature knows best, adaptation

# Hodja and the Mulberry Tree (Turkey)

Long ago, Hodja Nasrudin was sitting under a mulberry tree thinking about the world. He looked over at a garden where pumpkin vines were growing.

"How strange it is," thought Nasrudin, "that mulberry trees have strong branches and such tiny fruit, while pumpkins have large fruit and weak vines. One would think that Allah (God) would have put large fruit on strong plants and small fruit on weak ones."

Just then a ripe mulberry fell and splatted right on Nasrudin's forehead.

"Ah, now I see why things are as they are. Who would want a pumpkin to fall on his head! Truly the world is this way is for a reason!"

**Teller notes:** Nasrudin (NAZ-rue-deen) is a well-known "wise fool" in Islamic countries. The term *Hodja* or *Mulla* means "teacher" or "religious leader" in the Muslim world.

# Other Environmental Education Concepts

## Diversity Is the Key to Stability

*Themes:* diversity, food chain, nature knows best

*Pronunciation guide:*

Vainamoinen (VAIN-ah-MOY-nen)

Tuoni (too-ON-ee)

## The First Wolf (Finland)

The world didn't appear all at once. It came along a piece at a time. And in Finland, they tell of a powerful magician who had a hand in the making. His name was Vainamoinen, and he was already old at the beginning of time. They say he knew magic songs to make the world.

People say that Vainamoinen made the world, and when he was done making all of the rivers and lakes, the animals and the hills and the trees, he wanted to tell somebody about it.

And the first person he ran into was Tuoni, "the Lord of the Dead." Tuoni ruled the land across the Dead River, a dark and desolate place. But sometimes, he came into the land of the living to play tricks on the creatures there.

Old one-eyed Tuoni loved to criticize people, so when Vainamoinen bragged about his creation, Tuoni just frowned.

"You see those deer over there?" said Tuoni. "This winter they are going to eat all of the trees in your forest, and by spring, there will be nothing left."

"No, you're wrong, Tuoni. I made bear and snake to chase the deer out of the forests in the winter," said Vainamoinen.

"But don't bear and snake sleep during the wintertime, Vainamoinen?" said Tuoni.

"Whoops, I didn't think of that . . . say, Tuoni, since you have seen the problem, perhaps you can see your way clear to find a solution. Could you make a creature to chase the deer out of the forest in the wintertime?"

Tuoni smiled a yellow-toothed smile.

"Well, maybe I could do that for you, Vainamoinen," said Tuoni, stroking his thin gray beard and looking at the sky. "But you'll have to do something for me first. I need you to give me a magic word. As you know, my magic only kills things, it can't bring them to life, so you must give me some of yours."

"That's easy. All you have to say, once you complete your creature is 'up and devour the evil one.' Just say that and the creature will come to life," said Vainamoinen.

Tuoni walked away rubbing his hands and thinking of how he could play a trick on the old magician.

"Heh, heh, we'll see who gets devoured this time, Vainamoinen," thought Tuoni.

Tuoni walked down to a village of the humans to gather wood, nails, and two glowing coals. He went to the woods to gather stones and gray moss. He took all of these things across the Dead River, to the cave where he lived. With those pieces, Tuoni made a gray creature with sharp teeth and glowing yellow eyes.

When he finished the creature, Tuoni bent over it and whispered into its ear "up and devour the magician."

Nothing happened.

"Didn't you hear me?" he said, kicking the creature. "Up and devour Vainamoinen!"

Still, nothing happened.

"Well, Vainamoinen must have lied to me! Those aren't magic words at all. I'm going to have a talk with that wizard," he yelled.

Tuoni picked up the creature and stomped off toward Vainamoinen's house. When he arrived, he pounded on the door.

"Vainamoinen, get out here, I want to have a word with you!"

The door opened.

"Tuoni, you are back so soon," said Vainamoinen. "And is that the creature you made? It does look frightening, but, uh, Tuoni . . . it isn't moving."

"Of course it's not moving Vainamoinen. It's not moving because that magic word you gave me didn't even work."

"Well, that's strange," said Vainamoinen. "It has always worked for me. Why don't you say it again, so I can hear how you are saying it?"

Tuoni hadn't counted on this. He didn't really want Vainamoinen to hear the way he had said the magic words. So he leaned very close to the creature's ear, and whispered, as softly as he could "up and devour the magician." The creature didn't move.

"Tuoni, I see the problem. You see, you are pronouncing the last part of that last word incorrectly. What you should really be saying is 'up and devour the EVIL ONE.' "

The creature began to move. Its eyes glowed like the sun. But instead of devouring Vainamoinen, it headed straight for Tuoni. A growl rumbled like thunder from its throat.

Tuoni turned and began running for the woods. The creature was right behind him, growling and nipping at the heels on his black leather boots.

"Tuoni, what do you call the creature you made?" called Vainamoinen.

All that he heard from Tuoni was "stop, Wolf, stop, Wolf, stop."

Vainamoinen decided that the creature's name wasn't "stop," so it must be called "Wolf."

That night, Vainamoinen heard a sound he had never heard before.

"Ahoooooooooo."

It was the howl of the first wolf. From that first wolf came all the wolves that live here now.

To this day, grandmothers in Finland tell their children this story for a very important reason. They tell the story to teach their children that if they hear a wolf howling in the forest, they don't need to worry, because the wolves are only doing their jobs, chasing the deer out of the forests in the winter. And even if they aren't doing that, then they are doing their other job, chasing Tuoni, the evil one, keeping him moving all the time so he can't cause too much trouble in any one place. And some day, some day, the wolves might just catch him.

**Teller notes:**  I found pieces of this story in several different places and then reassembled them into this version of the story. One of the reasons that I like this story so much is that it reminds us that the animals in this world are here for a reason. Whether you believe the animals were created or evolved, they are here for a reason, even if we humans don't understand it.

Recent studies have shown that having large predators in an ecosystem actually increases the wildlife species diversity in that ecosystem. So it is a good thing that Tuoni made the wolves.

*Themes:* diversity, food chain

# Dutch Nightmare on Elmwood Street (Original Natural History)

It is hard to know how things travel sometimes, but it is clear that they do. In the 1950s, towns and forests in the Midwest were covered with the graceful arching branches of elm trees (*Ulmus americanus*). The elms grew so thick along the main street of my hometown that their branches interlaced over the street, making a tunnel of green leaves and shade on the hot summer days.

But then it happened. One day, a man walking down the street noticed that leaves on one tree were turning yellow in July, long before they should. Then more trees began changing color. The city forester looked closer at the trees and noticed tiny holes in the bark. Soon the yellow leaves were dropping from the elm tree branches. The forester took wood samples and sent them to a lab.

The forester began cutting down the sick trees, hoping that would stop the problem. The lab scientists found that a fungus had infected the elm trees. They called it "Dutch elm disease." The fungus came from Europe, probably on tree trunks or the backs of bark beetles. This fungus ate trees from the inside out. Bark beetles carried the fungus from elm tree to elm tree. Soon most of the elms in the town had turned yellow. Sunlight streamed down onto the streets. Urban forests of elm trees became a graveyard of dead trunks.

Now nature has its cycles. The elms were gone. But after the city forester cut down and burned the dead trees, he planted new trees in their place. But he didn't plant elms. He planted sugar maples and oaks and ash trees and spruce. Today, some of these trees are very large. They don't reach their branches over the street to make a shady tunnel in the summer, but they give us a bit of shade. When we asked the forester why he planted so many different kinds of trees in town, he looked at us and said, "diversity is the key to stability," and went on with his work. Never again has a disease stripped our town of its trees.

*Themes:* interdependence, diversity

# The Heaviest Burden (Adapted from Indonesia)

Long ago there was a huge apple tree growing at the edge of a forest. The tree was tall and proud of its branches and it carried large, round, red apples. One night, a whisper rose from the roots. It was the sound of complaining.

"We roots do all of the hard work around here!" said the Roots. "We're tired of it. We spend every day sucking up water and keeping you all rooted. We have to hold up the trunk and the branches and the leaves and the fruit. All the weight makes us sink into the ground, and we never get to feel the breeze or see the sun. We work day and night so the rest of you parts can take it easy. Look at the trunk. It has an easy life, just resting in the air and being lazy. Why can't we do that?"

"Easy? Is that what you think our work is?" said Trunk. "I work harder than anyone else. I hold the whole tree together. If I were to fall, it would be the end of you all. I have to stand against the storm winds. I have to pass water up and food down my body. And suffering? I know all about suffering. Animals scratch my bark. People break my branches for firewood. It's not me who has an easy life; it is the Leaves. Look at them, dancing in the sun. I wish I could be like them."

"That's garbage!" hissed the Leaves. "Our lives aren't easy. All day long we make sugar out of sun, soil, water, and air. Day and night we shade the rest of you from the hot sun and the hard rain. The wind tears us from the branches and blows us here and there. The bugs eat us and people burn us. Oh if only we were the Fruit. Fruit just hangs there and takes its ease in the sun.

"That's a lie!" growled the Fruit. "You air-head leaves know nothing! We do more than all the rest of you. Sure we grow fat, but it is for a good reason. We have to sacrifice ourselves for the rest of the tree. We are the reason that people don't chop the tree down for firewood. Do you think we like being eaten by deer and by bugs and by people? It is the seeds that have the easiest time of all. The seeds just wait inside me all summer long. They wait until they fall to the ground to sleep and grow. That is the job that I want."

"Shhh" whispered the Seeds, lying at the feet of the tree. "We should not argue, my friends. We each have a job to do and each of us needs the others. United we stand. When it is my time, I have work to do as well. I crack open and grow a new root and new sprout. Some day, my new tree might be as big as you are now, some day, some day."

Just then, a woman arrived to pick apples and the tree fell silent. Did the leaves and trunk and roots agree with the seed? What do you think?

**Teller notes:** I like this story because it shows us that every part of a tree, and by extension, every part of an ecosystem, has an important job to do. We often don't realize how important these natural jobs are until an animal or plant disappears and we have to find artificial ways to get the job done.

### Every Person Can Make a Difference (Stewardship)

*Theme:* stewardship

# It's in Your Hands (Jewish)

Long ago in a forest at the edge of a small village, there lived a Hermit. Most people avoided the Hermit. They thought he was strange. After all, who lives in the woods? Who lives on his own without family or friends? But people told stories about the Hermit. Some said that he understood the speech of animals. Others said he could just look at the sky and tell how long it would be before it rained.

Way back then, children were as they are today. There was one group of children who always liked tricking adults. One day, the older children gathered together.

"I've got a plan! I've got a great plan to fool that silly old hermit," said a boy named Abel. "First, we'll catch a bluebird. Then we'll go up to that hermit's hut. I'll put the bird behind my back and we'll ask that hermit what kind of bird it is. He can't possibly know what kind of bird it is. But if he does, then we'll ask him a second question that he can't possibly answer. We'll ask him: 'Is the bird alive or is it dead?' If he says that it is dead, I will just open my hand and let the bird fly into the air. If he says that the bird is alive, I will clench my fingers and crush the bird and then hold it out for him to see. No matter how he answers, he will be wrong!"

The older children thought this was a good idea. The younger children weren't sure, but they went along with the older ones and ran to catch a bird in the forest. That night, they crept out of their houses and walked into the woods. The children, even the older ones, felt a little frightened, but it was exciting, too. They were going to trick that stupid old man!

They saw a small light in the window of the hermit's hut as they walked up the path. They were almost close enough to knock on the door when the door opened. There stood the Hermit.

"Welcome children, I have been waiting for you. I understand that you have two questions for me."

"How did he know we were coming? How did he know we had questions?" whispered the children.

"Sh, sh, sh," called Abel. "Well old man, you think you're pretty smart, and we do have questions for you. You see, I have a bird behind my back and if you're so smart, tell me what kind of bird it is."

The Hermit looked at the children and stroked his white beard.

"Well child, I believe that you have bluebird behind your back."

"How did he know that? How did he know that?" whispered the children.

"Sh, sh, sh," called Abel.

"Well, I guess you know some things, old man. But answer me this. Is the bird alive, or is it dead?"

The old hermit looked into the wide eyes of each of the children. Then, very slowly he told him, "The answer to that question is in your hands."

**Teller notes:** I often use this as the closing story in a program.

*Theme:* cooperation

# The Difference Between Heaven and Hell (Adapted Jewish Tale)

Long ago, a man named William who had lived a particularly good life was growing old. One fall day he shared his meal with an old beggar at the side of the road. When they had finished their meal, the beggar looked at William and smiled.

"You see William, I am not a beggar at all, I am an angel, and because of your generosity, I will grant you a wish."

"Well Angel, I would like to see what I could expect in the afterlife."

"It's not a usual request, but you shall have it," said the Angel.

The Angel reached out and grabbed William's arm. There was a flash and in a moment, they were standing in a green grassy field on a pleasant summer day. In the middle of the field was a huge table laden with sausages and cake and pancakes and strawberries and oranges.

"This must be heaven," said William.

"Don't judge so fast," said the Angel.

William could see people walking toward the table. They wore strange white shirts that had long metal sleeves with no bend at the elbow.

It didn't take long for William to realize that with no bend in the elbows, the people couldn't bend their arms to feed themselves. It was then that William realized that the people's faces were gaunt and thin. They wore frowns and just stared at the sumptuous food on the table.

"This must be hell," said William.

The Angel smiled and touched William's arm. There was another flash. Suddenly they were standing in a green grassy field on a pleasant summer day. In the middle of the field was a huge table laden with sausages and cake and pancakes and strawberries and oranges. Once again William watched people with white shirts and metal sleeves walking to the table. But these people looked completely different. They had rosy round cheeks. They were smiling and laughing and talking together. When they reached the table, they sat down. And then each person turned to his or her neighbor, picked up some food and fed that neighbor. Everyone had plenty to eat.

The Angel turned to William.

"Now that you have seen what you can expect in the afterlife, I will let you choose. Where would you like to go when you die?"

William thought about what he had seen. Then his mouth broke into a wide grin.

"I want to go to hell . . . and teach those people how to feed each other."

*Themes:* persistence, cooperation

# Moving a Mountain (China)

Long ago, in a land far away, there lived two old farmers. People called them "the Wise One" and "the Fool." One day the Wise One was walking down the road when he came to the farm of the Fool. He saw the Fool and his children digging dirt and rocks from the side of a mountain.

"What are you doing?" said the Wise One.

"Oh, I am moving a mountain," said the Fool.

"You're doing WHAT?"

"Moving the mountain. You see this mountain hides the view from my house and when I have to go somewhere, it makes travel difficult. What is more, the landslides from the cliffs bury the road to my farm."

"Ha ha ha. YOU are moving a mountain? Let me tell you something you need to know. Moving mountains is beyond human power," said the Wise One.

"You may be right; but all the same, it must go."

"A man your age should have more common sense," said the Wise One.

"It has nothing to do with common sense. To succeed, I must travel in the direction of my goals," said the Fool.

"Do you think you can succeed?"

"I think nothing of the sort. Thinking sometimes kills imagination. And that is something no one can afford. With imagination and faith and persistence, I am sure the mountain will be gone some day," said the Fool.

"How can you believe such an impossible thing?"

"It is simple, you see. I devote myself to my work. When I have passed on, my sons and daughters will continue on, and their sons and daughters will continue on after them. Since the mountain doesn't grow and my children and grandchildren will continue on without rest, some day the mountain will be gone," said the Fool.

The Wise One hid his laughter and politely wished his friend good luck, thinking to himself, "the 'Fool' really deserves his name."

But later that day, a messenger from the Emperor of Heaven flew over the land and saw the work that the Fool and his family were doing. The Fool's dedication impressed the sky messenger. He told what he had seen to the Emperor of Heaven himself. Touched by the Fool's dedication, he flew over the farm. That night, the Emperor reached down from the sky and pulled the mountain from the ground and set it on the edge of the sea. There it would protect the farm from storms.

When the Wise One walked by the next day, he was amazed to see the Fool and his family playing in a beautiful field where that mountain had been.

"You see, I told you," said the Fool. "Imagination, faith, and persistence really can move mountains."

**Teller notes:** This story can cut both ways. Some might see it as permission to tear down mountains and change the land to suit human whims. But I like to think of the story as a metaphor. There are times when we all feel that the challenges in our lives are too great for us. It is those times that I feel we most need this story. It *is* possible to move mountains.

"Start by doing what is necessary. Then what is possible and suddenly, you will be doing the impossible"—St. Francis of Assisi, the patron saint of ecology.

# Build a Food Web Activity

**Grade Level:** 1–4

**Environmental Themes:** interdependence, food chain, adaptation, habitat

**Curriculum Areas:** science, visual arts

**Student Skills:** comprehension, inferring, modeling

**Materials:** cardstock paper, markers, copies of animal pictures and habitat features

## Instructions:

1.  Describe examples of a food web or food chain (Chapter 2). Ask students to draw an example of a simple (four-step) food chain in a forest or mountain area and a food chain from a city area.

2.  Once students have drawn pictures of their food chains, have them build a physical food chain mobile using cardstock paper, animal pictures, and yarn.

3.  Gather student food chains and tape them on the wall. Then link parts together to make food webs.

## Evaluation:

Discuss how these food chains and the more complicated food webs that we can build out of them demonstrate some of the interconnections in the natural world. Pull on one string in the food web and notice how it affects many parts of that web. The same thing is true in nature.

From Kevin Strauss, *Tales with Tails: Storytelling the Wonders of the Natural World.* Westport, CT: Libraries Unlimited, 2006.
Copyright © 2006 by Kevin Strauss.

# Making a Difference (Choose a Cause)

**Grade Level:** 5–8

**Environmental Themes:** stewardship

**Curriculum Areas:** science, social studies

**Student Skills:** comprehension, problem solving, inferring

**Materials:** paper and pencils, other materials depending on the project

## Instructions:

1. Talk with students about some of the environmental problems in the world today. Discuss how what people do in your community influences those environmental problems. Brainstorm what students could do in their own lives to help solve an environmental problem chosen by the class.

2. Work with school, library, or community officials to implement a plan that the students have come up with to address an environmental issue. Focus on concrete, hands-on projects with results that are achievable within four weeks. The point of this activity isn't really to create a recycling program at your school or have a "nature day" at the library, it is to demonstrate some of the steps that people go through as they plan to work on a community issue.

## Evaluation:

Was the group surprised by the results of their project? What went well in the planning and execution of the project? What went poorly? What have we learned that we can apply to future projects like this one?

From Kevin Strauss, *Tales with Tails: Storytelling the Wonders of the Natural World.* Westport, CT: Libraries Unlimited, 2006. Copyright © 2006 by Kevin Strauss.

# Chapter 14

## Story Sources

**Truth and Story (Jewish)**

This is one of my favorite stories about storytelling. You can find another retelling of this story as "Truth and Parable," on page 69 of Naomi Baltuck, *Apples from Heaven* (North Haven, CT: Linnet Books, 1995). 143pp. ISBN 0-208-02424-7; 0-208-02434-4pa.

A shorter version can be found on page 21 of Susan Strauss, *The Passionate Fact: Storytelling in Natural History and Cultural Interpretation* (Golden, CO: North American Press, 1996). 152pp. $16.95pa. ISBN 1-55591-925-1pa.

**Why Tell Stories (Jewish)**

I first heard this story told by storyteller Laura Sims. It appears on Laura Simms, *Making Peace, Heart Uprising (CD)* (Chicago: Earwig Music, 1993). 4925CD.

You can find a written version in an anecdote about the Preacher of Dubno on page 69 in Naomi Baltuck, *Apples from Heaven* (North Haven, CT: Linnet Books,1995).143pp. ISBN 0-208-02424-7; 0-208-02434-4pa.

**The Man, the Boy, and Their Donkey (Aesop)**

"The Man, the Boy, and the Donkey," on page 149 in Joseph Jacobs, ed., *The Fables of Aesop* (Mineola, NY: Dover Publications, 2002). 196pp. $2.50pa. ISBN 0-486-41859-6pa.

"The Miller, His Son and Their Ass," on page 269 in Jack Zipes, *Aesop's Fables* (New York: Signet Classic, 1992). 288pp. ISBN 0-451-52565-5pa.

**Prometheus and the Animals (Greek-inspired)**

In Greek mythology, Prometheus was the titan (giant) who had the job of giving all the animals their horns and teeth and claws. He also created humans and gave humans fire. I created this original tale based on that tradition.

Cheryl Evans and Anne Millard, *Greek Myths and Legends* (London: Usborne, 1985). 64pp. $10.95pa. ISBN 086020-946-6pa.

### Why Wolf Lives in the Forest (Aesop)

"The Dog and the Wolf" on page 70 in Joseph Jacobs, ed. *The Fables of Aesop* (Mineola, NY: Dover Publications, 2002). 196pp. $2.50pa. ISBN 0-486-41859-6pa.

"The Domesticated Dog and the Wolf," on page 50 in Jack Zipes, *Aesop's Fables* (New York: Signet Classic, 1992). 288pp. ISBN 0-451-52565-5pa.

### A Foolish Wolf Learns from His Mistakes (adapted from Finland)

"The Foolish Wolf," on page 450 in Aleksandr Afanas'ev, *Russian Fairy Tales* (New York: Pantheon, 1945). 662pp. ISBN 0-394-73090-9.

"The Stupid Wolf," on page 251 in James Cloyd Bowman and Margery Bianco, *Tales from a Finnish Tupa* (Morton Grove, IL: Albert Whitman & Company, 1964). 273pp. ISBN 8075-7756-1pa.

"The Stupid Wolf," on pages 116–117 in Mary Lou Masey, *Stories of the Steppes* (New York: David McKay Co., 1968). 142pp.

### Why Bear Has a Stumpy Tail (Sweden)

"How the Bear Got His Stubby Tail," on page 5 in Lone Thygesen Blecher and George Blecher, *Swedish Folktales and Legends* (New York: Pantheon Books, 1993). Pantheon Fairy Tale & Folklore Library. $25.00; $17.00pa. ISBN 0-394-54791-8; 0-697-75841-0pa.

"Bear Goes Fishing," on page 13 in Kaarina Brooks, *Foxy: Finnish Folk Tales for Children* (Beaverton, ON: Aspasia Books, 2002). $12.95pa. ISBN 0-9689054-7-1pa.

"Why the Bear's Tails Is Short," on page 11 in Babette Deutsch and Avrahm Yarmolinsky, *More Tales of Faraway Folk* (New York: Harper & Row, 1963). 93pp.

### Why Bear Has a Black Coat (adapted from Finland)

"The Vain Bear," on page 250 in James Cloyd Bowman and Margery Bianco, *Tales from a Finnish Tupa* (Morton Grove, IL: Albert Whitman & Company, 1964). 273pp. ISBN 8075-7756-1pa.

"Bear's Beautiful Fur Coat," on page 27 in Kaarina Brooks, *Foxy: Finnish Folk Tales for Children* (Beaverton, ON: Aspasia Books, 2002). $12.95pa. ISBN 0-9689054-7-1pa.

### Why Bear Sleeps Through the Winter (African American )

"Why the Bear Sleeps All Winter," on page 123 in Carolyn Sherwin Bailey, *Firelight Stories: Folk Tales Retold for Kindergarten, School and Home* (Springfield, MA: Milton Bradley, 1907). 192pp.

"Why Bear Sleeps All Winter," on page 73 in Maria Leach, *How the People Sang the Mountains Up: How and Why Stories* (New York: Viking Press, 1967). 160pp.

### Deer's Antlers (Aesop)

"The Hart and the Hunter," on page 65 in Joseph Jacobs, ed., The Fables of Aesop (Mineola, NY: Dover Publications, 2002). 196pp. $2.50pa. ISBN 0-486-41859-6pa.

"The Stag at the Pool," on page 259 in Jack Zipes, ed., *Aesop's Fables* (New York: Signet Classic, 1992). 288pp. ISBN 0-451-52565-5pa.

### Why Deer Has Split Hooves (adapted from the Philippines)

"Why the Carabao's Hoof Is Split," on page 58 in Elizabeth Hough Sechrist, *Once in the First Times: Folktales from the Philippines* (Philadelphia: Macrae Smith Company, 1949). 215pp.

"The Tortoise and the Reedbuck Run A Race," on page 95 in W. F. P. Burton, *The Magic Drum: Tales from Central Africa* (New York: Criterion Books, 1961). 127pp.

## Why Fox Has a White Tip on His Tail (Germany)

"Fox," on page 24 in Candace R. Miller, ed., *Tales from the Creature Kingdom: More Than 160 Multicultural Legends and Pourquoi Stories About Mammals, Insects, Reptiles and Water Creatures* (Lima, OH: Pourquoi Press, 1996). 94pp. $20.00pa. E-mail: naturelegends @wcoil.com

"Why the Fox Has a White-Tipped Tail," on page 17 in Kaarina Brooks, *Foxy: Finnish Folk Tales for Children* (Beaverton, ON: Aspasia Books, 2002). $12.95pa. ISBN 0-9689054-7-1pa.

## Fox Learns to Hunt (original)

Often, if an animal has an unusual tail or coloration, people tell stories about how the animal got that way. But the red fox seems to be an exception to this trend. I have found no traditional stories to explain how the fox got its bright red coat, so I developed this one.

## How Rabbit Got His Long Ears (African American)

"Why the Rabbit Has a Short Tail and Long Ears," on page 200 in Susan Kantor, *One Hundred and One African American Read-Aloud Stories* (New York: Black Dog & Leventhal Publishers, 1998). 416pp. $12.95. ISBN 1-57912-039-3.

"Why Brer Rabbit Is Bob-Tailed," on page 11 in Joel Chandler Harris, *The Favorite Uncle Remus* (Cambridge, MA: The Riverside Press, 1948). 310pp.

## How Rabbit Lost Her Tail (China)

"Rabbit's Tails Tale," on page 49 in Pleasant DeSpain, *Eleven Nature Tales: A Multicultural Journey* (Little Rock, AR: August House, 1996). 91pp. $10.75; $4.50pa. ISBN 0-87483-447-3; 0-87483-458-9pa.

"Rabbit Counts the Crocodiles," on page 54 in Martha Hamilton and Mitch Weiss, *How & Why Stories: World Tales Kids Can Read & Tell* (Little Rock, AR: August House, 1999). 96pp. $24.95; $14.95pa. ISBN 0-87483-562-3; 0-87483-561-5pa.

"The Sad Tales of the Rabbit's Tail," on page 33 in M. A. Jagendorf and Virginia Weng, *The Magic Boat and Other Chinese Folk Stories* (New York: Vanguard Press, 1980). 236pp. ISBN 0-8149-0823-3

## How Chipmunk Got Her Stripes (adapted from Mongolia)

"How the Chipmunk Got Its Stripes," on page 77 in Hillary Roe Metternich, *Mongolian Folktales* (Boulder, CO: Avery Press, 1996). 131pp. $19.95pa. ISBN 0-937321-06-0pa.

"How Chipmunk Got His Stripes," on page 75 in Maria Leach, *How the People Sang the Mountains Up: How and Why Stories* (New York: Viking Press, 1967). 160pp.

## Wolf and Mouse as Farmers (adapted from Egypt)

"The Partnership Between Wolf and Mouse," on page 192 in Hasan M. El-Shamy, ed., *Folktales of Egypt* (Chicago: University of Chicago Press, 1980). 347pp. ISBN 0-226-20624-6.

A similar "tops and bottoms" story can be found in several other sources, including: "Sharing Crops," on page 127 in Sharon Creeden, *Fair Is Fair: World Folktales of Justice* (Little Rock, AR: August House, 1994). 190pp. $19.95pa. ISBN 0-87483-400-7pa.

## Why Squirrels Live in Trees (Finland)

"Why the Squirrel Lives in Trees," on page 249 in James Cloyd Bowman, and Margery Bianco, *Tales from a Finnish Tupa* (Morton Grove, IL: Albert Whitman & Company, 1964). 273pp. ISBN 8075-7756-1pa.

"Old Sultan," on page 116 in Jacob Grimm and William Grimm, *Grimms' Complete Fairy Tales* (New York: Barnes & Noble Books, 1993). 628pp. ISBN 0-76070-335-3.

### Bat's Debt (Siberia)

"Bat," on page 9 in Candace R. Miller, ed., *Tales from the Creature Kingdom: More Than 160 Multicultural Legends and Pourquoi Stories about Mammals, Insects, Reptiles and Water Creatures* (Lima, OH: Pourquoi Press, 1996). 94pp. $20.00pa. E-mail: naturelegends @wcoil.com

"The Bat," on page 7 in Babette Deutsch, *More Tales of the Faraway Folk* (New York: Harper, 1963). 93pp.

"The Bat, the Birds and the Beasts," on page 62 in Joseph Jacobs, ed., *The Fables of Aesop* (Mineola, NY: Dover Publications, 2002). 196pp. $2.50pa. ISBN 0-486-41859-6pa.

### Hawk's Sewing Needle (Kenya)

I learned this story from a college friend, Chrissy Watson, when she was teaching English in Kenya with the Peace Corps in 1991. As a class project, Chrissy had her students collect traditional stories from their family members and then translate them into English.

### The Birds Choose a King (India)

"The Birds Elect a King," on page 104 in Krishna Dharma, *Panchatantra* (Badger, CA: Torchlight Publishing, 2004). $12.95pa. ISBN 1-887089-45-4pa.

"How the Birds Picked a King," on page 304 in Arthur W. Ryder, *The Panchatantra* (Chicago: University of Chicago Press, 1925).

### Why Owls Hunt at Night (Puerto Rico)

"How Owl Got His Feathers," on page 69 in Martha Hamilton and Mitch Weiss, *How & Why Stories: World Tales Kids Can Read & Tell* (Little Rock, AR: August House, 1999). 96pp. $24.95; $14.95pa. ISBN 0-87483-562-3; 0-87483-561-5pa.

"Owl Feathers," on page 20 in Anne Rockwell, *The Acorn Tree and Other Folktales* (New York: Greenwillow Books, 1995). 40pp. $16.00. ISBN 0-688-10746-X.

### How Birds Got Their Colors (original)

After realizing that I didn't like any of the bird color stories that I had read, I put together this story after learning that in German folklore, birds got their colors by flying through a rainbow.

### Robin's Red Breast (Ireland)

"The Robin," on page 165 in Richard Adams, *The Unbroken Web: Stories and Fables* (New York: Ballantine, 1980). 182pp. ISBN 0-345-30368-7pa.

"Robin," on page 58 in Candace R. Miller, ed., *Tales from the Bird Kingdom: More Than 160 Legends and Pourquoi Stories about Birds* (Lima, OH: Pourquoi Press, 1996). 94pp. $20.00pa. E-mail: naturelegends@wcoil.com

### The First Woodpecker (Romania)

"The Woodpecker," on page 48 in Richard Adams, *The Unbroken Web: Stories and Fables* (New York: Ballantine, 1980). 182pp. $3.95pa. ISBN 0-345-30368-7pa.

"Woodpecker," on page 75 in Candace R. Miller, ed., *Tales from the Bird Kingdom: More Than 160 Legends and Pourquoi Stories Aabout Birds* (Lima, OH: Pourquoi Press, 1996). 94pp. $20.00pa. E-mail: naturelegends@wcoil.com

"Why the Woodpecker Has a Long Beak," on page 544 in Robert Nye, ed., Classic Folk Tales from Around the World (London: Leopard, 1996). 605pp. ISBN 1-85891-330-6.

### The Talkative Turtle (adapted from India)

"The Talkative Turtle," on page 55 in Krishna Dharma, *Panchatantra* (Badger, CA: Torchlight Publishing, 2004). $12.95pa. ISBN 1-887089-45-4pa.

"The Turtle Who Couldn't Stop Talking," on page 49 in Martha Hamilton and Mitch Weiss, *How & Why Stories: World Tales Kids Can Read & Tell* (Little Rock, AR: August House, 1999). 96pp. $24.95; $14.95pa. ISBN 0-87483-562-3; 0-87483-561-5pa.

"The Wild Geese and the Tortoise," on page 45 in Lucia Turnbull, *Fairy Tales of India* (New York: Criterion Books, 1959).

### Turtle Wins at Tug-of-War (adapted African American tale)

"How the Tortoise Overcame the Elephant and the Hippopotamus," on page 9 in Robert Nye, ed., *Classic Folk Tales from Around the World* (London: Leopard, 1996). 605pp. ISBN 1-85891-330-6.

"Take up the Slack," on page 95 in Joel Chandler Harris, *The Favorite Uncle Remus* (Cambridge, MA: Riverside Press, 1948). 310pp.

### How Snake Lost Her Legs (original)

When I realized that all of the snake stories I could find showed snakes as villains, I figured it was time for a new snake story.

### How Snake Got Her Poison and Rattles (African American)

"How the Snake Got His Rattles," on page 22 in Julius Lester, *Black Folktales* (New York: Grove Press, 1969). 110pp. $9.95pa. ISBN 0-8021-3242-1pa.

"Snake, Rattlesnake," on page 49 in Candace R. Miller, ed., *Tales from the Creature Kingdom: More Than 160 Multicultural Legends and Pourquoi Stories about Mammals, Insects, Reptiles and Water Creatures* (Lima, OH: Pourquoi Press, 1996). 94pp. $20.00pa. E-mail: naturelegends@wcoil.com

"How the Snake Got Poison," on page 131 in Zora Neale Hurston, *Mules and Men* (New York: HarperCollins, 1990). 291pp. $29.50; $13.95pa. ISBN 0-25333-932-4; 0-25320-208-6pa.

### The Wide Mouth Frog (United States)

I first heard this story as a joke when I was working at a nature center in California. Since that time, I have heard several storytellers perform the story and seen it in a picture book. My version is rooted in a particular ecosystem and makes a point of teaching listeners about the foods that wild animals really eat. For other print versions, check out:

"The Big-Mouth Frog," on page 83 in Margaret Read MacDonald, *The Parent's Guide to Storytelling: How to Make Up New Stories and Retell Old Favorites,* 2d ed. (Little Rock, AR: August House, 2001). 120pp. $21.95; $11.95pp. ISBN 0-87483-619-0; 0-87483-618-2pa.

"Wide-Mouth Frog," on page 74 in Hiroko Fujita, *Stories to Play With: Kid's Tales Told with Puppets, Paper, Toys, and Imagination* (Little Rock, AR: August House, 1999). 96pp. $12.95pa. ISBN 0-87483-553-4pa.

### How Frog Lost Its Tail (Ashanti)

"Tadpole Loses His Tail," on page 65 in Roger D. Abrahams, ed., *Afro-American Folktales: Stories from Black Traditions in the New World* (New York: Random House, 1985). Pantheon Fairy Tale & Folklore Library. 327pp. $17.00; $11.95pa. ISBN 0-394-52755-0; 0-394-72885-8pa.

"Nyame's Well," on page 93 in Harold Courlander, *The Hat-Shaking Dance: And Other Ashanti Tales from Ghana* (New York: Harcourt, Brace & World, 1957). 115pp.

### Where Butterflies Come From (African American)

"How God Made Butterflies," on page 157 in Zora Neale Hurston, *Mules and Men* (New York: HarperCollins, 1990). 291pp. $29.50; $13.95pa. ISBN 0-25333-932-4; 0-25320-208-6pa.

"Butterflies," on page 11 in Candace R. Miller, ed., *Tales from the Creature Kingdom: More Than 160 Multicultural Legends and Pourquoi Stories About Mammals, Insects, Reptiles and Water Creatures* (Lima, OH: Pourquoi Press, 1996). 94pp. $20.00pa. E-mail: naturelegends @wcoil.com

"How God Made the Butterflies," on page 3 in Julius Lester, *Black Folktales* (New York: Grove Press, 1969). 110pp. $9.95pa. ISBN 0-8021-3242-1pa.

### The Ugly Worm (original)

I wrote this story after realizing that butterflies have more of a claim to the themes in Hans Christian Anderson's "Ugly Duckling" than even the swans do. This story was inspired by Anderson's well-known tale.

### Why Ants Are Everywhere (Burma)

"Why Ants Are Found Everywhere," on page 28 in Martha Hamilton and Mitch Weiss, *How & Why Stories: World Tales Kids Can Read & Tell* (Little Rock, AR: August House, 1999). 96pp. $24.95; $14.95pa. ISBN 0-87483-562-3; 0-87483-561-5pa.

"Why Ants Live Everywhere," on page 105 in Maria Leach, *How the People Sang the Mountains Up: How and Why Stories* (New York: Viking Press, 1967). 160pp.

"Ants," on page 5 in Candace R. Miller, ed., *Tales from the Creature Kingdom: More Than 160 Multicultural Legends and Pourquoi Stories About Mammals, Insects, Reptiles and Water Creatures* (Lima, OH: Pourquoi Press, 1996). 94pp. $20.00pa. E-mail: naturelegends @wcoil.com

### Who Has the Sweetest Blood? (Jewish)

"Swallow," on page 65 in Candace R. Miller, ed., *Tales from the Bird Kingdom: More Than 160 Legends and Pourquoi Stories About Birds* (Lima, OH: Pourquoi Press, 1996). 94pp. $20.00pa. E-mail: naturelegends@wcoil.com

Another retelling can be found on page 139 in Anthony S. Mercatante, *Zoo of the Gods: Animals in Myth, Legend and Fable* (Berkeley, CA: Seastone, 1999). $15.95. ISBN 1-56975-160-9.

### Mosquitoes and the Night Monster (original)

I developed this story as a way to talk about the importance of mosquitoes in the natural world. I felt that all of those stories that show mosquitoes as the tiny pieces of a blood-sucking giant weren't doing justice to these pestersome creatures. Any insect that provides food for gamefish and bright-colored warblers can't be all bad.

### The Hobgoblin's Revenge (Japan)

"Mosquitoes, Horseflies, Gnats," on page 34 in Candace R. Miller, ed., *Tales from the Creature Kingdom: More Than 160 Multicultural Legends and Pourquoi Stories About Mammals, Insects, Reptiles and Water Creatures* (Lima, OH: Pourquoi Press, 1996). 94pp. $20.00pa. E-mail: naturelegends@wcoil.com

A similar tale from the Ojibwa people of North America can be found in Douglas Wood, *The Windigo's Return: A North Woods Story* (New York: Simon & Schuster Children's, 1996). 32pp. ISBN 0-689-80065-7.

**Bees Get Their Sting (Aesop)**

"The Wages of Malice," on page 137 in S. A. Handford, *Aesop's Fables* (New York: Puffin, 1994). 212pp. ISBN 0-14-130929-6.

"Jupiter and the Bee," on page 124 in Jack Zipes, ed., *Aesop's Fables* (New York: Signet Classic, 1992). 288pp. ISBN 0-451-52565-5pa.

**Why Wasp Has a Small Waist (African American)**

"What Makes Brer Wasp Have Short Patience," on page 119 in Roger D. Abrahams, ed., *Afro-American Folktales: Stories from Black Traditions in the New World* (New York: Random House, 1985). Pantheon Fairy Tale & Folklore Library. 327pp. $17.00; $11.95pa. ISBN 0-394-52755-0; 0-394-72885-8pa.

"Why Brer Wasp Never Laughs," on page 121 in Susan Kantor, *One Hundred and One African American Read-Aloud Stories* (New York: Black Dog & Leventhal Publishers, 1998). 416pp. $12.95. ISBN 1-57912-039-3.

**The Little Pine Tree (Denmark)**

"The Pine Tree," on page 3 in Rose Dobbs, *One Upon a Time: Twenty Cheerful Tales to Read and Tell* (New York: Random House, 1950). 117pp.

"The Tiny Pine Tree's Wish," on page 107 in Mildred L. Kerr, and Frances Ross, *First Fairy Tales* (San Francisco: Charles E. Merrill Books, 1946). 128 p.

**Why Trees Are Evergreen (Denmark)**

"The Trees' Perpetual Penance," on page 43 in Time-Life Books, ed., *Magical Justice* (Alexandria, VA: Time-Life Books, 1986). Enchanted World Series. 143pp. ISBN 0-80945-269-3.

a similar story about evergreens receiving their year-round leaves for helping someone else (in this case baby Jesus) can be found in "The Trapper's Tale," on page 109 in Ruth Sawyer, *This Way to Christmas* (New York: Harper & Brothers, 1952). 165pp.

**The Rise of the Plants (original natural history)**

When I realized how difficult it was to help people understand how lowly lichens are responsible for the northwoods we have today, I figured a story would be a good way to take people back in time to see it happen. This story was the result.

**Alice Algae and Freddie Fungus (United States)**

I first heard this story working at a nature center in Minnesota. It is a well-known piece of environmental education folklore.

**Why Sun and Moon Live in the Sky (Efik-Ibibio, Nigeria)**

"A Home for Sun and Moon," on page 29 in Susan Kantor, *One Hundred and One African American Read-Aloud Stories* New York: Black Dog & Leventhal Publishers, 1998). 416pp. $12.95. ISBN 1-57912-039-3.

"Why the Sun and the Moon Live in the Sky," on page 41 in Paul Radin, ed., *African Folktales* (New York: Schocken Books, 1983). 322pp. ISBN 0-8052-0732-5pa.

**The Sky Wolves (Norse inspired)**

Both of the resources below provided information about Skoll and Hati, but neither contained the story that I finally developed to explain why the wolves chase the sun and moon across the sky.

Arthur Cotterell, *Norse Mythology* (New York: Lorenz Books, 2000). 96pp. $12.95. ISBN 1-85967-998-6.

"Skoll and Hati, The Swallowers," on page 27 in Susan Strauss, *Wolf Stories* (Hillsboro, NC: Beyond Words Publishing, 1993). 64pp. $7.95pa. ISBN 0-94183-184-1; 0-94183-188-4pa.

### The First Fire (Zaire)

"Starfire," on page 69 in Pleasant DeSpain, *Eleven Nature Tales: A Multicultural Journey* (Little Rock, AR: August House, 1996). 91pp. $10.75; $4.50pa. ISBN 0-87483-447-3; 0-87483-458-9pa.

"The Gift from a Star," on page 36 in Paola Caboara Luzzatto, *Long Ago When the Earth Was Flat: Three Tales from Africa* (New York: Collins, 1979). 44 p.

### Who Freed the Wind? (original)

I developed this story to answer the question of why the wind blows sometimes and doesn't blow other times.

### The Tinker's Clock (original)

I developed this story 10 minutes before a beaver ecology class when I wanted a story to talk about the importance of species in an ecosystem. I got the idea for the story from the Aldo Leopold quote that ends the story.

### The Frog Hunt (Zaire)

"All Things Are Linked," on page 103 in Harold Courlander, *The Crest and the Hide* (New York: Coward, McCann & Geoghehan, 1982). 137pp. ISBN 0-698-20536-7.

"All Things Are Connected," on page 13 in Pleasant DeSpain, *Eleven Nature Tales: A Multicultural Journey* (Little Rock, AR: August House, 1996). 91pp. $10.75; $4.50pa. ISBN 0-87483-447-3; 0-87483-458-9pa.

### The Parable of the Stomach (Aesop)

"The Belly and the Members," on page 72 in Joseph Jacobs, ed., *The Fables of Aesop* (Mineola, NY: Dover Publications, 2002). 196pp. $2.50pa. ISBN 0-486-41859-6pa.

"Belly and Members," on page 85 in Jack Zipes, ed., *Aesop's Fables* (New York: Signet Classic, 1992). 288pp. ISBN 0-451-52565-5pa.

### Just Enough . . . (Jewish)

"The Tailor," on page 2 in Nancy Schimmel, *Just Enough to Make a Story: A Sourcebook for Storytelling,* 3d ed. (Berkeley, CA: Sisters' Choice Press, 1992). 58pp. $14.75pa. ISBN 0-932164-03-X.

"The Tailor's Jacket," on page 94 in Margaret Read MacDonald, *Earth Care: World Folktales to Talk About* (North Haven, CT: Linnet Books, 1999). 162pp. $26.50; $17.50pa. ISBN 0-208-02416-6; 0-208-02426-3pa.

### Even Stones Go Somewhere (Jewish)

"Don't Throw Stones from Not Yours to Yours," on page 99in Harold Courlander, ed., *Ride with the sun; an anthology of folk tales and stories from the United Nations* (New York: Whittlesey House, 1955). 296pp.

"Don't Throw Stones from 'Not Yours' to 'Yours'," on page 112 in Margaret Read MacDonald, *Earth Care: World Folktales to Talk About* (North Haven, CT: Linnet Books, 1999). 162pp. $26.50; $17.50pa. ISBN 0-208-02416-6; 0-208-02426-3pa.

"Throwing Stones," on page 109 in Josepha Sherman, *Rachel the Clever and Other Jewish Folktales* (Little Rock, AR: August House, 1993). 171pp. $19.95; $10.95pa. ISBN 0-87483-306-X; 0-87483-307-8pa.

## Putting Feathers Back in the Pillow (Jewish)

"The Gossip," on page 143 in Ed Brody et al., ed., *Spinning Tales, Weaving Hope: Stories, Storytelling and Activities for Peace, Justice and the Environment* (Gabriola Island, BC: New Society Publishers, 2002). 281pp. $24.95 pa. ISBN 0-86571-447-9pa.

"Feathers," on page 59 in Corinne Stavish, ed., *Seeds from Our Past: Planting for the Future* (Washington, DC: B'nai B'rith Center for Jewish Identity, 1997). 96pp. $10pa. ISBN 0-910250-31-6pa.

## Why the Sky Is Up So High (Nigeria)

"Why the Sky Is Far Away," on page 80 in Jill Brand, *The Green Umbrella: Stories, Songs, Poems and Starting Points for Environmental Assemblies* (London: a & C Black, 1991). 106pp. $17.95pa. ISBN 0-7136-3390-5pa.

"Why the Sky Is High," on page 17 in Michael J. Caduto, *Earth Tales from Around the World* (Golden, CO: Fulcrum Publishing, 1997). 192pp. $17.95pa. ISBN 1-55591-968-5pa.

"Too Much Sky," on page 101 in Margaret Read MacDonald, *Earth Care: World Folktales to Talk About* (North Haven, CT: Linnet Books, 1999). 162pp. $26.50; $17.50pa. ISBN 0-208-02416-6; 0-208-02426-3pa.

## Four Who Made a Lion (India)

"The Four Wise People," on page 147 in Ed Brody et al., eds., *Spinning Tales, Weaving Hope: Stories, Storytelling and Activities for Peace, Justice and the Environment* (Gabriola Island, BC: New Society Publishers, 2002). 281pp. $24.95 pa. ISBN 0-86571-447-9pa.

"Four Who Made a Tiger," on page 161 in Michael J. Caduto, *Earth Tales from Around the World* (Golden, CO: Fulcrum Publishing, 1997). 192pp. $17.95pa. ISBN 1-55591-968-5pa.

"The Scholars Who Revived a Lion," on page 180 in Krishna Dharma, *Panchatantra* (Badger, CA: Torchlight Publishing, 2004). 201pp. $12.95 pa. ISBN 1-887089-45-4pa.

## The Goose That Laid the Golden Eggs (Aesop)

"The Goose with the Golden Eggs," on page 134 in Joseph Jacobs, ed., *The Fables of Aesop* (Mineola, NY: Dover Publications, 2002). 196pp. $2.50pa. ISBN 0-486-41859-6pa.

"The Goose with the Golden Eggs," on page 145 in Jack Zipes, ed., *Aesop's Fables* (New York: Signet Classic, 1992). 288pp. ISBN 0-451-52565-5pa.

## Big Daddy Frog (Aesop)

"The Frog and the Ox," on page 57 in Joseph Jacobs, ed., *The Fables of Aesop* (Mineola, NY: Dover Publications, 2002). 196pp. $2.50pa. ISBN 0-486-41859-6pa.

"The Frog and the Ox," on page 45 in Jack Zipes, ed., *Aesop's Fables* (New York: Signet Classic, 1992). 288pp. ISBN 0-451-52565-5pa.

## Hodja and the Mulberry Tree (Turkey)

"What Is It All For?" on page 165 in Indries Shah, *The Pleasantries of the Incredible Mulla Nasrudin* (London: Mulla Nasrudin Enterprises Ltd, 1968). 218pp.

"Nazrudin and the Mulberry Tree," on page 22 in Susan Strauss, *The Passionate Fact: Storytelling in Natural History and Cultural Interpretation* (Golden, CO: North American Press, 1996). 152pp. $16.95pa. ISBN 1-55591-925-1pa.

## The First Wolf (Finland)

"Why Is The Wolf Ferocious?" on page 135 in Denise Casey and Tim Clark, *Tales of the Wolf* (Moose, WY: Homestead Publishing, 1996). 320pp. $14.95. ISBN 0-94397-240-X.

"The Wolf with the Burning Eyes," on page 144 in Norma Livo and George Livo, *The Enchanted Wood and Other Tales from Finland* (Englewood, CO: Libraries Unlimited, 1999). 199pp. $33.50. ISBN 1-56308-578-X.

### Dutch Nightmare on Elmwood Street (original natural history)

This is a narrative account of how Dutch elm disease can change a town. Depending on how old you are, you probably have memories of similar things happening in your community.

### The Heaviest Burden (adapted from Indonesia)

"The Heaviest Burden," on page 93 in Jill Brand, *The Green Umbrella: Stories, Songs, Poems and Starting Points for Environmental Assemblies* (London: A & C Black, 1991). 106pp. $17.95pa. ISBN 0-7136-3390-5pa.

You can find a similar tales involving a house in "Those Who Quarreled," on page 82 in Elizabeth Hough Sechrist, *Once in the First Times: Folktales from the Philippines* (Philadelphia: Macrae Smith Company, 1949). 215pp.

### It's in Your Hands (Jewish)

"The Hermit and the Children," on page ix in Ed Brody, et al., eds., *Spinning Tales, Weaving Hope: Stories, Storytelling and Activities for Peace, Justice and the Environment* (Gabriola Island, BC: New Society Publishers, 2002). 281pp. $24.95pa. ISBN 0-86571-447-9pa.

"In Your Hands," on page 124 in Margaret Read MacDonald, *Earth Care: World Folktales to Talk About* (North Haven, CT: Linnet Books, 1999). 162pp. $26.50; $17.50pa. ISBN 0-208-02416-6; 0-208-02426-3pa.

### The Difference Between Heaven and Hell (adapted Jewish tale)

"The Difference Between Heaven and Hell," on page 80 in Elisa Davy Pearmain, *Doorways to the Soul* (Cleveland, OH: Pilgrim Press, 1998). 138pp. $9.95pa. ISBN 0-8298-1286-5pa.

"A Vision of Heaven and Hell," on page 82 in Todd Outcalt, *Candles in the Dark*: A *Treasury of the World's Most Inspiring Parables*. Hoboken, NJ: John Wiley & Sons, 2002. 237pp. $15.95pa. ISBN 0-471-43594-5pa.

"A Banquet in Heaven," on page 61 in Corinne Stavish, ed. *Seeds from Our Past: Planting for the Future* (Washington, DC: B'nai B'rith Center for Jewish Identity, 1997). 96pp. $10pa. ISBN 0-910250-31-6pa.

### Moving a Mountain (China)

"Old Man Stupidity," on page 26 in Cheou-Kang Sie, *A Butterfly's Dream & Other Chinese Tales* (Rutland, VT: Charles E. Tuttle Company, 1970). 91pp. ISBN 0-8048-0077-4.

"The Old Man Who Moved Mountains," on page 129 in Margaret Read MacDonald, *Three Minute Tales: Stories from Around the World to Tell or Read When Time Is Short* (Little Rock, AR: August House, 2004). 160pp. $24.95; $17.95pa. ISBN 0-87483-728-6; 0-87483-729-4pa.

# Bibliography

## Biology Information Resources

Bennet, Doug, and Tim Tiner. *The Wild Woods Guide: From Minnesota to Maine, the Nature and Lore of the Great North Woods.* New York: Houghton Mifflin, 2003. 436pp. $21.95. ISBN 0-06-093601-0pa.

Commoner, Barry. *The Closing Circle*: *Nature, Man, and Technology.* New York: Knopf, 1971. 326pp. ISBN 0-394423-50-X.

Easton, Thomas A., and Theodore D. Goldfarb, eds. *Taking Sides*: *Clashing Views on Controversial Environmental Issues.* 10th ed. Guilford, CT: McGraw-Hill, 2003. 437pp. $23.50. ISBN 0-07-293317-8pa.

McCarthy, Ann E. *Critters of Minnesota Pocket Guide.* Cambridge, MA: Adventure Publications, 2000. 126pp. $5.95. ISBN 1-885061-87-0.

McKinney, Michael, and Robert M. Schoch. *Environmental Science*: *Systems and Solutions.* St. Paul, MN: West Publishing Company, 1996. 639pp. $56.00pa. ISBN 0-314-06401-Xpa.

Scott, Michael. *The Young Oxford Book of Ecology.* New York: Oxford University Press, 1995. 160pp. $30.00. ISBN 0-19-521166-9.

Shedd, Warner. *Owls Aren't Wise & Bats Aren't Blind*: *A Naturalist Debunks Our Favorite Fallacies about Wildlife.* New York: Random House, 2000. 322pp. $14.00pa. ISBN 0-609-80797-8pa.

Stensaas, Mark. *Canoe Country Wildlife: A Field Guide to the Boundary Waters and Quetico.* Duluth, MN: Pfeifer-Hamilton Publishers, 1993. 221pp. $14.95pa. ISBN 0-938586-65-3pa.

Wells, Diana. *100 Birds and How They Got Their Names.* Chapel Hill, NC: Algonquin Books of Chapel Hill, 2002. 297pp. $18.95. ISBN 1-56512-281-X.

Wilson, Edward O. *The Future of Life.* New York: Alfred A Knopf, 2002. 229pp. $26.00. ISBN 0-67-945078-5.

Wright, Richard T., and Bernard J. Nebel. *Environmental Science: Toward a Sustainable Future.* 8th ed. Upper Saddle River, NJ: Pearson Education, 2002. 681pp. $25.00. ISBN 0-13-032538-4.

## Environmental Education Activity Resources

Acorn Naturalists Catalog, www.acornnaturalists.com or (800) 422-8886. A comprehensive catalog of environmental education books, puppets, props, and tools.

American Forest Foundation. *Project Learning Tree*: *Environmental Education Activity Guide, PreK–8.* Washington, DC: American Forest Foundation, 1993. 402pp.

Council for Environmental Education. *Project WILD K-12 Curriculum and Activity Guide.* Houston, TX: Council for Environmental Education, 2001. 537pp.

Lingelbach, Jenepher, ed. *Hands-On Nature*: *Information and Activities for Exploring the Environment with Children*. Woodstock: Vermont Institute of Natural Science, 1986. 233pp. $19.95pa. ISBN 0-9617627-0-5pa.

# Storytelling Books

Brand, Susan Trostl, and Jeanne M. Donato. *Storytelling in Emergent Literacy*: *Fostering Multiple Intelligences*. Albany, NY: Delmar, 2001. 354pp. $33.95pa. ISBN 0-7668-1480-7pa.

Bruchac, Joseph. *Roots of Survival: Native American Storytelling and the Sacred*. Golden, CO: Fulcrum Publishing,1996. 206pp. $24.95. ISBN 1-55591-145-5.

Geisler, Harlynne. *Storytelling Professionally*: *The Nuts and Bolts of a Working Performer*. Englewood, CO: Libraries Unlimited, 1997. 151pp. $25.00pa. ISBN 1-56308-370-1pa.

Haven, Kendall. *Super Simple Storytelling*. Englewood, CO: Teacher Ideas Press, 2000. 229pp. $25.00pa. $25.00. ISBN 1-56308-681-6pa.

Mooney, Bill, and David Holt. *The Storytellers Guide*: *Storytellers Share Advice for the Classroom, Boardroom, Showroom, Podium, Pulpit and Center Stage*. Little Rock, AR: August House, 1996. 208pp. $23.95pa. ISBN 0-87483-482-1pa.

Sima, Judy, and Kevin Cordi. *Raising Voices: Creating Youth Storytelling Groups and Troupes*. Teacher Ideas Press, 2003. 239pp. $32.50pa. ISBN 1-56308-919-Xpa.

Weaver, Mary, ed. *Tales as Tools*. Jonesborough, TN: National Storytelling Press, 1994. 213pp. $19.95pa. ISBN 1-879991-15-2pa.

# Folktale Book Resources

Abrahams, Roger D., ed. *Afro-American Folktales*: *Stories from Black Traditions* in *the New World*. (Pantheon Fairy Tale & Folklore Library). New York: Random House, 1985. 327pp. $17.00; $11.95pa. ISBN 0-394-52755-0; 0-394-72885-8pa.

Adams, Richard. *The Unbroken Web*: *Stories and Fables*. New York: Ballantine, 1980. 182pp. $3.95pa. ISBN 0-345-30368-7pa.

Aleksandr Afanas'ev. *Russian Fairy Tales*. New York: Pantheon, 1945. 662pp. ISBN 0-394-73090-9.

Bailey, Carolyn Sherwin. *Firelight Stories*: *Folk Tales Retold for Kindergarten, School and Home*. Springfield, MA: Milton Bradley, 1907. 192pp.

Baltuck, Naomi. *Apples from Heaven*. North Haven, CT: Linnet Books, 1995. 143pp. ISBN 0-208-02424-7; 0-208-02434-4pa.

Blecher, Lone Thygesen, and George Blecher. *Swedish Folktales and Legends*. (Pantheon Fairy Tale & Folklore Library). New York: Pantheon Books, 1993. $25.00; $17.00pa. ISBN 0-394-54791-8; 0-697-75841-0pa.

Bowman, James Cloyd, and Margery Bianco. *Tales from a Finnish Tupa*. Morton Grove, IL: Albert Whitman & Company, 1964. 273pp. ISBN 8075-7756-1pa.

Brand, Jill. *The Green Umbrella*: *Stories, Songs, Poems and Starting Points for Environmental Assemblies*. London: A & C Black, 1991. 106pp. $17.95pa. ISBN 0-7136-3390-5pa.

Brody, Ed, et al. *Spinning Tales, Weaving Hope: Stories, Storytelling and Activities for Peace, Justice and the Environment.* Gabriola Island, BC: New Society Publishers, 2002. 281pp. $24.95 pa. ISBN 0-86571-447-9pa.

Brooks, Kaarina. *Foxy: Finnish Folk Tales for Children.* Beaverton, ON: Aspasia Books, 2002. $12.95pa. ISBN 0-9689054-7-1pa.

Burton, W. F. P. *The Magic Drum: Tales from Central Africa.* New York: Criterion Books, 1961. 127pp.

Caduto, Michael J. *Earth Tales from Around the World.* Golden, CO: Fulcrum Publishing, 1997. 192pp. $17.95pa. ISBN 1-55591-968-5pa.

Caduto, Michael J., and Joseph Bruchac. *Keepers of the Earth.* Golden, CO: Fulcrum Publishing, 1988. 209pp. $26.95. ISBN 1-55591-027-0.

Casey, Denise, and Tim Clark. *Tales of the Wolf.* Moose, WY: Homestead Publishing, 1996. 320pp. $14.95. ISBN 0-94397-240-X

Cotterell, Arthur. *Norse Mythology.* New York: Lorenz Books, 2000. 96pp. $12.95. ISBN 1-85967-998-6.

Courlander, Harold. *The Crest and the Hide.* New York: Coward, McCann & Geoghehan, 1982. 137pp. ISBN 0-698-20536-7.

———. *The Hat-Shaking Dance: And Other Ashanti Tales from Ghana.* New York: Harcourt, Brace & World, 1957. 115pp.

Courlander, Harold, ed. *Ride with the Sun: An Anthology of Folk Tales and Stories from the United Nations.* New York: Whittlesey House, 1955. 296pp.

Creeden, Sharon. *Fair Is Fair: Wold Folktales of Justice.* Little Rock, AR: August House, 1994. 190pp. $19.95pa. ISBN 0-87483-400-7pa.

DeSpain, Pleasant. *Eleven Nature Tales: A Multicultural Journey.* Little Rock, AR: August House, 1996. 91pp. $10.75; $4.50pa. ISBN 0-87483-447-3; 0-87483-458-9pa.

Deutsch, Babette, and Avrahm Yarmolinsky. *Tales of Faraway Folk.* New York: Harper & Row, 1952. 68pp.

———. *More Tales of Faraway Folk.* New York: Harper & Row, 1963. 93pp.

Dharma, Krishna. *Panchatantra.* Badger, CA: Torchlight Publishing, 2004. 201pp. $12.95 pa. ISBN 1-887089-45-4pa.

Dobbs, Rose. *One upon a Time: Twenty Cheerful Tales to Read and Tell.* New York: Random House, 1950. 117pp.

El-Shamy, Hasan M. ,ed. *Folktales of Egypt.* Chicago: University of Chicago Press, 1980. 347pp. ISBN 0-226-20624-6.

Evans, Cheryl, and Anne Millard. *Greek Myths and Legends.* London: Usborne, 1985. 64pp. $10.95pa. ISBN 086020-946-6pa.

Forest, Heather. *Wisdom Tales from Around the World.* Little Rock, AR: August House, 1996. 156pp. $28.00; $17.95pa. ISBN 0-87483-478-3; 0-87483-478-3pa.

Fujita, Hiroko. *Stories to Play with: Kid's Tales Told with Puppets, Paper, Toys, and Imagination.* Little Rock, AR: August House, 1999. 96pp. $12.95pa. ISBN 0-87483-553-4pa.

Grimm, Jacob, and William Grimm. *Grimms' Complete Fairy Tales.* New York: Barnes & Noble Books, 1993. 628pp. ISBN 0-76070-335-3.

Hamilton, Martha, and Mitch Weiss. *How & Why Stories: World Tales Kids Can Read & Tell.* Little Rock, AR: August House, 1999. 96pp. $24.95; $14.95pa. ISBN 0-87483-562-3; 0-87483-561-5pa.

Han, Carolyn. *Why Snails Have Shells*: *Minority and Han Folktales of China*. Honolulu: University of Hawaii Press, 1993. 174pp. $7.95. ISBN 0-8248-1505-X.

Handford, S. A. *Aesop's Fables*. New York: Puffin, 1994. 212pp. ISBN 0-14-130929-6.

Harris, Joel Chandler. *The Favorite Uncle Remus*. Cambridge, MA: The Riverside Press, 1948. 310pp.

Hurston, Zora Neale. *Mules and Men*. New York: HarperCollins, 1990. 291pp. $29.50; $13.95pa. ISBN 0-25333-932-4; 0-25320-208-6pa.

Jacobs, Joseph ed. *The Fables of Aesop*. Mineola, NY: Dover Publications, 2002. 196pp. $2.50pa. ISBN 0-486-41859-6pa.

Jagendorf, M. A., and Virginia Weng. *The Magic Boat and Other Chinese Folk Stories*. New York: Vanguard Press, 1980. 236pp. ISBN 0-8149-0823-3.

Kantor, Susan. *One Hundred and One African-American Read-Aloud Stories*. New York: Black Dog & Leventhal Publishers, 1998. 416pp. $12.95. ISBN 1-57912-039-3.

Kendall, Carol, and Yao-wen Li. *Sweet and Sour*: *Tales from China*. New York: Seabury, 1978. 111pp. $7.95. ISBN 0-81643-228-7.

Kennerly, Karen. *Hesitant Wolf & Scrupulous Fox*: *Fables Selected from World Literature*. New York: Random House, 1973. 328pp. ISBN 0-304-46496-6.

Kerr, Mildred L., and Frances Ross. *First Fairy Tales*. San Francisco: Charles E. Merrill Books, 1946. 128 pp.

Leach, Maria. *How the People Sang the Mountains Up*: *How and Why Stories*. New York: Viking Press, 1967. 160pp.

Lester, Julius. *Black Folktales*. New York: Grove Press, 1969. 110pp. $9.95pa. ISBN 0-8021-3242-1pa.

Livo, Norma, and George Livo. *The Enchanted Wood and Other Tales from Finland*. Englewood, CO: Libraries Unlimited, 1999. 199pp. $33.50. ISBN 1-56308-578-X.

Luzzatto, Paola Caboara. *Long Ago When the Earth Was Flat*: *Three Tales from Africa*. New York: Collins, 1979. 44 pp.

Ma, Y. W., and Joseph S. M. Lau. *Traditional Chinese Stories*. New York: Columbia University Press, 1978. 603pp. ISBN 0-231-04058-X.

MacDonald, Margaret Read. *Earth Care*: *World Folktales to Talk About*. North Haven, CT: Linnet Books, 1999. 162pp. $26.50; $17.50pa. ISBN 0-208-02416-6; 0-208-02426-3pa.

———. *The Parent's Guide to Storytelling*: *How to Make up New Stories and Retell Old Favorites*. 2d ed. Little Rock, AR: August House, 2001. 120pp. $21.95; $11.95pp. ISBN 0-87483-619-0; 0-87483-618-2pa.

———. *Three Minute Tales*: *Stories from Around the World to Tell or Read When Time Is Short*. Little Rock, AR: August House, 2004. 160pp. $24.95; $17.95pa. ISBN 0-87483-728-6; 0-87483-729-4pa.

Masey, Mary Lou. *Stories of the Steppes*. New York: David McKay Co., 1968. 142pp.

Mercatante, Anthony S. *Zoo of the Gods*: *Animals in Myth, Legend and Fable*. Berkeley, CA: Seastone, 1999. $15.95. ISBN 1-56975-160-9.

Metternich, Hillary Roe. *Mongolian Folktales*. Boulder, CO: Avery Press, 1996. 131pp. $19.95pa. ISBN 0-937321-06-0pa.

Miller, Candace R., ed. *Tales from the Bird Kingdom*: *More Than 160 Legends and Pourquoi Stories about Birds*. Lima, OH: Pourquoi Press, 1996. 94pp. $20.00pa. E-mail: naturelegends@wcoil.com

———. *Tales from the Creature Kingdom: More Than 160 Multicultural Legends and Pourquoi Stories about Mammals, Insects, Reptiles and Water Creatures*. Lima, OH: Pourquoi Press, 1996. 94pp. $20.00pa. E-mail: naturelegends@wcoil.com

Nye, Robert, ed. *Classic Folk Tales from Around the World*. London: Leopard, 1996. 605pp. ISBN 1-85891-330-6.

Outcalt, Todd. *Candles in the Dark: A Treasury of the World's Most Inspiring Parables*. Hoboken, NJ: John Wiley & Sons, 2002. 237pp. $15.95pa. ISBN 0-471-43594-5pa.

Palmer, Marion. *Uncle Remus Stories*. New York: Golden Press, 1966.

Pearmain, Elisa Davy. *Doorways to the Soul*. Cleveland, OH: Pilgrim Press, 1998. 138pp. $9.95pa. ISBN 0-8298-1286-5pa.

Radin, Paul. ed. *African Folktales*. New York: Schocken Books, 1983. 322pp. ISBN 0-8052-0732-5pa.

Rockwell, Anne. *The Acorn Tree and Other Folktales*. New York: Greenwillow Books, 1995. 40pp. $16.00. ISBN 0-688-10746-X.

Ryder, Arthur W. *The Panchatantra*. Chicago: University of Chicago Press, 1925.

Sawyer, Ruth. *This Way to Christmas*. New York: Harper & Brothers, 1952. 165pp.

Schimmel, Nancy. *Just Enough to Make a Story: A Sourcebook for Storytelling*. 3d ed. Berkeley, CA: Sisters' Choice Press, 1992. 58pp. $14.75pa. ISBN 0-932164-03-X.

Sechrist, Elizabeth Hough. *Once in the First Times: Folktales from the Philippines*. Philadelphia: Macrae Smith Company, 1949. 215pp.

Serych, Jiri. *At the End of the Rainbow*. London: Orbis Publishing, 1984. 208pp. ISBN 0-85613-532-1.

Shah, Indries. *The Pleasantries of the Incredible Mulla Nasrudin*. London: Mulla Nasrudin Enterprises Ltd, 1968. 218pp.

Sherman, Josepha. *Rachel the Clever and Other Jewish Folktales*. Little Rock, AR: August House, 1993. 171pp. $19.95; 10.95pa. ISBN 0-87483-306-X; 0-87483-307-8pa.

Sie, Cheou-Kang. *A Butterfly's Dream & Other Chinese Tales*. Rutland, VT: Charles E. Tuttle Company, 1970. 91pp. ISBN 0-8048-0077-4.

Simms, Laura. *Making Peace, Heart Uprising (CD)*. Chicago: Earwig Music, 1993. 4925CD.

Stavish, Corinne, ed. *Seeds from Our Past: Planting for the Future*. Washington, DC: B'nai B'rith Center for Jewish Identity, 1997. 96pp. $10pa. ISBN 0-910250-31-6pa.

Strauss, Kevin. *Loon and Moon: And Other Animal Stories*. Ely, MN: Raven Productions, 2005. 48pp. $12.95pa. ISBN 0-9766264-3-8pa. www.naturestory.com.

———. *The Mountain Wolf's Gift* (CD). Ely, MN: Naturestory Productions, 2003. www.naturestory.com.

———. *The Song of the Wolf: Folktales and Legends from Around the World*. Wever, IA: Quixote Press, 2005. 182pp. $9.95pa. ISBN 1-57166-273-1pa. www.naturestory.com.

Strauss, Susan. *The Passionate Fact: Storytelling in Natural History and Cultural Interpretation*. Golden, CO: North American Press, 1996. 152pp. $16.95pa. ISBN 1-55591-925-1pa.

———. *Wolf Stories*. Hillsboro, NC: Beyond Words Publishing, 1993. 64pp. $7.95pa. ISBN 0-94183-188-4pa.

Temple, Olivia, and Robert Temple. *(Aesop's) Complete Fables*. New York: Penguin Classics, 1998. 288pp. $10.00. ISBN 0-14044-649-4.

Time-Life Books, ed. *Magical Justice*. (Enchanted World Series). Alexandria, VA: Time-Life Books, 1986. 143pp. ISBN 0-80945-269-3.

Turnbull, Lucia. *Fairy Tales of India*. New York: Criterion Books, 1959.

Weinreich, Beatrice Silverman. *Yiddish Folktales*. New York: Schocken Books, 1988. 413pp. $18.00pa. ISBN 0-8052-1090-3pa.

Wheeler, M. J. *Fox Tales*. Minneapolis, MN: Carolrhoda Books, 1984. 56pp. ISBN 0-87614-255-2.

Wood, Douglas. *The Windigo's Return*: *A North Woods Story*. New York: Simon & Schuster Children's, 1996. 32pp. ISBN 0-689-80065-7.

Zipes, Jack. *Aesop's Fables*. New York: Signet Classic, 1992. 288pp. ISBN 0-451-52565-5pa.

# Proverb Sources

Bartlett, John, and Justin Kaplan, eds. *Bartlett's Familiar Quotations*. 17th ed. Boston: Little, Brown, 2002. 1472pp. $50.00. ISBN 0-31608-460-3.

Forest, Heather. *Wisdom Tales from Around the World*. Little Rock, AR: August House, 1996. 156pp. $28.00; $17.95pa. ISBN 0-87483-478-3; 0-87483-478-3pa.

MacDonald, Margaret Read. *Earth Care*: *World Folktales to Talk About*. North Haven, CT: Linnet Books, 1999. 162pp. $26.50; $17.50pa. ISBN 0-208-02416-6; 0-208-02426-3pa.

# Index

# About the Author

Naturalist storyteller Kevin Strauss tells nature stories and world folktales for listeners of all ages. Kevin performs storytelling concerts and workshops at schools, nature centers, libraries, and community events across the Midwest. He serves on the Northlands Storytelling Network's board of directors and is artistic director for the "Moose Is Loose Storytelling Festival" in Ely, Minnesota. Kevin has performed storytelling workshops at the Midwest Environmental Education Conference, the Northlands Storytelling Network Conference, and the National Storytelling Network Conference. He has published a collection of wolf folktales, *The Song of the Wolf,* and a children's book of folktales and animal stories, *Loon and Moon.* For more information on Kevin's programs, visit him at www.naturestory.com.